DANCING GIRLS, "LOOSE" LADIES, *and* WOMEN OF "THE CLOTH"

DANCING GIRLS, LOOSE LADIES, and WOMEN of the CLOTH

The Women in Jesus' Life

F. SCOTT SPENCER

continuum

NEW YORK • LONDON

www.continuumbooks.com

The Continuum International Publishing Group, 15 East 26th Street, New York, NY 10010

The Continuum International Publishing Group Ltd, The Tower Building, 11 York Road, London SE1 7NX

Cover art: Furrini, Francesco (1603–1646). Saint Mary Magdalen. Kunsthistorisches Museum, Vienna. Erich Lessing/Art Resource, NY

Cover design: Corey Kent

Library of Congress Cataloging-in-Publication Data

Spencer, F. Scott (Franklin Scott)
  Dancing girls, "loose" ladies, and women of "the cloth" : the women in Jesus' life / F. Scott Spencer.
    p. cm.
  Includes bibliographical references and index.
  ISBN 0-8264-1612-8 (pbk.)
  1. Women in the Bible. 2. Bible. N.T. Gospels—Feminist criticism. 3. Bible. N.T. Acts—Feminist criticism. I. Title.
  BS2445.S62 2004
  226'.0922'082—dc22
                    2004009121

Printed in the United States of America

04 05 06 07 08 09   10 9 8 7 6 5 4 3 2 1

To the Courageous Women of "the Cloth" at BTSR

CONTENTS

PREFACE

A crowd was sitting around him; and they said to him, "Your mother and your brothers and sisters are outside, asking for you." And he replied, "Who are my mother and my brothers?" And looking at those who sat around him, he said, "Here are my mother and my brothers! Whoever does the will of God is my brother and sister and mother." (MARK 3:32–35)

While the New Testament Gospels consistently portray Jesus as single and celibate throughout his earthly life and in close company with twelve male followers during his years of itinerant ministry, the passage above affirms that by no means was Jesus misogynistic, gynophobic, or isolated from women in any extraordinary sense for a typical Jewish man in first-century Palestine. There were numerous women in his life.

Like everybody else, Jesus had a mother, and like many men he apparently had sisters as well. We may also assume that within his extended kinship and neighborhood network in Nazareth he had female aunts, cousins, and possibly nieces and even friends and acquaintances among "girls next door" (not strictly blood relatives)—in other words, all the normal relationships males have with females, except for those of husband/wife and father/daughter.

To be sure, according to the gospel narratives, Jesus does not always treat his mother, sisters, and other women in his life like they want to be treated. In pursuing his vocation to advance the kingdom of God, he leaves his family behind and is not all that receptive to his mother and sisters when they come seeking an audience with him in Capernaum (the background for the above text); and later in Mark, Jesus appears to be even more annoyed by the intrusion of another mother—a woman from Syrophoenicia pleading for her daughter's health—upon his time and energy (7:24–30). Jesus is no model of the sensitive male or a feminist advocate, whatever those labels might mean in our day. But Jesus does welcome into his wider circle of fellowship, indeed, into the very household of God, *any* ("whoever") woman who follows God's will; and he welcomes such women not as his inferior subjects and subordinates, but as his intimate family and friends—as "my mother and my sisters." In fact, such spiritual kin includes some of the same women he otherwise resists—like his own natural mother, who reemerges in both Luke and John as an exemplary woman of God, and the Syrophoenician woman in Mark, whom Jesus eventually honors for her persistent faith.

This book explores the stories of several of these notable women in Jesus' life featured in the four canonical gospels as well as some women who help carry on the legacy of Jesus' work in the book of Acts. The women I have selected to study are those most active and influential, provocative and controversial in Jesus' life—women of remarkable passion and purpose—including Jesus' maternal ancestors on his father's side as well as his own mother Mary and a number of other women who, like the Syrophoenician, press themselves physically upon Jesus in some fashion (women who touch—or try to touch—Jesus' body or clothing) or express themselves verbally in some way to or about Jesus (women who speak—or try to speak—to Jesus or in Jesus' name).

Four of these studies have appeared elsewhere in different form. I have revised and expanded each of them for this volume, mostly in terms of updated annotations. A version of chapter 2 may be found in *Are We Amused?: Humour About Women in the Biblical Worlds* (ed. Athalya Brenner; T & T Clark, 2003); versions of chapters 4 and 7 appear in the respective volumes on John and Acts in the Feminist Companion to the New Testament series edited by Amy-Jill Levine (with the help of Marianne Blickenstaff; T & T Clark, 2003–2004); and a version of chapter 6 was published in *Biblical Interpretation* 7 (1999): 133–55. Chapters 1, 3, and 5 appear here in print for the first time. Portions of chapters 3 and 5 were aired at national meetings of the Society of Biblical Literature and the Catholic Biblical Association. My thanks go out to the members of those societies for graciously hearing and commenting on the papers.

I particularly thank a number of exceptional women New Testament scholars who have kindly read parts of my work, gently pointed out places where I just didn't "get it," and unfailingly encouraged me to keep trying. They include Beverly Roberts Gaventa, Elizabeth Struthers Malbon, Sandra Hack Polaski, Kathy Chambers (Williams), Marianne Blickenstaff, and B. Diane Wudel. Special thanks for this project goes to Amy-Jill Levine, a scholar of uncommon intelligence and insight, wit and wisdom, passion and purpose (who will probably groan at this alliterative tribute). In the field of New Testament women's studies, we are all in her debt for her own key contributions in numerous publications and lectures as well as her expert editorial oversight of the multivolume Feminist Companion to the New

Testament series. The nature of the essays in the present volume adds extra force to the usual prefatory disclaimer: I will not pull an Adam and blame these women for any of the deficiencies in this book; the blunders and bungles are mine alone. I'm grateful for the many wise "fruits" of scholarship shared by a host of feminist interpreters; if some have turned sour in these studies, that's my doing.

I also extend special thanks to a remarkable man of passion and purpose, Henry Carrigan, whose personal support and editorial vision sustained this project from start to finish. Henry, it has been a genuine pleasure to work with you again.

Finally, I thank the principal women in my life—Janet (let's go another thirty), Lauren (go IU), and Meredith (go "dancing girl")—my deepest passions in life. It's tacky to dedicate another book to you three, and Lord knows I'm tacky enough as it is. So I am happy to dedicate this volume to another group of women who enrich my life immeasurably and for whom I wish the best of everything as they seek to discern and fulfill the call of God upon their lives: the courageous women of Baptist Theological Seminary at Richmond, where I am privileged to serve.

CHAPTER 1

Getting into Focus:
Reading with Feminist Lenses

A variety of critical approaches—literary, narratological, historical, sociological, cultural, intertextual, ideological, and deconstructive—inform this collection of studies. Such an eclectic, multifaceted methodology seems appropriate in light of both the wide array of fruitful interpretive strategies currently employed in biblical scholarship and the rich, intricate texture of the New Testament narratives (the Gospels and Acts) under investigation. To analyze these complex texts through only a single lens would potentially yield myopic and reductive readings.[1] However, while cognizant of this mono-focal danger, all of these essays cohere under an overarching interest in *feminist criticism*. Simply put, these studies represent exercises in feminist biblical interpretation in reading, that is, with feminist lenses selected texts from the Gospels and Acts that feature provocative women characters.

The apparent inconsistency of merging one dominant interpretive scheme with a multiplicity of other approaches is considerably eased if the primary paradigm is expansive and inclusive enough to embrace a spectrum of supporting perspectives. And if feminist biblical interpretation has emerged as anything over recent decades, it is just that: a colorful, sprawling "big top" under which all voices and viewpoints—including (especially) those of the disenfranchised—may be heard. Amy-Jill Levine, editor of the wide-ranging, multivolume Feminist Companion to the New Testament and Early Christian Writings series, likens the current state of feminist biblical scholarship to a symphonic orchestra:

> "[F]eminist biblical studies" is now a symphony. It acknowledges the different concerns social location and experience bring to interpretation and recognizes the tentativeness and partiality of each conclusion: no

instrument alone is complete; no two musicians play the same music alike. Feminist readers of Christian origins are so diverse in terms of *approach* (literary, historical, sociological, text-critical, ideological, cross-cultural . . .), *focus* (imagery, characterization, genre, plot, Christology, ethics, politics, polemic . . .), *hermeneutics* (of suspicion, of recovery . . .), *identity* (Womanist, Latina, African, Evangelical, lesbian, Jewish, Catholic . . .) and *conclusions*—namely, it is just like most biblical studies and indeed like most academic disciplines in the humanities and social sciences—that any single definition of what constitutes a "feminist reading" is necessarily reified.[2]

But like a symphony, the multi-tonal, distinctive strains of feminist analysis still work together to comprise a fundamental harmony; within their diverse specialties, the various practitioners of feminist criticism, both female and male, remain "in tune" with each other on basic principles and priorities integral to the feminist enterprise. A brief discussion of this common feminist agenda and its appropriation by male biblical scholars sets the stage for the present collection of feminist readings of New Testament narratives.

Feminism Is for Everybody

In her pointed and passionate book *Feminism Is for Everybody: Passionate Politics,* written at the dawn of the new millennium (2000), influential cultural critic and black feminist thinker bell hooks reaffirmed her understanding of feminism as an equal opportunity political movement:

> Simply put, feminism is a movement to end sexism, sexist exploitation, and oppression. This was a definition of feminism I offered in *Feminist Theory: From Margin to Center* more than 10 years ago. It was my hope at the time that it would become a common definition everyone would use. I liked this definition because it did not imply that men were the enemy. By naming sexism as the problem it went directly to the heart of the matter. Practically, it is a definition which implies that all sexist thinking and action is the problem, whether those who perpetuate it are female or male, child or adult. It is also broad enough to include an understanding of systemic institutionalized sexism. As a definition it is open-ended.[3]

Similarly, in a steady flow of writings running against the main/male-stream of "objective," positivist biblical scholarship, Walter Wink has "named" (defined) and "unmasked" (exposed) the diabolical "power" of "domination systems" operative both within the biblical world and among its interpreters. He defines "domination system" as "a social system characterized by hierarchical power relations, economic inequality, oppressive politics, patriarchy, ranking, aristocracy, taxation, standing armies, and war. Violence became the preferred means for adjudicating disputes and getting and holding power."[4]

Hooks' and Wink's statements properly implicate patriarchy in the network of unjust sexism and domination but do not make it carry the full load. While most dominators in the history of human civilization have been men and while most men are socialized in some measure to dominate women, children, and less powerful men, gender identity is but one element combining with a range of economic, ethnic, religious, geographical, environmental, and other sociopolitical factors to create lethal systems of oppression. Therefore not all men dominate equally, and not all women are equally dominated. Both theoretically and practically, men can be and are subordinated (sometimes brutally) to more powerful men; and women of privilege can and do lord their superior status over lesser women and men. This is not to say that subaltern men perfectly identify with oppressed women and know exactly how they feel or that dominant women are blissfully free of discrimination. To put it baldly, the beleaguered man beaten down on the job might compensate by beating his wife when he gets home; and the aristocratic woman remains more vulnerable to perils of rape and violence than her male counterparts. But the fact that domination systems do not function absolutely along fixed gendered lines gives some hope for at least some women and men joining together in a common liberation cause.

And that cause might just as well be labeled "feminism," conceived as a comprehensive political critique—in both rhetoric and praxis—of established domination systems, with the expressed aim of dismantling such structures and fostering dignity and equality for all persons. Feminist biblical critic Pamela Thimmes helpfully unpacks this dual political thrust of exposition (critique) and reconstruction (transformation) of "oppressive structures of society":

> I understand feminism as both a political term and as a political category because it is, essentially, a liberation movement that not only *critiques the oppressive structures of society,* but, by its various voices and approaches, works for *transformation.* . . . Just as feminism affirms and promotes the full humanity and equality of women, it rejects and denies anything that diminishes the full humanity and equality of women, as well as sexism, racism, classism, ageism, or any other dominance pattern that seeks to alienate, separate, and oppress.[5]

Thimmes further avers that mature feminism, while sprouting from the soil of women's experiences, advocates the interests of *all* dominated persons, male as well as female. By the same token, men as well as women can participate in feminist cultural critique and textual interpretation, though not without difficulty.

> For me, then, what makes a feminist reading feminist has less to do *today* with the gender of the person offering the reading and more to do with the coherence the reading has with a feminist ideology. However, I make this statement well aware that there are serious problems inherent in both the appropriation of feminism by men, and with the assumption that men can read like women.[6]

Apart from the more "innocent" difficulty of well-meaning males presuming they know how women and other oppressed groups really feel (premature identification), more insidious "serious problems" of male involvement in feminism may include patronization (showing the girls how it's done), colonization (getting in on a popular trend and taking over), cooptation (bemoaning the terrible burden of being the "man in charge"), and neutralization (subverting the resistance movement from within).[7] Is it fruitful to use such terms as "male feminist" or "pro-feminist male," or are such monikers hopelessly futile, confused, oxymoronic, or just plain moronic? Echoing the title of an important Modern Language Association panel in the mid-1980s, should we speak of "men *in* feminism," with all that such loaded language implies regarding men's "entering," "penetrating," "invading" women's space?[8] Or can we follow Joseph Boone's more sanguine suggestion that "'being *in*' isn't the only relation possible between men/feminism and redirect our attention to the *possibilities* (rather than impossibilities) inherent in the potential conjunction of men *and* feminism"?[9] I throw my hat in with Boone in hopes that the present studies open up rather than shut down "possibilities" for the "conjunction of men *and* feminism" and the liberation of marginalized women *and* men.

Since women are both socialized from birth into a predominantly patriarchal system and may, in certain situations, act themselves (wittingly or blindly) as agents of oppression, they are not automatically feminists by virtue of being female. Until the cultural tide shifts and most children are raised by feminist-conscious mothers (and fathers), most girls still need to *learn* feminism, to become conscious themselves of stifling structures that engulf them.[10] And so we may distinguish "female feminists" from women unaware of and/or unresistant to the strictures of traditional socialization.

Moreover, since men, too, are socialized, not naturalized, into a male-dominated world, and since feminism is a global political movement, not a parochial sexual agenda, there is room for men to resist the status quo and to pursue liberationist aims—in other words, to become "male feminists" or "pro-feminist males" (however awkward those terms might be). Far from being a mere possibility, one could argue that the political "feminization" of men is a bare necessity for lasting social change.[11] Apart from a utopian or apocalyptic vision of supernatural intervention, the full liberation of humanity cannot take place without women and men cooperating together.

Feminism Is for Men Who Interpret the Bible

Feminist study of the Bible is not a passing fad or politically correct flavor of the month.[12] It has been going strong since the 1970s, gathering steam, and branching out in new directions ever since; and it shows no signs of abating in the new century. Despite the tendency of many male (and a few female) scholars to keep their heads in the sand (ignorance) or to fire potshots from a distance (intolerance), feminist analysis—in a variety of forms—has emerged as a major critical movement in biblical interpretation.[13]

Sometimes it takes an astute observer outside the guild to point out the obvious. In *The Word According to Eve: Women and the Bible in Ancient Times and Our Own*, managing editor of *The Atlantic Monthly* Cullen Murphy trains a keen journalistic eye on the burgeoning feminist movement in biblical studies, tracking the key players and their contributions to understanding the Jewish and Christian scriptures.[14] He tackles this project for two reasons: one personal, the other professional. On the personal side, he writes with the recent memory of his "daughter's first communion in a denomination that still restricts the role of women . . . in the expectation that with regard to the position of women, matters will not remain—will simply not be able to remain—as in some places we see them now; in the expectation, to employ a biblical turn, that the present way's days are numbered."[15] I, too, have been deeply affected by the women closest to me—my wife, best friend, and academic colleague of thirty years and our two remarkable daughters (all daughters are remarkable) whom we are trying to nurture in a different denomination than Murphy's, which in large part (though not wholly) also sadly throttles women's leadership.[16]

On the professional side, Murphy contends that feminist study of the Bible must be taken seriously by scholars and laypersons alike, because it represents nothing short of a major "intellectual revolution" in the history of biblical interpretation, on a par with the Reformation and the Enlightenment in terms of its creative, disruptive, and reorienting potential.[17] Of course, only time will tell whether "feminism" will become the standard designation for this current period of methodological ferment, but whatever term is adopted ("liberationism" is perhaps a more likely, more inclusive, candidate),[18] it seems certain that feminist concerns will be at the forefront of this paradigm shift. Although certain reactionary religious groups will doubtless continue to resist this movement as they have the Enlightenment, feminism is here to stay, and to ignore its seismic influence on biblical interpretation is to be profoundly obscurantist and, dare we say, *unenlightened*.

Murphy devotes most of his attention to the work of female biblical scholars such as Phyllis Trible, Elisabeth Schüssler Fiorenza, Carol Meyers, Tikva Frymer-Kinsky, Mieke Bal, Amy-Jill Levine, Kathleen Corley, Bernadette Brooten, Karen King, Karen Jo Torjesen, Elaine Pagels, and Ross Kraemer. And that is how it should be: women scholars have blazed the feminist trail and opened up new vistas for biblical interpretation. But since the rise of the "women's liberation" movement in the 1960s and '70s, a handful of male scholars have also focused on "women in the Bible" and, more recently, an increasing number would happily describe themselves as "feminist" or "pro-feminist."

Curiously, the main "token male"[19] featured in Murphy's book is neither a feminist critic nor a biblical scholar, but rather the eminent Yale church historian Jaroslav Pelikan, who, by his own admission, has been in "the Mary business" for forty years, beginning with the revised "Mary" entry to *Encyclopaedia Britannica* in the 1950s and culminating with the monograph *Mary through the Centuries: Her Place in the History of Culture* in 1996.[20] While such scholarly "devotion" to Mary is notable and in some respects revolutionary—not least because Pelikan is Protestant as well as male—and while Pelikan is sensitive to the biblical roots of Mariology, he is by no means the model of a modern major male feminist exegete.

Murphy also includes a brief discussion of the works of Leonard Swidler and Ben Witherington III. Swidler wrote a number of articles and monographs from 1971 to 1988 promoting the liberating teaching and ministry of a "feminist" Jesus;[21] such studies, however, were beset by blatant anachronism (feminism, as we know it, would have been inconceivable in first-century Palestine, by Jesus or by anyone else) and latent anti-Judaism (the liberating, "feminist" Jesus was constructed at the expense of a caricatured, repressive Judaism). Still, Swidler makes no claims to having all the answers and should be given his due for helping spur exegetes to take the role of women in the biblical world more seriously. He is not a professional biblical scholar but rather a Catholic theologian who, in an interview with Murphy, offers a rather whimsical (but still provocative) assessment of his "feminist" biblical ventures: "Why did it take a fourth-rate biblical scholar like me to look at what the Gospels have to say about women?"[22] Why indeed?

Unlike Pelikan and Swidler, Ben Witherington III is a professional biblical scholar with two Cambridge monographs on women and the New Testament to his credit (1984, 1988)[23] framed by two key articles: the first treatment of Luke 8:1–3 "in any scholarly journal of the last hundred years" (1979),[24] and the signature article on "Women, New Testament" in the prestigious *Anchor Bible Dictionary* (1992).[25] The latter offers a convenient synopsis of Witherington's major works, showcased in a leading reference work in biblical studies. The fact that the editors of *ABD* selected Witherington for this article is a tribute to the scope and quality of his work; yet it represents a somewhat surprising selection, given the number of qualified female scholars working in the field by this period. Even more puzzling— particularly in comparison with Phyllis Bird's companion article on "Women, Old Testament"[26]—is the dearth of references to feminist and other female scholars in Witherington's bibliography. Out of the twenty-five authors cited, by far most are men. To be fair, Witherington argues for a largely "positive portrayal" of women's roles in the Jesus movement and early church and does not (explicitly) argue against feminist interpretations. But if feminist criticism has taught us anything, it is that women are most effectively effaced by simple neglect. By going unmentioned, they become easily forgettable—"unmentionable" in the loaded sense of the word. "Women *in* the Bible" Witherington attends to carefully; "women *and* the Bible"—that is, what women scholars have to say about biblical women—is scarcely on his radar.

In contradistinction to some scholars who detect considerable tension within the New Testament's portrayals of women, Witherington perceives a "consistent trajectory" from Jesus to Paul and the early church endorsing "the new freedom and roles women can assume in Christ," without, however, advocating a full-blown social revolution. Overall, the New Testament "shows an attempt at *reformation,* not *repudiation,* of the patriarchal structure of family and society evident in the 1st century."[27] Ironically, many feminist interpreters would concur with this assessment of the New Testament evidence—albeit from a sharply critical perspective distinct from Witherington's Evangelical commitment to biblical authority. More problematic is Witherington's contention that, while Jesus was no first-century feminist revolutionary (contra Swidler), nonetheless, with respect to the "restrictive context" of ancient Palestinian *Jewish* society, "Jesus' relationship with women must have seemed radical indeed" (pace Swidler).[28] Supposedly,

Jesus' traveling with female disciples and transgressing purity laws pertaining to women (e.g., permitting a menstruating woman to touch him) would have particularly shocked the Jews of his day. However, as Ross Shephard Kraemer and other Jewish scholars have persuasively argued, this approach by Witherington—and a host of other Christian New Testament interpreters, male and female, conservative and liberal—is both historically suspect and politically lethal.[29] (In chap. 3, "Shall We Dance?" I examine the social and religious status of the hemorrhaging [menstruating?] woman in Mark.) Often misassumptions about oppressive, gyno-restrictive Jewish life in the first century are drawn from uncritical usage of later rabbinic materials and from a priori judgments regarding Jesus' uniqueness and supremacy. Jesus' saving, liberating, redeeming vision for women and other marginalized persons is purchased at the price of a legalistic, myopic, and misogynistic bowdlerization of Judaism.

In spite of these critical limitations of Witherington's work from our current vantage point, Levine points out that Witherington "is to no small extent responsible for reintroducing gospel women to the academic mainstream" and has been especially influential in opening the minds of many conservative, biblically rooted Evangelicals to greater women's freedom in the life of the church.[30] That is no mean achievement—believe me.

The most recent substantial investigation of women in the Gospels by a male scholar comes from the pen of Professor Richard Bauckham of St. Andrew's University, Scotland.[31] Apart from a treatment of Mary and Elizabeth in Luke 1, these studies focus primarily on lesser-known, named female characters associated with Jesus, such as the genealogical foremothers in Matt 1, Mary of Clopas, the two Salomes, and Joanna, the wife of Herod's steward Chuza. About a third of the book (almost one hundred pages) attempts to track the career of Joanna from a follower of Jesus in Luke 8:1–3 (the same passage examined by Witherington) to an apostolic partner of Paul in Rom 16:7 (Bauckham argues that Joanna = Junia).[32]

Bauckham describes his method as "historically rigorous and imaginatively literary" or, vice versa, as "literarily rigorous and imaginatively historical."[33] But on the whole, historical interests outweigh the literary, consistent with Bauckham's formidable expertise in Second Temple Jewish literature and culture. His stark confession—"I find inexhaustibly fruitful the pursuit of a kind of detailed, even meticulous, historical investigation that not many New Testament scholars now trouble to undertake"[34]—serves as an important reminder to interpret biblical texts in their original contexts, since, whatever surplus of meaning(s) they may spawn, they contain no less than that which derives from the ancient settings that produced them. While my own studies of women in New Testament narratives lean more toward the literary side, with regard to women's vocations (prostitute, slave-girl, seamstress, dyer, leatherworker) and Jewish values (kinship ties, purity concerns), for example, I endeavor to maintain a proper historical perspective. Moreover, along with Bauckham, I also find it fruitful to explore intertextual links between the testaments, aided by the creative and stimulating insights of Hebrew Bible/Old Testament scholars (feminist and otherwise). Although we come to different conclusions, Bauckham and I both investigate the complex literary interplay between the Old Testament and Matthew's gospel around the figures of Tamar, Rahab, Ruth, and Bathsheba in Jesus' genealogy (see chap. 2).[35]

With respect to feminist hermeneutics, on the one hand, Bauckham applauds the work of feminist historians and archaeologists of early Judaism, like Tal Ilan,[36] and his sympathetic interest in neglected biblical women clearly aligns with feminist calls for recovery. But on the other hand, in terms of reading the gospel texts with feminist-critical lenses, while Bauckham says he is "far from depreciating" this approach, he comes awfully close. He registers a personal suspicion of the "blinkered use of a feminist hermeneutic of suspicion" that seeks to expose the Bible's embedded patriarchal-androcentric bias at every turn.[37] While not denying the male-dominated thrust of many biblical texts, Bauckham feels that feminist critics have done their job and it's time to move on. No need to get too uptight, too obsessive, too bogged down in "one-issue exegesis."

> Although I might easily be misunderstood here, I suspect that part of the problem lies in "one-issue exegesis": the issue of patriarchal oppression of women is the only interest the exegete brings to the text and therefore the feminist hermeneutic of suspicion is the only exegetical tool that is employed. It is hard to attend fairly and openly to a text unless one is genuinely interested in all that the text is about, and unless one takes the trouble to approach it with the rich resources of interpretation available in the form of historical and literary methods that are designed to open up the text for its own sake and not just for ideological illustration.[38]

As I see it, the misunderstanding runs in the direction of Bauckham's blinkered assessment of feminist biblical interpretation. His critique suffers from abstraction, citing no specific culprits of "one-issue" exegetical felony. The vast majority of feminist critics I know come to the Bible with deep respect for its rich complexity, religious profundity, and cultural legacy, having invested years and years in professional study of its language, history, theology, ethics, and interpretation. The desire to unmask harmful assumptions about women's subordinate status in the biblical world goes hand in glove with appreciating the Bible's enormous iconic power to influence contemporary society for good—and ill. Krister Stendahl's challenge that the Bible potentially poses a serious "public health" hazard—especially for women—still rings true today.[39] When people quit using the Bible to oppress and disenfranchise women, to justify holy war and ethnic cleansing, to foment anti-Judaism and other political hatreds—then maybe we can stop being suspicious. Beyond recognizing the persisting validity of feminism's hermeneutic of suspicion, we should also be reminded (see above) that this strategy is but one device (not the "only tool," as Bauckham avers) in a multipurpose exegetical toolbox, one instrument in a full-fledged analytical orchestra.

On a more positive note, Bauckham argues that a hyper-suspicious hermeneutic can blind the reader to some genuinely women-oriented, gynocentric bright spots in the biblical text—places where women's voices may truly be heard and women's perspectives realistically represented. Of course, these viewpoints may not be overtly critical of patriarchal structures (women in the biblical era, like some modern women, may have been relatively content—or at least not consciously discontent—with their station in life) and may derive from male writers. But Bauckham sees "no reason to deny to a male author in ancient Israel the imaginative capacity to adopt a woman's perspective that modern male novelists such as [André] Brink display."[40] Banner examples of gynocentric biblical texts include the books of Ruth and Song of Songs in the Old Testament, and the song of Mary and dialogue with Elizabeth in Luke 1. These samples provide a "gynocentric interruption of the dominant androcentricity of Scripture."[41] While not displacing or subverting the biblical canon, "gynocentric texts . . . can function canonically as a critical counterbalance to the androcentricity of others" and can even "authorize gynocentric reading of otherwise androcentric texts."[42] For example, Luke's mention of Mary Magdalene, Joanna, and other women as Jesus' followers early in his itinerant mission (8:2–3) and later at his empty tomb (24:10) invites interpreting the intervening material from these women's perspectives, even though they explicitly appear in only these two places. Thus, sympathetic readings of gospel narratives through female lenses can go "with the grain of the text as a whole, even though it may run against the grain of androcentric parts of the text."[43]

While encouraging men to try to read male-dominated biblical texts from a woman's point of view is all to the good, I still worry that Bauckham is too optimistic about the interpretive enterprise and the salutary effects of biblical authority. He does not adequately address the problems of cooptation, colonization, and patronization (suggested above) that inevitably arise when dominant male authors and readers attempt to speak for and about women's experiences. Nor does he give sufficient weight to the silence and absence of women that still haunt the New Testament narratives. The parallels with gynocentric Old Testament books like Ruth and Song of Songs break down at key points. Female characters (Ruth and Naomi) propel the action *throughout* the story, from start to finish, albeit not in a way that challenges or "mocks" (Bauckham's term)[44] the patriarchal environment they inhabit (at the end of the story, Ruth gives birth to a son, the grandfather of the mighty King David: "David" is and has the last word, 4:22). By contrast, Mary and Elizabeth—while certainly inspired by the Spirit and attuned to each other and to God's purposes—*begin* the action in Luke's gospel by giving birth to notable sons, John and Jesus, who then dominate the story from that point on. After Luke 2, Mary and Elizabeth are never seen or heard from again.[45] These women do not name their sons (as was the case with Ruth's child, Obed, 4:17), and in a narrative so completely devoted to extolling the "Son of the Most High God," one can scarcely imagine Mary or any other woman in Luke being valued "more than seven sons," as Ruth was (4:15). "Blessed . . . *among women*"—yes, as Elizabeth says to Mary (Luke 1:42)—but not blessed *above sons*.

The Song of Songs also stands out for featuring a woman's voice throughout the book. The work presents a series of poetic exchanges between two heterosexual lovers, marked by deep mutuality and authenticity. The female speaks as much and as passionately to her beloved as he does to her, in an idiom that female readers have recognized as true to women's erotic experience.[46] The memorable refrain—"My beloved is mine and I am his" (2:16)/"I am my beloved's, and his desire is for me" (7:10)—epitomizes the woman's strong individual voice amid her voluntary mutual relationship with a male lover that seems to reverse the patriarchal "curse" of Gen 3:16 ("your desire shall be for your man, and he shall rule over you").[47] Although all is not bliss for the Shulammite (she must still beware the threat of male violence, 5:7),[48] she remains a shining star of vocal biblical women. But she has no true counterpart among New Testament women, although some women in the Fourth Gospel come close to holding their own in conversation with Jesus (see chap. 4 below). The sensuous woman in Luke 7 who anoints Jesus' feet resembles the Song's lover in some respects (see chap. 5 below)—but certainly not in her volubility, since she remains totally silent throughout the scene! And with a few exceptions where Luke teases us with the possibility of women's prophetic speech, throughout his two-volume narrative women mostly play the role of passive listener to the powerful male preachers: John, Jesus, Peter, Stephen, Philip, and Paul. While it is nice to notice Mary Magdalene and Joanna framing the ministry and resurrection of Jesus in Luke and interesting to read the intervening material *as if* they were there taking in and commenting on the entire experience, the fact is that they are *not there* between the two brief references. The Lukan writer ignores them for a long stretch of story time. They appear as mere window dressing around the travel and passion narratives, they are given no lines to speak, and when their witness (to the empty tomb) is reported indirectly, it is promptly treated as an "idle tale" by the male apostles (Luke 24:11). Of course, the men are wrong in this judgment, but the message of Jesus' resurrection does not go forward in Luke's account until the men accept and announce it.

While Witherington and Bauckham go about their work of investigating women in the New Testament independently, for the most part, of feminist-critical scholars, other male biblical scholars are much more sympathetic and more personally engaged with the kaleidoscope of feminist biblical interpretation. By way of example and as model for my own work, I mention three scholars.

In a brief but incisive article, "On Becoming a Male Feminist Biblical Scholar," Marc Brettler recounts writing a doctoral dissertation in the 1980s on divine kingship in the Hebrew Bible "without ever considering that such an androcentric metaphor might have raised a problem for ancient Israelite women, or wondering if they might have had an alternative metaphor for God."[49] A small crack in his critical armor developed in the course of preparing for a comprehensive examination at Brandeis University on the book of Judges. Here Brettler began to see that his traditional philological and historical-critical approach left much to be desired in accounting for the important roles, both positive and negative, of women like Deborah, Jael, Jephthah's daughter, and the Levite's concubine. He did little to remedy this deficiency, however, until several years later, as a professor at Brandeis, he served on a women's studies program committee and taught "Women and the Bible"—"the first-ever Women's Studies course" in his department. Engaging now with trenchant feminist interpretations of Judges offered by Phyllis Trible and Mieke Bal, with innovative readings of the Decalogue by Judith Plaskow and of the Song of Songs by Marcia Falk, and with challenging questions and comments by bright female students in his courses, a whole new thought-world opened up for Brettler.

> From my experience in teaching Women and the Bible, I have begun to understand that gender, the study of socially created differences between

men and women, can be as relevant to biblical studies as ancient near eastern texts are, as Hebrew philology is. It is now a different Bible I teach. To paraphrase 1 Samuel 10:6, I have become a different person.[50]

My dissertation was also male-centered, focusing on the figure of Philip the evangelist in the book of Acts and his relationship with Peter, Paul, Simon Magus, and the Ethiopian eunuch—all men, as it happens, although the last example raises interesting gender questions that I hinted at, but did not explore until a later article.[51] Further, while I acknowledged in passing the presence of Philip's four prophetic daughters in Acts 21:9, it did not bother me then, as it did later, that they do not actually do any prophesying in the narrative (that is handled by the visiting male prophet, Agabus, in 21:10–11), despite the explicit Pentecostal expectation that "your daughters will prophesy" (Acts 2:17). As Brettler came to a new appreciation of women's roles in Judges, so did I with respect to Luke's writings. I acquiesced with the party line that Luke was women's best friend in the New Testament—because of the large number of female characters he included—until I started paying attention to how those characters were actually portrayed. I noticed that many if not most Lukan women are silent and submissive. There are a fair number of demons and derelicts inhabiting Luke's story as well. Numbers don't tell the whole tale. Three of the articles in this volume wrestle with the "double message," as Turid Karlsen Seim calls it, toward women in Luke's double narrative.[52] As with Brettler, much of this new perspective for me was crystallized in my serving on the Women's Studies Task Force and teaching the "first-ever" course on "Women and the Bible" at my university. I'm certain I learned more than the students each of the four times I taught it.

Another leading Hebrew Bible scholar, David Gunn, offers a more extensive reflection on his pilgrimage with feminist interpretation. Whereas Brettler's foundational work focused on God the King, Gunn has been preoccupied for over twenty years with David the king. His earlier work, *The Story of King David: Genre and Interpretation* (1978), represented a pioneering effort in formalist, literary criticism of biblical narrative (sometimes dubbed "narrative criticism").[53] However, not content to ride one major paradigm shift (which is more than most folks can handle), Gunn soon began to notice holes in his tidy "new critical" methodology, which he quickly took steps to fill with less tidy, more textured feminist and deconstructive insights.[54]

On the feminist side, once again Phyllis Trible made her mark. Although he admits to ignoring Trible's landmark *God and the Rhetoric of Sexuality* when it first appeared (the same year as his *Story of King David*), within a couple of years, from his post as editor of JSOT Press, Gunn published a collection of women's caucus papers from the centennial meeting of the Society of Biblical Literature, edited by Trible, on "The Effects of Women's Studies on Biblical Studies."[55] From that time on, Gunn confesses, "it began to dawn on me that I had to learn to read and write differently."[56] Especially appreciating Trible's astute blend of intricate literary criticism and perceptive feminist critique, Gunn returned to the David story with new lenses. He began to see the many women, named and unnamed, wrapped up in David's "heroic" career—and it was not a pretty picture. To change the image from the artistic to the gastronomic: the despicable treatment of Michal and David's concubines "particularly stuck in my gullet."[57]

On the deconstructive side, Gunn started to drift away from the formalist literary-critical tradition of F. R. Leavis toward a freer engagement with elements of ambiguity (à la William Empson), openness, and indeterminacy in the biblical text. Multiple problematic readings began to overwhelm and undermine definitive, univocal interpretations. Tables were turned, paradoxes given fuller play, as in the case of Gunn's "exploration of the demonic in God" displayed in God's often capricious and callous dealings with Samson and Saul as well as God's unabashed alliance with David's oppressive regime.[58] Although aware that deconstructive criticism can degenerate into an irresponsible, amoral, almost flippant play of ideas inimical to feminism's serious political agenda, Gunn contends that the two methods can still form "a powerful alliance" around their mutual interests in "destabilizing" and "undermining" established hierarchies and domination systems.[59]

Apart from the influences of monographs, journal articles, book reviews, and professional meetings that drive the scholarly enterprise, Gunn has been shaped by "memorable and invaluable collaboration" with female scholars and students in the classroom and in writing projects.[60] The rich fruit of this interaction may be sampled in joint publications with Danna Nolan Fewell on the book of Ruth, the broad Genesis-Kings saga, and other biblical narratives.[61] These writings reflect a lively, sophisticated, and challenging combination of close literary, feminist, and deconstructive readings of biblical stories that I suspect could only be achieved by sustained interaction between a female and male biblical scholar. It seems to me that such collegial, intellectual intercourse provides the most hopeful avenue for substantive, lasting change.[62] The journey will still be long and hard, largely because of male ignorance and resistance, but some women and a few men think it's worth the hassle: "I struggled to confront some of the deep-seated problems of trying to be 'a man in feminism'. My students, Danna [Nolan

Fewell], Jeanne [Stevenson Moessner] and others encouraged me to keep trying."[63]

If Gunn, like most of us, had to grow into an appreciation of feminist and deconstructive approaches to the Bible, Stephen Moore seems to have been born in such an environment and, in any event, comes as close to fluency in these critical discourses as any male biblical critic that I know of, and he has done it on the typically more conservative New Testament side of the scholarly divide. Thus Moore mirrors the experience of a growing number of male secular literary critics "for whom," as Andrew Ross avers, "the *facticity* of feminism, for the most part, goes without saying; in other words there are men [like Ross] who are young enough for feminism to have been a primary component of their intellectual formation."[64] Although the impact of feminism on the New Testament field lags behind other disciplines in the humanities, the prospects of catching up with Ross and Moore are more promising, with a current crop of male Ph.D. candidates studying under leading feminist scholars at top institutions.[65]

I make no attempt to cover all of Moore's mind-stretching methodological forays into New Testament narratives. Two examples will suffice on the feminist front. In 1992, Moore collaborated with feminist scholar Janice Capel Anderson in editing a set of groundbreaking essays in *Mark and Method: New Approaches in Biblical Studies.* They coauthored the introduction and separately wrote the articles on deconstruction (Moore) and feminism (Anderson), which appeared back-to-back in the collection.[66] (Anderson's feminist reading[s] of "The Dancing Daughter" in Mark 6:14–29 informs my essay in chap. 3.) Their introduction groups deconstructive and feminist analyses with narrative and reader-response criticisms under the heading "How Mark Lost His Grip on the Text."[67] Each of these methods, to one degree or another, shifts the locus of meaning from writer to reader, from authorial intent to audience interpretation. Deconstruction and feminism share a further shift to ideological concerns, stressing the self-interested, power-laden dimensions of all encounters with multi-vocal, supercharged texts. Moore and Anderson describe deconstructive criticism as especially attuned to the "unpredictable and uncontrollable excess of meaning that simmers within every text, always ready to spill over."[68] This spillage (think oil spill or nuclear leak) inevitably affects the social and political ecosystem in a host of ways, not least for women.

Two years later Moore himself brought together feminist and deconstructive approaches in a fascinating treatment of Jesus' meeting with the Samaritan woman at the well.[69] This study proved most stimulating to my own reading of the story in "'You Just Don't Understand' (or Do You?): Jesus,

Women, and Conversation in the Fourth Gospel" (chap. 4). Fully conversant with feminist interpretation, Moore identifies two streams of thought: one, exemplified by Gail O'Day and Sandra Schneiders, accentuating the positive characterization of the Samaritan woman as an astute believer, witness, and interlocutor with a receptive and affirming Jesus; the other, much less sanguine about the liberating effects of Jesus and the Gospels, following Susan Durber's assessment that "there is no evidence at all that he [Jesus] mounted a critique of the position of women in his society" and little hope of reclaiming biblical texts—all written "by men and for men"—for women's benefit.[70] Although poles apart in their value judgments, both perspectives assume that Jesus is the superior figure and standard-setter in the Gospels. However, Moore's mix of deconstruction and feminism leads him to consider an innovative third option, "capsizing" and "drowning" oppositional hierarchies between male and female, Jesus and the woman at the well, in John 4. "What if the Samaritan woman were found to be the more enlightened partner in the dialogue from the outset? What if her insight were found to exceed that of Jesus all along?"[71] Teasing out affirmative answers to these questions, Moore attempts to demonstrate "that deconstruction, in particular, can enable us to read against the grain of the biblical authors' intentions in ways that affirm women."[72]

While I aim to use an eclectic methodology (see above), the following essays on female characters in New Testament narratives betray a much closer affinity to the approach of Gunn and Moore than to that of Witherington and Bauckham. If I had to pick a label limited to a single hyphen, I would characterize these studies as "literary-feminist." The literary strand focuses on New Testament narratives as complex, interwoven tapestries of plot, rhetoric, and characterization.[73] I consider the individual stories of selected biblical women as integral parts of the larger stories of the books in which they appear and of the still larger epic narratives of the Old Testament that form their canonical heritage. I look for connecting stitches, intertwined knots, and coordinating patterns, both inner- and inter-textu(r)al, between New Testament women and other biblical figures. But I also look for loose threads, places where women disrupt the story's tempo and set their own pace (dancing girls) and where they threaten to bust their narrative stays ("loose" ladies) and don't quite fit the standard New Testament pattern (women of "the cloth"). Thus my literary method combines both narratological and deconstructive approaches.

The feminist strand builds on common images of sewing and weaving (see chap. 7)—both positively, as a dynamic vision of feminist creativity, designing a new quilt-world of possibilities for women out of torn and worn-out materials—and negatively, as a bitter reminder of women's oppression and lack of opportunity. As Anne Sullivan, Helen Keller's brilliant teacher, so candidly remarked: "Sewing and crocheting are inventions of the devil. I'd rather break stones on the king's highway than hem a handkerchief."[74] How are women on King Jesus' highway treated in the New Testament narratives? These studies uncover a patchy path: sometimes refreshingly liberating, at other times drably conventional. The devil (pace Sullivan) lurks in the details of biblical stories, threatening to muffle women's voices and stifle women's vocations. A feminist-critical perspective helps to unravel the good from the bad, the redemptive from the destructive.

What Do Feminists Want?

"Again and again," writes bell hooks, "men tell me they have no idea what it is feminists want. I believe them. I believe in their capacity to change and grow. And I believe that if they knew more about feminism they would no longer fear it, for they would find in feminist movement the hope of their own release from the bondage of patriarchy."[75] In short, they would become "comrades in struggle":

> Visionary feminists have always understood the necessity of converting men. We know all the women in the world could become feminists but if men remain sexist our lives would still be diminished. . . . Those feminist activists who refuse to accept men as comrades in struggle—who harbor irrational fears that if men benefit in any way from feminist politics women lose—have misguidedly helped the public view feminism with suspicion and disdain. . . . It is urgent that men take up the banner of feminism and challenge patriarchy. The safety and continuation of life on the planet requires feminist conversion of men.[76]

"And what do feminists want?" asks Alice Jardine, in response to a panel of male literary critics interested "in feminism."

> If you will forgive me my directness, we do not want you to *mimic* us, to become the same as us; we don't want your pathos or your guilt; and we don't even want your admiration (even if it's nice to get it once in a while). What we want, I would even say what we need, is your *work*. We need you to get down to serious work. And like all serious work, that involves struggle and pain. . . .

You see, you have all of your work before you, not behind you. We as
feminists need your work. . . . We need you as traveling *compagnons* into
the twenty-first century.[77]

Jardine proceeds to sketch several specific tasks that male academic *compagnons* might fruitfully carry out in the service of feminist causes, including: 1) reading, teaching, and writing about women's writings; 2) supporting
and promoting women students; 3) recognizing one's scholarly "debts" to
feminist criticism in publications; 4) exposing male colleagues' neglect and
misunderstanding of feminism; and 5) "the most important, you yourselves
could stop being *reactive* to feminism and start being *active* feminists—your
cultural positionality as men allows you to!"[78]

I offer the following essays as modest tokens of my comradeship (hooks)
and companionship (Jardine) with women students and scholars on the
feminist road. As with any scholarly enterprise, they involve a healthy measure of hard work and struggle—although mostly from the comfort of my
private study. I cannot say that I have suffered or sacrificed in any apprecia-
ble way for this project. Rolling up one's sleeves to thumb through a hefty
bibliography and to type out one's thoughts strains the back a bit, but hardly
breaks it. Without question, there is much active work and struggling still to
be done—at least in the ecclesiastical and societal contexts where I operate—
to realize the full equality of women and men. Consider these studies a first
installment on a lifelong project.

Notes

---

1. As Robert Tannehill, a leading pioneer of narrative criticism, observes in the introduction to his commentary on Acts: "I do not understand narrative criticism to be an exclusive
method, requiring rejection of all other methods. Methodological pluralism is to be encouraged,
for each method will have blind spots that can only be overcome through another approach."
The Narrative Unity of Luke-Acts: A Literary Interpretation (vol. 2 *of The Acts of the Apostles;* Minneapolis: Fortress, 1990), 4. Cf. F. Scott Spencer, "Acts and Modern Literary Approaches," in *The
Book of Acts in Its Ancient Literary Setting* (ed. Bruce W. Winter and Andrew D. Clarke; vol. 1 of
The Book of Acts in Its First-Century Setting; ed. Bruce W. Winter; Grand Rapids: Eerdmans,
1993), 414.

2. Amy-Jill Levine, "Introduction," in *A Feminist Companion to Matthew* (ed. Amy-Jill
Levine; Feminist Companion to the New Testament and Early Christian Writings 1; Sheffield,
UK: Sheffield Academic Press, 2001), 14 (emphasis mine). Cf. also the assessment of Harold W.
Attridge, "'Don't Be Touching Me': Recent Feminist Scholarship on Mary Magdalene," in *A Fem-
inist Companion to John* (ed. Amy-Jill Levine; vol. 2; FCNT 5; London: Sheffield Academic Press,
2003), 165: "[F]eminist exegesis is hardly a monolithic or uniform movement. The program to

read the New Testament from a feminist perspective has produced an impressive body of literature, one that shows no signs of diminishing in intensity or scope. In the process it has produced results sometimes playful, sometimes profound, sometimes insightful and sometimes silly; in other words, it is like most other types of scholarly discourse."

3. bell hooks, *Feminism Is for Everybody: Passionate Politics* (Cambridge, MA: South End, 2000), 1; see also *Feminist Theory: From Margin to Center* (Cambridge, MA: South End, 1984).

4. Walter Wink, *When the Powers Fall: Reconciliation in the Healing of Nations* (Minneapolis: Fortress, 1998), 4. His "Powers" trilogy includes: *Naming the Powers: The Language of Power in the New Testament* (Philadelphia: Fortress, 1984); *Unmasking the Powers: The Invisible Forces that Determine Human Existence* (Philadelphia: Fortress, 1986); and *Engaging the Powers: Discernment and Resistance in a World of Domination* (Minneapolis: Fortress, 1992).

5. Pamela Thimmes, "What Makes a Feminist Reading Feminist? Another Perspective," in *Escaping Eden: New Feminist Perspectives on the Bible* (ed. Harold C. Washington, Susan Lochrie Graham, and Pamela Thimmes; New York: New York University Press, 1999), 134–35 (emphasis mine).

6. Ibid., 138 (emphasis hers).

7. On the problem of men's coopting and patronizing women's experience, see Daniel Patte, *Ethics of Biblical Interpretation* (Louisville, KY: Westminster/John Knox, 1995), 23–27; using the language of "colonizing" to make the same point, see Stephen Heath, "Male Feminism," in *Men in Feminism* (ed. Alice Jardine and Paul Smith; New York: Methuen, 1987), 1.

8. Essays from the panel were collected and published in Jardine and Smith, eds., *Men in Feminism*. Subsequent collections of essays dealing with the same issue include: Joseph A. Boone and Michael Cadden, eds., *Engendering Men: The Question of Male Feminist Criticism* (New York: Routledge, 1990); Steven P. Schacht and Doris W. Ewing, eds., *Feminism and Men: Reconstructing Gender Relations* (New York: New York University Press, 1998); Tom Digby, ed., *Men Doing Feminism* (New York: Routledge, 1998).

9. Joseph A. Boone, "Of Me(n) and Feminism: Who(se) Is the Sex That Writes?" in Boone and Cadden, eds., *Engendering Men*, 12 (emphasis his).

10. Building on the work of bell hooks (*Feminism Is for Everybody*, 7–12), Elisabeth Schüssler Fiorenza calls for a renewed emphasis on consciousness-raising (or "conscientization," as she prefers) regarding gender realities and inequities: "Like bell hooks, I envision the revitalization of revolutionary consciousness-raising in and through the creation of feminist wisdom/Wisdom groups that come together to engage in biblical interpretation as a spiritual practice of conscientization, conversion, and commitment to walking in Wisdom's ways of justice." *Wisdom Ways: Introducing Feminist Biblical Interpretation* (Maryknoll, NY: Orbis, 2001), 17; also see pp. 15–17, 93–98, 151–61.

11. As bell hooks forcefully argues: "Feminist consciousness-raising for males is as essential to revolutionary movement as female groups. . . . Males of all ages need settings where their resistance to sexism is affirmed and valued. Without males as allies in struggle feminist movement will not progress" (*Feminism Is for Everybody*, 11–12). "Until men share equal responsibility for struggling to end sexism, feminist movement will reflect the very sexist contradiction we wish to eradicate. Separatist ideology encourages us to believe that women alone can make feminist revolution—we cannot. Since men are the primary agents maintaining and supporting sexism and sexist oppression, they can be successfully eradicated only if men are compelled to assume responsibility for transforming their consciousness and the consciousness of society as a whole." "Men: Comrades in Struggle," in Schacht and Ewing, eds., *Feminism and Men*, 278; the entire article, pp. 265–79, is reprinted from chap. 15 of hooks, *Feminist Theory*.

12. Cf. Patte, *Ethics of Biblical Interpretation*, 54, 70n44.

13. See the helpful surveys of feminist biblical scholarship in Carolyn Osiek, "The Feminist and the Bible: Hermeneutical Alternatives," in *Feminist Perspectives on Biblical Scholarship* (ed. Adela Yarbro Collins; Atlanta: Scholars Press, 1985), 93–105; Pamela J. Milne, "Feminist Interpretations of the Bible: Then and Now," *Bible Review* (October 1992): 38–43, 52–55; Janice

Capel Anderson, "Mapping Feminist Biblical Criticism: The American Scene, 1983–1990," in *Critical Review of Books in Religion* (ed. Eldon Jay Epp; Atlanta: Scholars Press, 1991), 21–44; and Yvonne Sherwood, "Feminist Scholarship," in *The Oxford Illustrated History of the Bible* (ed. John Rogerson; Oxford: Oxford University Press, 2001), 296–315.

14. Cullen Murphy, *The Word According to Eve: Women and the Bible in Ancient Times and Our Own* (Boston: Houghton Mifflin, 1998); see also his "Women and the Bible," *The Atlantic Monthly,* August 1993, 39–63.

15. Murphy, *Word According to Eve,* xiii.

16. Murphy is Roman Catholic. My background is Southern Baptist, although I currently teach in a "moderate" Baptist seminary with ties to the Cooperative Baptist Fellowship, Alliance of Baptists, Baptist World Alliance, and other groups. The revised "Baptist Faith and Message," adopted by the Southern Baptist Convention on June 14, 2000, added specific statements in its sections on "Church" and "Family" restricting the role of women: "While both men and women are gifted for service in the church, the office of pastor is limited to men as qualified by Scripture" (Section VI. The Church). "A wife is to submit herself graciously to the servant leadership of her husband even as the church willingly submits to the headship of Christ" (Section XVIII. The Family).

17. Murphy, *Word According to Eve,* xi, identifies feminism as "the Bible's fifth intellectual revolution," following the formation of Israel and the Hebrew Bible, the birth of the Christian testament, the Reformation, and the Enlightenment. He also cites a conversation with theologian David Tracy, who affirmed feminism's impact on religious thought as "the next intellectual revolution."

18. The section on "Contemporary Interpretation" in the recent *Oxford Illustrated History of the Bible* (pp. 293–355) contains four articles: one on "Feminist Scholarship" grouped with three on "Liberation Theology" in different regions (Latin America, Africa, and Europe); in *The Human Being: Jesus and the Enigma of the Son of Man* (Minneapolis: Fortress, 2002), 10, Walter Wink regards "efforts to construct a new, liberating Jesus-myth" as "the most important theological enterprise since the Protestant Reformation, urgently to be pursued"; and an important series on "The Bible and Liberation," edited by Norman K. Gottwald and Richard A. Horsley for Orbis Books, includes monographs on feminist interpretation with other studies of a "liberated Bible."

19. The phrase is from Jack Miles's blurb on the back jacket of Murphy's book. Miles applauds Murphy's "judicious pick of the most interesting feminist Bible scholars now writing, plus Jaroslav Pelikan as (golden) token male."

20. Jaroslav Pelikan, *Mary through the Centuries: Her Place in the History of Culture* (New Haven: Yale University Press, 1996); Murphy, *Word According to Eve,* 165–71.

21. See, e.g., Leonard Swidler, "Jesus Was a Feminist," *Catholic World* (January 1971): 177–83; *Women in Judaism: The Status of Women in Formative Judaism* (Metuchen, NJ: Scarecrow, 1976); *Biblical Affirmations of Woman* (Philadelphia: Westminster, 1979); *Yeshua: A Model for Moderns* (Kansas City: Sheed & Ward, 1988).

22. Murphy, *Word According to Eve,* 142.

23. Ben Witherington III, *Women in the Ministry of Jesus: A Study of Jesus' Attitudes to Women and Their Roles as Reflected in His Earthly Life* (Society for New Testament Studies 51; Cambridge, UK: Cambridge University Press, 1984) *Women in the Earliest Churches* (SNTSMS 58; Cambridge, UK: Cambridge University Press, 1988).

24. Ben Witherington III, "On the Road with Mary Magdalene, Joanna, Susanna, and Other Disciples—Luke 8.1–3," *ZNW* 70 (1979): 243–48; repr. pages 133–39 in *A Feminist Companion to Luke* (ed. Amy-Jill Levine; FCNT 3; London: Sheffield Academic Press, 2002). The citation is from p. 133.

25. Ben Witherington III, "Women, New Testament," *Anchor Bible Dictionary,* vol. 6 (ed. D. N. Freedman; 6 vols.; New York: Doubleday 1992), 957–61.

26. Phyllis A. Bird, "Women, Old Testament," *ABD* 6:951–57.

27. Witherington, "Women, New Testament," 960 (emphasis his).

28. Ibid., 957.

29. See the critique of Witherington in Ross Shepard Kraemer, "Jewish Women and Christian Origins: Some Caveats," in *Women and Christian Origins* (ed. Ross Shepard Kraemer and Mary Rose D'Angelo; New York: Oxford University Press, 1999), 35–49; Murphy, *Word According to Eve*, 142–43.

30. Amy-Jill Levine, "Introduction," in *A Feminist Companion to Luke*, 12.

31. Richard Bauckham, *Gospel Women: Studies of the Named Women in the Gospels* (Grand Rapids: Eerdmans, 2002).

32. Ibid., 109–202.

33. Ibid., xviii.

34. Ibid., xviii.

35. Ibid., xii–xiii, 1–46, 51–55.

36. Ibid., xii. Key works by Tal Ilan include: *Jewish Women in Greco-Roman Palestine* (Peabody, MA: Hendrickson, 1995); *Integrating Women into Second Temple History* (Peabody, MA: Hendrickson, 1999).

37. Bauckham, *Gospel Women*, xv–xvii.

38. Ibid., xv.

39. Krister Stendahl, "Ancient Scripture in the Modern World," in *Scripture in the Jewish and Christian Traditions: Authority, Interpretation, Relevance* (ed. Frederick E. Greenspahn; Nashville, TN: Abingdon, 1982), 202–14.

40. Bauckham, *Gospel Women*, 3. The Brink novel (discussed on pp. 1–3) is *The Wall of the Plague* (New York: Summit, 1984). The author is a male Afrikaner who narrates in the first-person voice of a mixed-race South African woman.

41. Bauckham, *Gospel Women*, 13.

42. Ibid., xix–xx.

43. Ibid., xx, 199–202.

44. "The book of Ruth is not polemical. Its stance toward men is not adversarial or even satirical. . . . The parallel between the opening (1:1–2) and the closing of the book, neither of which reflects the gynocentric perspective of the narrative between them, is valid so far as it goes, but 'mocking' is not true to the tone of Ruth" (Ibid., 10–11).

45. A brief general reference to Mary appears in Luke 11:27, as an anonymous woman in the crowd cries out to Jesus: "Blessed is the womb that bore you and the breasts that nursed you!" But Jesus quickly neutralizes this maternal privilege in the next verse: "Blessed rather are those who hear the word of God and obey it" (11:28). Mary also pops up with "certain women" in Acts 1:14, but plays no role thereafter in Luke's story of the early church.

46. See Marcia Falk, *Love Lyrics from the Bible: The Song of Songs. A New Translation* (New York: HarperCollins, 1993), xiii–xxii.

47. See Phyllis Trible, *God and the Rhetoric of Sexuality* (Overtures to Biblical Theology; Philadelphia: Fortress, 1978), 144–65.

48. Sparked by feminist perspectives, Marc Brettler describes his new awareness of and struggle with this more sinister side of Song of Songs in "On Becoming a Male Feminist Bible Scholar," *Bible Review* (April 1994): 45.

49. Ibid., 44.

50. Ibid., 45.

51. My revised dissertation was published as *The Portrait of Philip in Acts: A Study of Roles and Relations* (Journal for the Study of the New Testament: Supplement Series 67; Sheffield, UK: Sheffield Academic Press, 1992). My further study of the Ethiopian eunuch is "The Ethiopian Eunuch and His Bible: A Social-Science Analysis," *Biblical Theology Bulletin* 22 (1992): 155–65.

52. Turid Karlsen Seim, *The Double Message: Patterns of Gender in Luke and Acts* (Nashville, TN: Abingdon; Edinburgh, UK: T and T Clark, 1994).

53. Gunn's trailblazing forays into biblical "narrative criticism" include: *The Story of King David: Genre and Interpretation* (Journal for the Study of the Old Testament: Supplement Series 6; Sheffield, UK: JSOT, 1978); *The Fate of King Saul: An Interpretation of a Biblical Story* (JSOTSup 14; Sheffield, UK: JSOT, 1980); "Joshua and Judges," in *The Literary Guide to the Bible* (ed. Robert Alter and Frank Kermode; Cambridge, MA: Harvard University Press, 1987), 102–21; "Narrative Criticism," in *To Each Its Own Meaning: An Introduction to Biblical Criticisms and Their Application* (ed. Steven L. McKenzie and Stephen R. Haynes; Louisville, KY: Westminster/John Knox, 1993), 171–95.

54. Gunn recounts his hermeneutical pilgrimage in a refreshingly honest and insightful article: "Reflections on David," in *A Feminist Companion to Reading the Bible: Approaches, Methods, Strategies* (ed. Athalya Brenner and Carole Fontaine; Sheffield, UK: Sheffield Academic Press, 1997), 548–66.

55. Phyllis Trible, ed., "The Effects of Women's Studies on Biblical Studies," JSOT 22 (1982), 3–71.

56. Gunn, "Reflections on David," 553.

57. Ibid., 559.

58. Ibid., 550–53.

59. Ibid., 555.

60. Ibid., 560.

61. Danna Nolan Fewell and David M. Gunn, *Compromising Redemption: Relating Characters in the Book of Ruth* (Literary Currents in Biblical Interpretation; Louisville, KY: Westminster/John Knox, 1990); *Gender, Power, and Promise: The Subject of the Bible's First Story* (Nashville, TN: Abingdon, 1993); *Narrative in the Hebrew Bible* (Oxford Bible Series; Oxford: Oxford University Press, 1993).

62. I look forward to my own fruitful scholarly exchange with Amy-Jill Levine on *The Women Who Walked with Jesus,* forthcoming from University of South Carolina Press, 2006.

63. Gunn, "Reflections on David," 560.

64. Andrew Ross, "No Question of Silence," in Jardine and Smith, eds., *Men In Feminism,* 86 (emphasis his); see also Boone, "Of Me(n) and Feminism," 22.

65. To name a few leading feminist New Testament scholars currently supervising doctoral students at prominent institutions: Schüssler Fiorenza at Harvard; Levine at Vanderbilt; Kraemer at Brown; O'Day at Emory; Beverly Roberts Gaventa at Princeton; and Carolyn Osiek at TCU/Brite Divinity School.

66. Janice Capel Anderson and Stephen D. Moore, eds., *Mark and Method: New Approaches in Biblical Studies* (Minneapolis: Fortress, 1992). "Introduction: The Lives of Mark" appears on pp. 1–22; Moore's article on "Deconstructive Criticism: The Gospel of the Mark" appears on pp. 84–102, followed by Anderson's study of "Feminist Criticism: The Dancing Daughter" on pp. 103–34. More recently, Anderson and Moore have collaborated on the other side of gender studies, dealing with issues of masculinity. See, e.g., their "Taking It Like A Man: Masculinity and 4 Maccabees," *Journal of Biblical Literature* 117 (1998): 249–73; and "'O Man, Who Art Thou . . . ?': Masculinity Studies and New Testament Studies" and "Matthew and Masculinity" in *New Testament Masculinities* (ed. Stephen D. Moore and Janice Capel Anderson; Semeia Studies; Atlanta: SBL, 2003), 1–42, 67–91. I draw on these masculinity studies in the last part of chap. 5.

67. Anderson and Moore, "Introduction," 12–16.

68. Ibid., 14.

69. Stephen D. Moore, *Poststructuralism and the New Testament: Derrida and Foucault at the Foot of the Cross* (Minneapolis: Fortress, 1994), 43–64.

70. Ibid., 46–52; the Durber citation on p. 51 derives from her "The Female Reader of the Parables of the Lost," *JSNT* 45 (1992): 59–60.

71. Moore, *Poststructuralism,* 50.

72. Ibid., 52.

73. See Joanna Dewey, "Mark as Interwoven Tapestry: Forecasts and Echoes for a Listening Audience," *Catholic Biblical Quarterly* 53 (1991): 221–36; Vernon K. Robbins, *The Tapestry of Early Christian Discourse: Rhetoric, Society, and Ideology* (London: Routledge, 1996); *Exploring the Texture of Texts: A Guide to Socio-Rhetorical Interpretation* (Valley Forge, PA: Trinity Press International, 1996).

74. Cited by Cynthia Ozick, "What Helen Keller Saw: The Making of a Writer," *The New Yorker,* June 16 and June 23, 2003, 189.

75. hooks, *Feminism Is for Everybody,* ix.

76. Ibid., 115–16; see also 10–12, 67–71; and "Men: Comrades in Struggle," in Schacht and Ewing, eds., *Feminism and Men,* 265–79.

77. Alice Jardine, "Men in Feminism: Odor di Uomo Or Compagnons de Route?" in Jardine and Smith, eds., *Men and Feminism,* 60–61 (emphasis hers).

78. These are similar to four "pathways for men to become feminist" sketched by Schacht and Ewing, "Many Paths of Feminism," in Schacht and Ewing, eds., *Feminism and Men,* 132–38.

CHAPTER 2

Those Riotous—yet Righteous—
Foremothers of Jesus:
Exploring Matthew's Comic Genealogy

Two centuries ago, a German romantic poet named Friedrich von Sallet dubbed biblical genealogies, like that which Matthew begins his story of Jesus, as "this barren page [dry leaf, *dürre Blatt*] in the Holy Book"—a candid assessment shared in thought, if not word, by countless Bible readers, both devout and indifferent.[1] What can be gained from plowing through a long list of distant ancestors except perhaps some impish delight in pronouncing tongue twisters like Jehoshaphat and Zerubbabel without stumbling? At least the Priestly redactors of the Torah had the good sense to open with a stirring hymn exalting God's creation, followed by intriguing tales of rebellion and fratricide, before introducing a genealogy in Gen 5.

But maybe Matthew's genesis is not as arid as it appears. For one thing, with all that "begetting" going on, it can hardly be described as "barren." But more importantly, Matthew creates interest by linking Jesus with some interesting figures from Israel's past. While we might pass over Jehoshaphat and Zerubbabel without notice, epic heroes like Abraham and David are not easily ignored. And then, among this great host of patriarchs, four foremothers randomly appear (1:3, 5–6). The tantalizing question, posed by Raymond Brown in uncharacteristically colloquial style, begs for an answer: "Why bring on the ladies?"[2] Or better put, "Why bring on *these* ladies?"—Tamar, Rahab, Ruth, and the wife of Uriah.

The standard answers are well known and worn thin. First, although sin and shame swirl around the situations involving these women, they themselves are not remembered, as many have suggested, as *sinners*. Quite the contrary, starting with Judah's final assessment of Tamar—"She is more in the right than I" (Gen 38:26)—the women are all respected for their righteous actions.[3] If Matthew's genealogy features a prototypical evildoer to set the stage for Jesus' redemptive mission, fore*father* Manasseh—the worst king Judah ever had (for fifty plus years!)—fits the bill better than any of the women.[4] Second, although the stories surrounding these women are rather strange, it is not certain that the women themselves are all *strangers* (foreigners, non-Jews): Rahab the Canaanite and Ruth the Moabite, yes (although Jewish tradition regards them as proselytes, fully incorporated into the covenant);[5] Tamar (Aramean?) and Bathsheba (Hittite?), maybe, but we can't be sure.[6] Again, if Matthew needs genealogical warrant for the church's outreach to Gentiles, Abraham is foundation enough, considering God's promise to bless all peoples of the earth through him.[7]

A third approach focuses on the "irregular," "anomalous," or even "scandalous" nature of the four women's stories (scandalous in the sense of provocative and unconventional, not lascivious and immoral), preparing the way for the most extraordinary case of all—Mary's nonsexual conception of Jesus out of wedlock. While this perspective isolates an important common thread among Jesus' maternal ancestors cited by Matthew, it doesn't go far enough. To call the episodes surrounding Tamar, Rahab, Ruth, and the wife of Uriah "irregular" is a gross understatement (see Gen 38:1–30; Josh 2:1–24; Ruth 1–4; 2 Sam 11:1–26; 1 Kgs 1:11–37; 2:13–25). They are among the wildest, weirdest incidents depicted anywhere in the Bible—in fact, they border on the bizarre; and for those with eyes to see and ears to hear, unfettered by puritanical presumptions concerning the proper tone and subject matter of holy writ, they are downright hilarious. These are riotous as well as righteous women.

The purpose of this study is to explore the comic features of these women's stories and the link between comedy and piety in Matthew's gospel that they portend. An immediate problem is a framework for defining humor. Scholars readily acknowledge what everybody already knows—how slippery and subjective humor is. Cue a laugh track and someone's bound to respond, "What's so funny about that?"—to which another answers amid bouts of reverie, "Oh come on, that's a hoot!" Add the component of cultural relativity (societies often differ on comedic conventions), and the matter becomes even more complicated.[8] Humor is in the eye of the beholder, the ear of the auditor. Still, we need some heuristic parameters. We all admit some things *aren't* funny, even if we don't agree on what those things are.

Catching the Eel: Detecting Humor in the Bible

Philosophers and literary critics from ancient times, along with social scientists, physicians, theologians, and biblical scholars more recently,[9] have tried to get a tentative handle, if not a firm grasp, on this "slippery eel" of humor and laughter.[10] Some have concentrated on stock comic characters. Ovid, for example, observed that the popularity of the Greek comic playwright Menander would persist "as long as tricky slave, hard father, treacherous bawd, and wheedling harlot shall be found."[11] Many others could be added to the list. Our Old Testament ancestral narratives do feature a couple of sneaky prostitutes (Rahab, Tamar?) and one rather cold and callous father (Judah). But this identification doesn't get us very far. Not all cunning courtesans are comic (at the end of the day, Samson was not amused by Delilah [Judg 16]) and not all firm fathers are funny (just ask Jephthah's daughter [Judg 11]).

Another approach attempts to pinpoint typically humorous content, subject matter, or plot lines. Hebrew Bible critic Francis Landy suggests "the content of humour is frequently terrible, centered around man's obsessive preoccupations, sexual failure and fear of death."[12] We laugh about other things, too, but sex and death are indeed fertile territories for comedy (we laugh to keep from crying). As it happens, these elements feature prominently in all four of our stories, but that doesn't automatically make them funny. Landy puts it right—"sex and death are always *potentially* laughable."[13] It all depends on how these subjects are treated—which leads us to consider more general characteristics of comedic discourse.

What elements tend to characterize funny stories? In the *Anchor Bible Dictionary* article on "Humor and Wit," Edward Greenstein, drawing on "a common theory," highlights "three factors [that] together occasion humor: a sense of the incongruous, a relaxed or lightheaded mood or attitude, and an effect of suddenness or surprise."[14] He then exposes each of these characteristics in the Gen 18 scene where Sarah laughs at the preposterous prospect that she will give birth: 1) the incongruity comes in the ridiculous notion that a barren, nonagenarian woman might get pregnant; 2) the happy mood is associated with the feast prepared for Abraham's mysterious three visitors who promise that Sarah will produce a son; and 3) the surprise factor emerges with both Sarah's accidental hearing of the birth news and the Lord's hearing her laughter, which she supposedly kept "to herself."[15]

I want to adapt these three elements slightly and add four others to provide a fuller framework for detecting humor in the Bible, starting with Sarah's case and then moving to the four women in Matthew's genealogy. The preliminary focus on Sarah sets up a contrastive as well as a comparative model, because in fact Matthew does *not* highlight Sarah (it's all Abraham) among the ancestresses of Jesus. Is there something about the four fore- mothers' laughable situations—distinct from Sarah's—that suits Matthew's purpose?

In a word, the first humorous element—indeed, the dominant charac- teristic noted by contemporary critics—is *incongruity*. Humor arises in the ironic cracks of a narrative where something doesn't fit conventional expec- tations of how life works—or, in Sarah's case, how life starts.[16] Second is the element of *festivity*, which includes not only the amusement of eating and drinking stressed by Greenstein, but also the familiar climax of the happy ending.[17] Break out the champagne: Abraham and Sarah are finally going to have a son. All's well that ends well. The third feature is *spontaneity*, the pre- sentation of some incongruous, joyous bit of news in a strikingly sudden, unexpected fashion. A prediction of her own fertility was the last thing Sarah expected to hear while eavesdropping on her husband and visitors' conversation.

Fourth, expanding beyond Greenstein, is the element of *ingenuity*. We are typically diverted by witty speech or clever schemes played out in a story. As is well known, the narratives surrounding the birth of Isaac repeatedly pun on the word for "laughter." Here *God* functions as the shrewd orchestra- tor of the comic routine, divining Sarah's secret chuckle ("Oh yes, you did laugh!" Gen 18:15) and dramatically having the last laugh by causing Sarah to conceive and bear *Yitzchaq*, the embodiment of laughter (21:1–7).

The fifth comic marker is *inferiority*, the flip side of the so-called "supe- riority theory" of humor advanced by thinkers from Plato to Hobbes to Freud.[18] In Hobbes's terms, we laugh as an expression of the "sudden glory" we feel at the expense of "some deformed thing in another" that makes us look good in comparison.[19] Humor trades on our base human tendency toward *schadenfreude*. Accordingly, in humorous tales someone normally plays the fool, the butt of the joke, the one delightfully outmaneuvered by smart characters and smug readers. In Sarah's saga, the laughing woman plays the fool whom we instinctively laugh at, because, of course, we want to align ourselves with God. How silly, even shameful, of Sarah not to believe in God's power.

Sixth, I borrow from Henri Bergson the notion of *inelasticity*. Bergson theorizes that we especially laugh at people who are trapped in a box of "*mechanical inelasticity*, just where we would expect to find the wide-awake adaptability and the living pliableness of a human being."[20] At our best, we are flexible, innovative creatures. Thus, when people are portrayed as unthinking machines or automatons, we find them odd, out of kilter, freakishly funny—

eliciting our nervous laughter. In short, Bergson concludes: "rigidity is the comic, and laughter is its corrective."[21] In the Genesis story, Sarah again represents the comic character: this time the inflexible figure caught in the rut of biological mechanics (old ladies don't normally have babies), but not beyond the realm of God's creative possibilities. Sarah laughs at God in mocking disbelief. We laugh at Sarah in hopeful disavowal of her closed mind as well as womb.

The seventh and final characteristic of comic narratives is *imperceptibility* or hiddenness. Infants squeal with delight at that most primitive of all games, peek-a-boo; older kids continue this comic tradition in their adventures of hide-and-seek, and children of all ages through adulthood laugh with glee over the now-you-see-it-now-you-don't legerdemain of master illusionists. Philosopher John Morreall notes that such responses are more involuntary-reflex reactions to a sudden perceptual change than a conscious, cognitive realization of a humorous situation.[22] That may be true, but this instinctive impulse to laugh at lost-and-found phenomena carries over into more discerning amusement over matters hidden and revealed. Thus comic stories throughout the ages exploit characters in disguise or otherwise concealed from the view of other characters, to the delight of knowing readers. We watch and listen with pleasure as the hidden Sarah overhears the incredible birth announcement and as the hidden God, from Sarah's viewpoint, suddenly exposes her private thoughts.

Tracking Jesus' Riotous Foremothers

We turn now to apply the comic characteristics of Sarah's story to the stories of Jesus' maternal ancestors highlighted by Matthew.

TAMAR

Following the tragic, premature deaths of Tamar's first two husbands (Judah's eldest sons), her subsequent isolation as a childless widow, as well as Judah's loss of his own wife, comedy breaks through and ultimately triumphs (Gen 38). All the elements are in place. *Incongruity* emerges as Tamar breaks out of her widow's role to seduce her father-in-law, even as the product of their "irregular" union (Perez) breaches the womb to squirt past his twin brother (Zerah).[23] Still, Judah eventually concedes Tamar's higher righteousness (38:26): she does what she has to do to survive. Since Judah balked at giving a third son to Tamar, as levirate law demanded, she must take matters into her own hands. She waits for a *festive* occasion. After a period of mourning his deceased wife, Judah heads to the annual sheep-shearing festival in Timnah, with his good Canaanite friend Hirah, for some much-needed diversion (38:12–13).[24] Tamar positions herself along the road to Timnah *disguised* behind a veil (whatever else she is wearing—or not wearing—is anybody's guess).[25] Judah takes the bait and unwittingly impregnates his daughter-in-law. Tamar has thus *ingeniously* compelled Judah to provide her with progeny. But the most clever—and comic—move comes with her securing Judah's signet, cord, and staff—his driver's license and credit cards, as Alter quips, symbols of his patriarchal authority[26]—and producing them *spontaneously* at the precise moment Judah sentences her to be burned to death (38:16–26).

By his own admission, Judah fits the part of the *inferior* fool. Whether he thought Tamar was a common whore (*zonah*) or cult prostitute (*qedeshah*),[27] the fact remains that he has shamefully "uncovered the nakedness of his daughter-in-law," in violation of the Holiness Code (Lev 18:15). The irony of Judah's blunder intensifies in light of his recent scheme to sell brother Joseph into slavery and dupe father Jacob—with the aid of a doctored garment[28]—into believing Joseph had died. He now receives his comeuppance for abusing both Joseph and Tamar as the latter tricks him with her own masquerade. Judah also exemplifies Bergson's characteristic of *inelasticity,* as he consistently refuses to entertain alternative judgments about Tamar until forced to do so. In his rigid viewpoint, Tamar had to be responsible for killing his first two sons (even though the narrative indicates that "the Lord put [them] to death," 38:7, 10), and her pregnancy must mean that she had become irreparably defiled.[29]

While Tamar's tale matches all seven comic elements found in Sarah's story, their particular roles are markedly different. Whereas Sarah portrays the surprised, set-in-her-ways fool discomfited by the controlling deity, Tamar shines as the shrewd protagonist, thoroughly upstaging the bungling patriarch Judah, all the while *God remains hidden*—concealed behind his own veil of anonymity.

RAHAB

Next we consider Rahab's story (Josh 2:1–24; cf. 6:17–25), another tale riddled with *incongruity* revolving around a most unlikely hero with three strikes against her, as Fewell and Gunn observe: Rahab is woman, foreigner, and prostitute (a full-time professional, not a one-night pretender, like Tamar).[30] Isn't it funny how the Bible depicts such a triple threat as a paragon of faith in action? Though battle looms, the immediate situation is *festive,* even frivolous. Diverted from their assigned mission, the two young male spies[31] come to Jericho to have a good time. They seem more interested in recreation than reconnaissance, indulgence than intelligence. Instructed by Joshua, "Go, view the land, especially Jericho," the pair of secret agents made a beeline for the "red lamp district,"[32] where they "entered the house of a prostitute whose name was Rahab, and spent the night there" (2:1)—not exactly the expedition Joshua had intended. Pious suggestions that a brothel was a perfect place to get gossip or a good night's sleep without being detected seem flimsy and naïve. (As Josephus tells it, Rahab ran a sort of "holiday inn" to which the spies retired after a hard day of inspecting the city—wishful thinking with scant textual support.[33]) The fact is, our "heroes" ask no questions, gain no information, and find themselves suddenly summoned by the king of Jericho who knows exactly where they are. They get caught, rather literally it seems, with their pants down.[34]

But have no fear: a woman shall save them.[35] Rahab steps in as a remarkable model of *spontaneity, ingenuity,* and *imperceptibility.* Without skipping a beat, she springs into action, hiding the spies under a rooftop flax stack and cleverly misdirecting the king's messengers: "True, the men *came* to me [note the sexual innuendo],[36] but I did not know where they came from . . . [and] where the men went I do not know" (2:4). The undercover hijinks continue, as Rahab, after dispatching the messengers, returns to the roof "before [the spies] went to sleep" (there's a cute picture: two guys lying together in the hay), strikes a deal with them, arranges for their escape, and finally instructs them to *hide* in the hill country for three days until the coast is clear (2:8–16). Rahab's running the show. She seems much more adept at the spy business than Joshua's agents. Indeed, the two putative spies come off as the *inferior* and *inelastic* dolts in the story (along with the king of Jericho and his messengers, deceived by Rahab and destined for destruction). Apart from indulging base sexual desires in the midst of a holy military campaign (Samson will show the same weakness)[37] and functioning as hapless "marionettes"[38] driven by Rahab's will and dangling from her window, when the two men finally assert themselves as spies and soldiers, they do so in a ridiculously pedantic and pontificating manner. Following Rahab's remarkable confession of faith in the God of Israel, her reasonable plea for mercy during the upcoming siege, and her courageous engineering of the spies' escape, the two men, apparently shouting up at Rahab from outside the wall, lay down three strict conditions for sparing her and her family: 1) "Tie this crimson cord in the window"; 2) keep all your relatives indoors; and 3) (repeating what they had said before climbing down the wall) don't tell anyone "this business of ours" (which business, we might ask—the spying or the whoring?) (2:17–20). Instead of spontaneously responding to Rahab with deep gratitude and commitment—they owe her their lives, after all—they mechanically impose a set of rules and regulations in a pathetic last-ditch effort to reclaim some of the dignity and authority they've forfeited throughout the story. They might have even hoped Rahab would slip up so they would no longer be indebted to a Canaanite prostitute.[39]

For those attuned to the ironic humor of the narrative, Rahab remains the bold and wise protagonist; Joshua's spies and the king of Jericho's messengers are the fools. And, once again, Rahab's heroics, like Tamar's, are of *her own making.* The Lord God, whose dramatic displays of power permeate the battle scenes of Joshua, takes a backseat on this occasion while Rahab drives the plot.

RUTH

Third, we come to the story of Ruth in the book that bears her name. Phyllis Trible identifies the story as "a human comedy," largely because "beginning in deepest despair [it works] its way to wholeness and well-being."[40] However, Ruth evinces many other comic features besides a happy ending. *Incongruity* emerges once again, similar to that featured in the two previous stories. As with Rahab, Ruth's suspicious foreign status makes her a highly atypical heroine. Worse than being a Canaanite, Ruth is a *Moabite woman,* which recalls in the biblical record nothing but bad memories of incest (the original Moab, Gen 19:30–38), immorality, and idolatry (the Baal-Peor incident, Num 25:1–5).[41] Deuteronomic law flatly excluded Moabites from the covenant community (23:3). Like Tamar, who is explicitly remembered in Ruth 4:12, Ruth is a childless widow who secures progeny by dressing up and seducing a reluctant elderly male relative.[42] Again, Ruth is more admired than admonished for her trickery, evoking laughter rather than lament.

Much of the humor in Ruth focuses on the famous threshing-floor "bed-trick"[43] in chap. 3. *Festivity* and *spontaneity* certainly characterize the scene. Instead of sheep shearing, it's barley baling, but whatever the task, Boaz tops the day off with plenty of refreshment and crashes in a "contented" stupor at the edge of the grain pile (3:2–7). Unlike Judah, who seemed to be looking for female companionship, the groggy Boaz is thoroughly "startled" at midnight by a woman, of all things, lying at his feet, of all places. Ruth has come to Boaz "stealthily" or *imperceptibly,* masked in her finest clothing and make-up, and initiating a chain of covert—that is, under-cover and cover-over—operations (3:3, 7–8). It's not entirely clear what Ruth bares—her body (on linguistic grounds, van Wolde argues for the possibility of a "midnight striptease")[44] or Boaz's feet; but either way, there are sexual implications, consistent with the provocative language of "knowing," "lying," "coming," and "spreading over" throughout the narrative.[45] The scene climaxes with Ruth's proposal that Boaz cover her with his cloak—that is, that they both get undercover(s) together (3:9). What precisely happens here is left to the imagination, but enough happens that Boaz continues the cloak-and-dagger routine by insisting that Ruth stay the night but leave early before breakfast so as not to rouse suspicion: "It must not be *known* that the woman *came* to the threshing floor"—and spent the whole night (3:13–14). I guess not!

More than just a pretty face who plays "footsy" with Boaz, Ruth appears as a wise, courageous woman, an *ingenious* initiator. The plan starts with Naomi, but Ruth carries it out and takes it further. She ventures out at night by herself—a brazen move for a single woman[46]—lies at Boaz's feet, and instead of waiting for Boaz to tell her what to do, as Naomi had instructed, Ruth tells Boaz what to do ("spread your cloak over your servant," 3:9), clev-erly echoing Boaz's own words, which he had spoken to her earlier in the field: "May you have a full reward from the Lord, the God of Israel, under whose wings [or cloak] you have come for refuge" (2:12). Ruth both chal-lenges and entices Boaz to put his faith into action, to do God's will, to be the human agent of divine redemption.

Boaz doesn't fully fit the role of the embarrassed fool meriting mockery (the *inferiority* factor). He may be a little slow to respond and need to be "tricked" into commitment—not exactly a tower of "strength" befitting his name[47]—but his reluctance is not born of bitter malice against Ruth or obstinate violation of levirate law, as we found with Judah and Tamar. Boaz is not Ruth's brother-in-law, father-in-law, or even closest kinsman; he has no obligation here, no axe to grind.[48] But Boaz may be viewed as an amusing example of *inelasticity* with his insistence on the rigmarole of the strange sandal ceremony with the next-of-kin. It's not clear why this is necessary: Ruth and Boaz are both legally free, it seems, to marry whom they please. Why not embrace the passionate bond struck on the threshing floor? Why reduce legitimate love to a bureaucratic transaction (even in a patriarchal world, love was a powerful force: remember Jacob's love for Rachel)?[49] Could it be that Boaz is having second thoughts about Ruth and needs some public reassurance of propriety? Could wanting "all the assembly of my people [to] know that you [Ruth] are a *worthy woman*" (3:11) mask residual traces of

Boaz's own inflexible, intolerant assessment of Moabite women? Old preju-
dices die hard.

In contrast to Sarah, Ruth continues the Tamar-Rahab line of clever,
active women who take care of themselves and fulfill God's plan, but with little help from God himself. The book of Ruth invokes the Lord's name a good
bit, but Ruth (and Naomi) do most of the work—*until* the closing verses
delineating the genealogy of David. Ruth suddenly becomes—very much
like Sarah—the passive recipient (literally, the receptacle) of divine intervention: "*the Lord made her conceive,* and she bore a son" (4:13).[50] And, retro-
spectively, the Lord is also given a more active role in Tamar's situation:
"through the children that *the Lord will give you* by this young woman, may
your house be like the house of Perez, whom Tamar bore to Judah" (4:12).

BATHSHEBA

Finally we come to the story of Bathsheba, which may seem the least likely to
fit the comic genre. The main incident that springs to mind is doubtless
David's notorious seizure[51] and insemination of the wife of Uriah the Hittite.
Although the scene where David futilely plies Uriah with drink to get him to
go home to Bathsheba (a ploy to cover up David's paternity of her unborn
child) provides almost farcical comic relief between the horrors of adultery/
rape and murder (2 Sam 11:6–13), the story is not a funny one overall and
for Bathsheba in particular. As Adele Berlin observes, Bathsheba the victim is
hardly acknowledged at all: "Throughout the entire story the narrator has
purposely subordinated the character of Bathsheba. He has ignored her feelings and given the barest notice of her actions. . . . All this leads us to view
Bathsheba as a complete non-person. She is not even a minor character, but
simply part of the plot."[52] Quite a contrast to Tamar, Rahab, and Ruth. But
that is not the end of Bathsheba's story. Although often forgotten in popular
interpretation, she reemerges in the opening two chapters of 1 Kings as a
major player in Solomon's succession to David's throne. And here is where
the humor comes in, beginning with the delicious *incongruity* of Bathsheba's
remarkable transformation in the Samuel-Kings saga: the abused, aban-
doned "non-person" becomes the mighty, manipulative queen mother.[53]

Two scenes further the comic plot: 1) Solomon's appointment over
brother Adonijah and 2) his assassination of Adonijah. Although in both
cases Bathsheba acts at the behest of male initiators, she *ingeniously* impro-
vises and holds her own,[54] exposing the foolish *inferiority* of Adonijah, in
particular, but also, the feeble King David. The once youthful and vigorous

ruler has become both impotent and ignorant in his old age. The narrative accentuates two vital matters David *does not know*: sexually, he "does not know" the beautiful young virgin, Abishag, warming his bed; and politically, he "does not know" that Adonijah has already usurped the throne (1 Kgs 1:1–4, 11). Bathsheba exploits this situation aided by the prophet Nathan. Nathan makes the first move, suggesting that Bathsheba present herself before David, with the subtle reminder, "Did you not, my lord the king, swear to your servant, saying: Your son Solomon shall succeed me as king, and he shall sit on my throne? Why then is Adonijah king?" (1:12). Bathsheba takes up Nathan's plan but boldly shifts the mood from interrogative to indicative.[55] She flatly *tells* the king: "My lord, *you swore* . . . Your son Solomon will succeed me as king, and he shall sit on my throne. But now suddenly Adonijah *has become king,* though you, my lord, the king, *do not know it*" (1:17–18). Having played up the elements of *spontaneity* and *imperceptibility* (there has "suddenly" been a coup which you "don't know" about), Bathsheba also describes the atmosphere of *festivity*: Adonijah is throwing a big party celebrating his coronation.[56] Of course, all of this rhetoric is designed to get David to spoil Adonijah's shindig and appoint Solomon as king. The plan succeeds brilliantly: after Nathan confirms Bathsheba's message, the king "summons Bathsheba" and announces *to her* that Solomon will succeed "as I swore *to you*" (1:28–30).

A last bit of irony should not be missed: there is no record that David ever swore any such thing. Bathsheba seems to exploit David's senility: poor king can't remember what he had for breakfast, much less what he had decreed about his successor. Though none of us has perfect memories, we tend to snicker at the forgetfulness of the aged and feebleminded. Bergson closely relates "absentmindedness" to his understanding of *inelasticity*. The absent-minded person, incapable of correlating past and present and adapting to new stimuli, suffers, in Bergson's terms, "a certain inborn lack of elasticity of both senses and intelligence" and provides irresistible fodder for the comic imagination.[57]

Though derailed by Solomon's appointment, Adonijah is not through scheming. He asks Bathsheba to arrange for Abishag, David's bedmate, to be his wife. Bathsheba cautiously attends to Adonijah's plea[58] and agrees "to speak to the king on your behalf," or, more literally, "about you" (1 Kgs 2:13–18).[59] What Adonijah represents is more important to Bathsheba than what he requests. She approaches Solomon, who promptly rises, bows, and seats her on a throne at his right hand. Bathsheba is no Esther, wary about imposing on the king's presence: she knows where she stands with her son. And so she presents Adonijah's proposal, but with certain telling rhetorical flourishes.[60] She wants merely "one small favor" from Solomon, which she trusts he will "not refuse" (2:20), the implication being that if Solomon does regard the request as a "larger" issue, he might react adversely. Well, whatever Adonijah's precise motives (to save face? to stake another claim to the throne?), in the world of ancient royal politics, his desire for his father's concubine was no "small matter" (remember Absalom, 2 Sam 16:20–23). And Bathsheba, herself a victim of royal lust, knows this better than most and doubtless knows that Solomon knows this too. Although an influential queen mother, Bathsheba must still operate shrewdly in a man's world. So she baits Solomon and rouses his indignation against his rival brother. Adonijah dies, and Abishag disappears from the story. We may take Bathsheba's silence as consent, if not secret pleasure. She has cleverly manipulated the situation to eliminate a male competitor to her son's throne and a female intruder into her husband's bed. Is this finally sweet revenge for the crimes against her and Uriah?

However we might judge the methods, motives, and morality of this court intrigue, from a biblical perspective the will of God has been fulfilled. Solomon, alias Jedidiah, "the beloved of the Lord," is God's choice to extend the Davidic covenant (2 Sam 12:24–25). But the chief actor in the succession drama is not God, but Bathsheba, acting in a wily way on God's—and her—behalf.

Understanding Matthew's Comedic Purpose

In sum, all four stories surrounding Jesus' foremothers in Matthew's genealogy satisfy our seven-point criteria for humor or comedy. So Matthew starts us off laughing. But for what purpose? Surely more than breaking the ice, like beginning a speech with a joke that has nothing to do with what follows. Matthew strategically designs the genealogy to prepare the way for the ensuing story of Jesus.[61] Why bring on *these* funny ladies, then? And further, why not also include the humorous story involving Sarah? I suggest that the distinction in character roles is critical. Sarah is the butt of the joke, the passive pawn in the ingenious comic plot engineered by God. By contrast, the other women are all active agents, upstaging and outsmarting a variety of foolish male characters—typically those in positions of authority; and, while these women advance God's will, they do so (with the exception of Ruth's conception) without God's assistance. While engaging in a variety of humorous hiding operations, they manage to hide God's hand as well: all of his work is behind the scenes.[62]

Here Jane Schaberg has it right: "The stories [of Jesus' foremothers] show a significant *lack* of miraculous, divine intervention on the part of

God. . . . [They] are instead examples of the divine concealed in and nearly obliterated by human actions, and they share an outlook which stresses God as creator of the context of human freedom. Matthew leads his reader to expect a story which will continue this subtle theologising."[63] So far, so good. However, Schaberg's case breaks down when applied to the opening story of Jesus' birth in 1:18–25, immediately following the genealogy. She assumes that the four ancestresses function as prototypes for Mary, who, like them, carries on the messianic line in scandalous fashion outside the bonds of legitimate marriage. Certain facts of Mary's case are clear: while betrothed to Joseph, she becomes pregnant by someone other than Joseph; an angel of the Lord intervenes, however, and explains Mary's perplexing condition to Joseph as the product of a virgin's conception sanctioned by the Holy Spirit. Not to worry, then: Joseph can honorably take Mary and the son she will bear into his household. By virtue of the parallels with Tamar and the other foremothers, Schaberg interprets this virginal conception as a *natural, human activity* wrought under suspicious circumstances (adultery or rape), and the Spirit's generative agency as a "figurative" or "symbolic" expression of God's life-giving power, as might be said of any conception (e.g., the psalmist's affirmation: "You knit me together in my mother's womb," 139:13). As with the four Old Testament women, Mary is not the beneficiary of any extraordinary divine miracle.[64]

Among various problems plaguing Schaberg's correlation of Jesus' genealogy and conception is the fact that Mary appears as a completely *passive* figure, a non-subject: "she *was found* to be with child by the Holy Spirit" (Matt 1:18). As such, she is the polar opposite of the four pro-active Old Testament women. She mirrors Ruth, whom "the Lord made to conceive," but shows nothing of Ruth's remarkable initiative to get to this point. She also resembles Bathsheba, who conceived in 2 Sam 11 as a victim of imposed power (David's lust), but without Bathsheba's show-stealing curtain call in 1 Kgs 1–2.[65] Mary initiates no action, comedic or otherwise. Schaberg acknowledges Mary's passivity but regards it as Matthew's means of placing her under patriarchal (Joseph's) authority. But the other women are also contained within patriarchal structures without denying their remarkable achievements within the system.[66] Also downplayed in Schaberg's reading is Matthew's continuing interest in God's supernatural intervention as well as human faith in action. Matthew likes spectacular splashes of God's kingdom on earth. It should not surprise us that a story that ends with rock-splitting earthquakes, open tombs, and dead men walking, should begin with a wondrous, Spirit-empowered birth apart from human paternity.[67]

So we confront apparent discontinuity between the lively, assertive fore-mothers and the "flat" character Mary. Or should we say incongruity? Matthew creates his own humorous anomaly: isn't it funny how God, who sometimes takes a back seat and lets widows, prostitutes, foreigners, and adulteresses drive his messianic plan, also steps in at a unique moment and dynamically intervenes in the life of an unsuspecting young Jewish virgin? Go figure. Beyond this surprising characterization of Mary is a further, even more amusing incongruity—with *Joseph*. For as Amy-Jill Levine has observed, the role of the righteous actor in unusual circumstances of life and death—prefigured by the four women in the Hebrew Bible—is played by the *male* Joseph in Matthew's birth narrative.[68] To be sure, he has special divine assistance (multiple dreams) where the women had none, but Joseph still acts in ways reminiscent of his foremothers (they are his ancestors, after all, not Mary's). The humor comes in Joseph's liminal status: he does not per-form the masculine duty of "begetter" in chap. 1 and assumes the role of "female savior" in chap. 2, thwarting the malevolent intention of a powerful male ruler.

We first encounter the "righteous" Joseph embroiled in a terrible fix con-cerning his unlawfully pregnant fiancée: should he expose her publicly or dismiss her quietly? He chooses the latter course (1:19). While this may seem similar to Judah's "dismissal" of Tamar, in fact, it is quite different. Judah, we may recall, utterly disregarded his legal duty to Tamar and then peremptorily demanded her execution upon discovering her (seemingly) illegitimate preg-nancy. The conscientious Joseph is "more in the right," not to mention more charitable than Judah, and more sympathetically aligned with Tamar. More-over, when Joseph awakes from his dream, he exhibits none of the groggy Boaz's hedging about a potentially problematic marriage; rather, he promptly "did as the angel of the Lord commanded him; he took her as his wife" (1:24). And more surprisingly, he "had no marital relations with her until she had borne a son" (1:25). One can scarcely imagine David being so restrained.[69] In short, Joseph shows up his inferior, inelastic forefathers by acting in rather un-masculine fashion. He's not all that clever in the process but does show a measure of courage and a commitment to righteousness.

Soon after Jesus' birth, Joseph faces another crisis, this time in the form of a threatened king who retaliates with violence. King Herod, Rome's client-ruler of the Jews, becomes paranoid over the birth of a potential rival and orders the slaughter of all youngsters two years and under in the Bethlehem area (2:16). While most reminiscent of Pharaoh's brutal plot against baby Moses and the children of Israel, Herod's conduct also recalls the machinations of other nervous royals, like the king of Jericho and Adonijah. Once again, the king and his sidekicks bungle the cloak-and-dagger operation in humorous fashion.[70] As Pharaoh had his wizards, the king of Jericho his messengers, and Adonijah his cronies, Herod has his "chief priests and scribes" (2:4). And let's not forget the fabled "wise men," who are not very wise at all[71] and not terribly helpful in thwarting Herod's hunt for the Christ-child—not unlike the stooges[72] Joshua sent to spy out Jericho.

Nobody quite knows what they're doing: any fool could have followed the signs to the birthplace of the newborn Messiah, but not these guys. The magi are given a blazing star to guide them, and what's the first thing they do when they hit the country? They forget the star and head straight to the current "king of the Jews" and inquire: "Where is the child who has been born king of the Jews?" (2:2). (Our stargazers aren't any too bright.) Herod then gets all worked up and calls an emergency meeting of the priestly security council to determine: "Where can we find this messiah?" Finally, somebody has a clue: the priests go to their manual and pinpoint the target as Bethlehem of Judea (2:4–6). Why, then, doesn't Herod just charge into Bethlehem with all the king's horses and all the king's men and find this messianic upstart? Bethlehem was not that large or far away (perhaps Herod is thrown by his advisors' misquote of Mic 5:2, reversing Bethlehem's "little town" status).[73] Rather than take direct action, Herod "secretly" summons the wise men and dispatches them to "search diligently" for the child (2:7–8). A major intelligence mission is launched with not very intelligent agents. Our wise guys blithely follow Herod's orders and discover the child's location—not because of a "diligent search," however, but because the star leads them to the spot (why didn't they follow the star in the first place?) (2:9–10). After worshiping the Christ-child, they are "warned in a dream not to return to Herod" (2:12). Without the dream, would they have actually headed back to Herod? Nothing in the story thus far suggests otherwise, and I think the narrator's later comment concerning Herod's fury over being "tricked by the wise men" (2:16) is doubly ironic: the wise men in this tale couldn't trick a fool, but a fool is exactly what Herod is.

He is a ruthless, maniacal fool, however, who takes out his frustrations on Bethlehem's infants. There is nothing funny about such cold-blooded carnage, especially for the bereft mothers. Weeping and wailing are all they can manage (2:18). So how dare we laugh in the face of such lament? Why on earth might Matthew embed such a tragic episode in a comic narrative?[74] An obvious answer appealing to the stock device of "comic relief" does not do justice to the flow of Matthew's story. The amusement surrounding the actions of Herod, the magi, and Joseph does not relieve or interrupt the tension as much as swallow or engulf it. The heinous and horrible scene of infanticide is the aberration breaking into an otherwise humorous and hopeful account. Again, we laugh to keep from crying hopelessly, incessantly. We laugh in the hope that God has the last laugh—that God's affirmation of life and goodness will ultimately overwhelm the destructive forces of evil.

Matthew's story pins its hopes for a merciful and just world on God's revelation in Jesus Christ. Thus the Christ-child, the true "King of the Jews," escapes Herod's clutches. But he does it, strangely enough, through the agency of his human stepfather Joseph, who springs into action once again in response to an angelic prompt. The narrator uses a series of action verbs to describe Joseph's movements: "he *got up, took* the child and his mother by night, and *went* to Egypt, and *remained* there until the death of Herod" (2:14–15). And similarly, when instructed to return, "he *got up, took* the child and his mother, and *went* to the land of Israel" (2:21). Like Jochebed and Miriam, who hid the threatened baby Moses, and Pharaoh's daughter who rescued him (Exod 2:1–10); like Rahab, who hid the spies from the king of Jericho and sent them on their way; and like Bathsheba, who saved herself and her son by hiding key bits of information, Joseph successfully hides Mary and Jesus from a predatory king. Though lacking his foremothers' flair for the dramatic and requiring repeated cues from backstage, Joseph plays his female savior role pretty well.[75]

Do we have then in Matthew's narrative an early Christian (ef)feminist manifesto where all the good men act like women or at least not like typical men? In the gospel that uniquely extols the virtue of becoming "eunuchs for the sake of the kingdom of heaven" (19:11), the whole notion of masculinity is fraught with ambiguity, if not "profound contradictions."[76] Levine suggestively extends my reading of Matthew's genealogy and the subsequent Joseph story "as promoting celibacy (a Matthean interest), even as it undermines the value of both marriage and procreation in wedlock, the two major elements of patriarchal society."[77] Neither Judah nor Joshua's spies nor Boaz nor David (by Bathsheba) nor Joseph show any great commitment to procreation or impregnation; indeed, in the cases of Judah, David, and Joseph, such a result is most unwelcome. Levine elaborates with respect to Judah:

> Poor Judah: with a sire who sires left and right, he has only three offspring. Compared to Jacob, his siring leaves much de-sired; compared to Simeon's six and Benjamin's ten children, his three seem minimal; and, worse, he shows no interest in producing more. Now he must face the undesirable awkwardness of admitting to being the father of twins.

Unlike the patriarchal ideal, sons are the last things he wants, and now he has two more. No wonder "he did not lie with her again" (Gen 38:26). The point fits Matthew's text perfectly for only in this gospel does Jesus praise those who "make themselves eunuchs for the kingdom of heaven" (19:12).[78]

Matthew's main male figure—Jesus of Nazareth—takes his patriarchal ancestors' bungling cues and "perfects" them into a life of total celibacy. He is the model "eunuch" for God's kingdom. How, though, does Jesus relate to his *matriarchal* predecessors and to his stepfather Joseph's *feminist* affinities? A full examination of Matthew's portrait of Jesus is not possible here, but we consider briefly one story that recalls the genealogical foremothers: Jesus' encounter with a desperate Canaanite woman, an ethnic sister to Rahab and cousin to Ruth the Moabite, Uriah the Hittite, and possibly Tamar (15:21–28). The woman reverently, even righteously, we might say—without guile or trickery—petitions Jesus to heal her demon-harassed daughter. Jesus, however, first ignores her and then rebuffs her (15:23–24)—not the Joseph-like empathy we might expect. Indeed, as Levine notes, Jesus' insensitive inaction casts him more "in the role of Judah, the Israelite spies, Boaz, and David: he remains consistent in his role as patriarch."[79] While some have tried to soften Jesus' retort comparing the woman to a dog as an endearing "half-humorous" quip delivered with a "twinkle in the eye,"[80] this is not the funny moment of the story from a feminist point of view (women are rarely amused by "bitch" comments). The humor emerges when the Canaanite woman, like Tamar with Judah and Ruth with Boaz, boldly positions herself *at Jesus' feet*, where he must notice and deal with her,[81] and cleverly—with more than a pinch of sarcasm—turns Jesus' words against him ("Yes, Lord, yet even dogs are useful in licking the floors clean," 15:27).[82] She has now turned into a righteous trickster worthy of Jesus' foremothers. But what does this make Jesus if not the fool of the scene, the inferior, inelastic male authority who must be persuaded to conform to woman's will, which happens to conform with God's will (the perspective of faith, as Jesus himself acknowledges, 15:28)?

We who are Christians are not accustomed to viewing Jesus as a fool (Paul, maybe, who dubs himself as a fool, but not Jesus). But, then again, we are not accustomed to reading the biblical narratives in the humorous, at times riotous, spirit in which they were written. But isn't that a symptom of our own stuffy self-righteousness, a tendency to hide behind our own masks of piety, which are just that—comic masks disguising our own hypocrisy? And isn't that what Matthew's Jesus is intent on exposing above all else in the

Sermon on the Mount and other speeches, including the one immediately preceding his encounter with the Canaanite woman (15:1–20; cf. 6:1–18; 23:1–36)? Perhaps, then, a healthy sense of humor, especially at one's own expense, is the first step toward the higher righteousness that Jesus emphasizes and embodies—sometimes with women's encouragement.

Notes

1. "Genealogies, plumply inserted by the limited sense of morons. . . . I tear you out. What is this dry leaf doing in the Holy Book full of fresh splendors of palms? What is it whether John begat Joe, down to him who made the world free?" Cited in Ulrich Luz, *Matthew 1–7: A Commentary* (trans. W. C. Linss; Hermeneia; Minneapolis: Fortress, 1989), 112–13; cf. H. Hempelmann, "'Das dürre Blatt im Heilgen Buch': Mt 1, 1–17 und der Kampf wider die Erniedrigung Gottes,' *Theologische Beiträge* 21 (1990): 6–23.

2. Raymond E. Brown, *The Birth of the Messiah: A Commentary on the Infancy Narratives in Matthew and Luke* (London: Geoffrey Chapman, 1977), 71–74.

3. See Amy-Jill Levine, "Matthew," in *Women's Bible Commentary* (ed. Carol A. Newsom and Sharon H. Ringe; 2nd ed.; Louisville, KY: Westminster/John Knox, 1998), 340–41.

4. See 2 Kgs 21:1–18; David E. Garland, *Reading Matthew: A Literary and Theological Commentary on the First Gospel* (New York: Crossroad, 1993), 18.

5. Cf. Amy-Jill Levine, "Rahab in the New Testament," in *Women in Scripture: A Dictionary of Named and Unnamed Women in the Hebrew Bible, the Apocryphal/Deuterocanonical Books, and the New Testament* (ed. Carol Meyers; Grand Rapids: Eerdmans, 2000), 141–42.

6. *Jubilees* 41:1 associates Tamar with "the daughters of Aram" (cf. *Testament of Judah* 10:1), and Bathsheba is identified as the wife of a Hittite, which may or may not mean that she was a Hittite as well. In support of the primary Gentile identity of these women, see Richard Bauckham, "The Gentile Foremothers of the Messiah" in his *Gospel Women: Studies of the Named Women in the Gospels* (Grand Rapids: Eerdmans, 2002), 17–46.

7. See Gen 12:1–3. Matthew's birth narrative also features the Messiah's appeal to Gentiles in the visit of the Eastern magi in 2:1–12.

8. Cf. R. Alan Culpepper, "Humor and Wit: New Testament," *Anchor Bible Dictionary* 3:333: "[Humor and wit] are often expressed by means of verbal subtleties, indirection, and clever turns of phrases. Consequently, humor and wit do not translate well from one culture, age, or language to another."

9. For a sampling of analyses of humor in biblical scholarship, see *On Humour and the Comic in the Hebrew Bible* (ed. Y. T. Radday and A. Brenner; Sheffield, UK: Almond, 1990); J. Jónsson, *Humour and Irony in the New Testament* (BZRGG, 28; Leiden, Neth.: Brill, 1985).

10. In *Laughing Matters: The Paradox of Comedy* (Amherst: University of Massachusetts Press, 1986), 3–4, S. C. Shershow develops the "slippery eel" image, drawing on both ancient Roman (Plautus) and modern American (W. C. Fields) sources:

What happens when he [a conniving slave] is caught in the act? He slips away like an eel. (Plautus)

The funniest thing about comedy is that you never know why people laugh. I know *what* makes them laugh, but trying to get your hands on the *why* of it is like trying to pick an eel out of a tub of water. (W. C. Fields)

11. Ovid, *Amores* 1.15.17–18; cited in Shershow, *Laughing Matters*, 10.

12. Frances Landy, "Humour as a Tool for Biblical Exegesis," in Radday and Brenner, eds., *On Humour and the Comic*, 104.

13. Ibid., 105 (emphasis mine).

14. E. L. Greenstein, "Humor and Wit: Old Testament," *ABD* 3:330.

15. Ibid., 330–31.

16. Frank M. Cross observes, with respect to the Rahab incident in Josh 2, "there is here a juxtaposition of incompatibles, an element of ironic incongruity which is often at the heart of humor." Cross, "A Response to Zakovitch's 'Successful Failure of Israelite Intelligence,'" in *Text and Tradition: The Hebrew Bible and Folklore* (ed. Susan Niditch; Society of Biblical Literature Symposium Series; Atlanta: Scholars Press, 1990), 102.

17. Cf. the assessment of W. D. Howarth, "Introduction: Theoretical Considerations," in *Comic Drama: The European Heritage* (ed. W. D. Howarth; New York: St. Martin's Press, 1978), 6: "Of all the attributes which help to define comedy, the happy ending is perhaps the most unequivocal and the least disputed."

18. See the collection of primary readings by Plato, Hobbes, and Freud (among others) and the helpful discussion of "superiority theory" in humor by John Morreall, "A New Theory of Laughter," all gathered in *The Philosophy of Laughter and Humor* (ed. John Morreall; Albany: State University of New York, 1987), 10–13, 19–20, 111–16, 128–38. Cf. also, Howarth, "Introduction," 12–13.

19. Thomas Hobbes, *Leviathan*, Part 1, chap. 6; excerpted in Morreall, ed., *Philosophy of Laughter*, 19.

20. Henri Bergson, "Laughter: An Essay on the Meaning of the Comic," in *Comedy* (ed. W. Sypher; trans. C. Brereton and F. Rothwell; New York: Doubleday, 1965), excerpted in Morreall, ed., *Philosophy of Laughter*, 121 (emphasis in the original). See another excerpt in R. W. Corrigan, ed., *Comedy: Meaning and Form* (2nd ed.; New York: Harper & Row, 1981), 328–32.

21. Bergson, "Laughter," excerpted in Morreall, *Philosophy of Laughter*, 125.

22. Morreall, "New Theory of Laughter," 134–38.

23. The name "Perez" (Gen 38:29) means "breach" and reinforces the boundary-breaking elements of the story. Cf. Danna Nolan Fewell and David M. Gunn, *Narrative in the Hebrew Bible* (Oxford Bible Series; Oxford: Oxford University Press, 1993), 44: "Perez is . . . like his mother who, breaking all the rules of social respectability, breached the walls of the prison to which Judah had consigned her and punctured the patriarch's veneer of righteousness."

24. Cf. Phyllis A. Bird, *Missing Persons and Mistaken Identities: Women and Gender in Ancient Israel* (Overtures to Biblical Theology; Minneapolis: Fortress, 1997), 204: "Judah is needy and therefore vulnerable. At the point where the critical action begins, he is depicted as recently bereaved and hence in need of sexual gratification or diversion. . . . He is also a traveler, away from home, desiring entertainment and free to seek it in a strange place. Prostitution is typically offered (and organized) as a service to travelers, a tourist attraction."

25. All we are told in Gen 38:14 about Tamar's appearance is that "she put off her widow's garments, put on a veil, wrapped herself up, and sat down at the entrance to Enaim, which is on the road to Timnah." Cf. Bird, *Missing Persons*, 203: "The language is deliberately opaque and suggestive. The narrator does not say that Tamar dressed as a harlot. That is the inference that Judah makes—and is intended to make—but the narrator leaves it to Judah to draw the conclusion."

26. Robert Alter, *Genesis: Translation and Commentary* (New York: Norton, 1996), 221; and *The Art of Biblical Narrative* (New York: Basic Books, 1981), 8–9.

27. The first term (*zonah*) is used by the narrator in 38:15 to identify what Judah privately "thought her [Tamar] to be." Later in the story, when Judah sends his friend Hiram to pay Tamar and recover his pledge, Hiram searches (unsuccessfully) for "the temple prostitute [*qedeshah*] who was at Enaim by the wayside" (38:21). Apparently, Judah had revised his assessment of Tamar's role, perhaps because he thought it more publicly acceptable among his Canaanite neighbors to engage the services of a cultic prostitute (hierodule) than a common harlot. On the

difficult issue of distinguishing types of prostitutes in the Bible, see Bird, *Missing Persons,* 199–208; Gail Corrington Streete, *The Strange Woman: Power and Sex in the Bible* (Louisville, KY: Westminster/John Knox, 1997), 43–51.

28. The use of deceptive garments to outwit unsuspecting targets in both Gen 37:29–34 and 38:14–19 is noted by Alter, *Genesis,* 220; *Art of Biblical Narrative,* 10–12.

29. Does Judah consider the pregnant Tamar an unwed single woman who has "committed a disgraceful act in Israel by prostituting herself in her father's house" (Deut 22:21) or an adulteress unfaithful to her betrothed (Judah's third son)? Either way, the penalty, according to Deut 22:20–24, would be death by stoning. Execution by burning was reserved for "the daughter of a priest [who] profanes herself through prostitution" (Lev 21:9). Cf. the discussion in Streete, *Strange Woman,* 45–46; and Susan Niditch, "The Wronged Woman Righted: An Analysis of Genesis 38," *Harvard Theological Review* 72 (1979): 145–48.

30. Danna Nolan Fewell and David M. Gunn, *Gender, Power, and Promise: The Subject of the Bible's First Story* (Nashville, TN: Abingdon, 1993), 119.

31. Josh 6:23 describes the spies as "young men" or "young lads." Cf. Fewell and Gunn, *Gender,* 117. Y. Zakovitch opines that the characterization of the spies as anonymous juveniles suggests that "Joshua does not select the well-bred or even soldiers as his spies; he may have simply grabbed the first two lads who happened to be near his tent when he went out to dispatch spies—sheer irresponsibility!" "Humor and Theology or the Successful Failure of Israelite Intelligence: A Literary-Folkloric Approach to Joshua 2," in *Text and Tradition: The Hebrew Bible and Folklore* (ed. Susan Niditch; Atlanta: Scholars Press, 1990), 81. In turn, however, Cross, "Response," 101, regards Zakovitch's imaginative reading as irresponsible "midrash."

32. Fewell and Gunn, *Gender,* 118. Cf. the query in Bird, *Missing Persons,* 213: "Was the red cord a permanent sign of an ancient red-light district, or only specific to this narrative?"

33. Josephus, *Jewish Antiquities* 5.1.2. Cf. discussion in Zakovitch, "Humor," 81–82, who is critical of Josephus's "humorless" report.

34. Contra Zakovitch, "Humor," 82, who thinks "it is clear that nothing happened" sexually between Rahab and the spies. Actually, the narrative does not clarify exactly how Rahab and her visitors pass the time, but her primary identity as a prostitute narrows the options. Although downplaying their sexual misadventures, Zakovitch still appreciates the spies' basic role as "first-class bunglers" (p. 85).

35. Zakovitch, "Humor," 79–96, links this incident to a network of biblical-type scenes featuring women as rescuers of imperiled men: see, e.g., 1 Sam 19:9–17; 2 Sam 17:17–22.

36. Cf. Bird, *Missing Persons,* 211–12.

37. On the strict requirements of sexual purity during military campaigns, see Deut 23:9–14; 1 Sam 21:5; and 2 Sam 11:11.

38. I borrow this felicitous image from Zakovitch, "Humor," 91: "This manner of escape again emphasizes the passivity of the spies. Like marionettes they are dependent on Rahab's graces, their lives hanging in the balance every moment."

39. Cf. Fewell and Gunn, *Gender,* 119–20.

40. Phyllis Trible, *God and the Rhetoric of Sexuality* (OBT; Philadelphia: Fortress, 1978), 195.

41. On the Moabite stigma, see Amy-Jill Levine, "Ruth," in Newsom and Ringe, eds., *Women's Bible Commentary,* 84–85; and Fewell and Gunn, "'A Son Is Born to Naomi!': Literary Allusions and Interpretation in the Book of Ruth," in *Women in the Hebrew Bible: A Reader* (ed. Alice Bach; New York: Routledge, 1999), 235–36.

42. On the Tamar-Ruth connection, see Ellen van Wolde, "Intertextuality: Ruth in Dialogue with Tamar," in *A Feminist Companion to Reading the Bible: Approaches, Methods, and Strategies* (ed. Athalya Brenner and Carole Fontaine; Sheffield, UK: Sheffield Academic Press, 1997), 426–51; and Fewell and Gunn, "A Son Is Born," 236–38.

43. Edward L. Greenstein, "Reading Strategies and the Story of Ruth," in Bach, ed., *Women in the Hebrew Bible,* 220–22, citing and discussing the study of Harold Fisch, "Ruth and the Structure of Covenant History," *VT* 32 (1982): 425–37.

44. van Wolde, "Intertextuality," 444–46.

45. See Kathleen A. Robertson Farmer, "The Book of Ruth: Introduction, Commentary, and Reflections," in *The New Interpreter's Bible* (vol. 2; Nashville, TN: Abingdon, 1998), 924–30.

46. Cf. Song of Songs 5:6–7; Fewell and Gunn, "A Son Is Born," 237.

47. On the ironic association of Boaz's name with "strength" in the book of Ruth, see Mieke Bal, *Lethal Love: Feminist Literary Readings of Biblical Love Stories* (Bloomington: Indiana University Press, 1987), 78–79. Cf. the discussion and critique of Bal's reading in Greenstein, "Reading Strategies," 222–23.

48. Fewell and Gunn, "A Son Is Born," 236, suggest that Naomi, rather than Boaz, plays a Judah-like role, resistant (at first) to arranging remarriage for her widowed daughter-in-law: "Might she [Naomi] perhaps be like Judah, not expressing her suspicion directly to the young women [Ruth and Orpah], but insisting nevertheless that they belong not with her but their own families in Moab? Ruth, then, would be to Naomi as Tamar is, to Judah, an albatross around her neck."

49. Rachel's story is explicitly recalled in Ruth 4:11.

50. In "Ruth," 85, Levine notes that this marks the only direct action by God in the entire book: "With all the language of piety, God appears actively only once in the book—in allowing Ruth to conceive (4:13). With this divine intervention the depiction of Ruth shifts from active agent to one in the power of God."

51. On possible ways of understanding Bathsheba as a victim of violent rape, see J. Cheryl Exum, *Fragmented Women: Feminist (Sub)versions of Biblical Narratives* (Valley Forge, PA: Trinity Press International, 1993), 170–76.

52. Adele Berlin, *Poetics and Interpretation of Biblical Narrative* (Winona Lake, IN: Eisenbrauns, 1994), 26–27.

53. On this shift in characterization, see Berlin, *Poetics*, 27–30; Joanna A. Hackett, "1 and 2 Samuel," in Newsom and Ringe, eds., *Women's Bible Commentary*, 98.

54. Note the assessment of Bathsheba's role by Claudia V. Camp, "1 and 2 Kings," in Newsom and Ringe, eds., *Women's Bible Commentary*, 105: "Though the initiative for her action appears to come from Nathan, she possesses her own power, skills, and motives for her role. At stake for her is the position of supreme female power in the land, that of queen mother." On Bathsheba's improvising of Nathan's scheme to her own advantage, see S. Bar-Efrat, *Narrative Art in the Bible* (Journal for the Study of the Old Testament: Supplement Series 70; Bible and Literature 17; Sheffield, UK: Almond, 1989), 164–65.

55. See Choon-Leong Seow, "The First and Second Books of Kings: Introduction, Commentary, and Reflections," in *The New Interpreter's Bible* (vol. 3; Nashville, TN: Abingdon, 1999), 19.

56. Bathsheba exaggerates the extent of Adonijah's celebration by adding to the narrator's previous description that Adonijah "has sacrificed oxen, fatted cattle, and sheep *in abundance*" (1:19; cf. 1:9); cf. Bar-Efrat, *Narrative Art,* 164.

57. Bergson, "Laughter," excerpted in Morreall, *Philosophy of Laughter,* 120–22.

58. Berlin, *Poetics,* 29, notes that Bathsheba's repeated, guarded encouragement of Adonijah to "go on" or "say on" (2:14, 16) hints "that she is considering at each step what it all means and where it might lead."

59. Cf. Seow, "First and Second Books of Kings," 32.

60. Cf. Berlin, *Poetics,* 29.

61. Though not pursuing a humorous or comedic thread, the following studies all agree that Matthew's genealogy is an integral component of the larger Matthean narrative: Bauckham, *Gospel Women,* 17–46; David R. Bauer, "The Literary and Theological Function of the Genealogy in Matthew's Gospel," in *Treasures New and Old: Contributions to Matthean Studies* (ed. David R. Bauer and Mark Allan Powell; Society of Biblical Literature Symposium Series 1; Atlanta: Scholars Press, 1996), 129–59; E. D. Freed, "The Women in Matthew's Genealogy," *Journal for the Study of the New Testament* 29 (1987): 3–19; John Paul Heil, "The Narrative Roles of

the Women in Matthew's Genealogy," *Biblica* 72 (1991): 538–45; Herman C. Waetjen, "The Genealogy as the Key to the Gospel According to Matthew," *Journal of Biblical Literature* 95 (1976): 205–30.

62. This is not to say that God's work is not important, for God is the ultimate life-giver who opens these women's wombs and carries on the messianic line according to divine purpose. On the tension between these women's activity and God's sovereignty, see Janice Capel Anderson, "Mary's Difference: Gender and Patriarchy in the Birth Narratives," *Journal of Religion* 67 (1987): 186–90.

63. Jane Schaberg, "The Foremothers and the Mother of Jesus," *Concilium* 206 (1989): 114.

64. Ibid., 112–19.

65. The parallel between Mary and Rahab is also weakened by the fact that we know nothing about the circumstances surrounding Rahab's maternity. Further, Mary is not a Gentile or a prostitute or a widow, as are one or more of the four Old Testament ancestresses.

66. On abiding tensions between women's freedom and containment within patriarchal biblical narratives, see Janice Capel Anderson, "Matthew: Gender and Reading," *Semeia* 28 (1983): 3–27.

67. See Matt 27:51–54. For further critique of Schaberg's reading, see Craig L. Blomberg, "The Liberation of Illegitimacy: Women and Rulers in Matthew 1–2," *Biblical Theology Bulletin* 21 (1991): 145–50.

68. Levine, "Matthew," 340–41.

69. Another possible link between Joseph and his foremothers may be his naming of Jesus (1:25), just as the women of Bethlehem named Ruth's son, Obed (Ruth 4:17).

70. Two studies note ironic dimensions of this episode, but they do not exploit any humorous overtones. Blomberg, "Liberation," 147–49, focuses on Herod's "illegitimacy" as "King of the Jews," his title notwithstanding. Dorothy Jean Weaver ("Power and Powerlessness: Matthew's Use of Irony in the Portrayal of Political Leaders," in Bauer and Powell, eds., *Treasures New and Old,* 179–87) exposes King Herod's ironic "powerlessness" in the narrative: "The revelation that 'the king is terrified of the child' signals to the reader not only that Herod's position as 'king over Judea' is being challenged but also that Herod's power itself is more appearance than reality" (p. 185).

71. Challenging popular interpretations of the magi or "wise men," see the lively, incisive study by Mark Allan Powell, *Chasing the Eastern Star: Adventures in Biblical Reader-Response Criticism* (Louisville, KY: Westminster/John Knox, 2001), 131–84; esp. pp. 148–56.

72. I owe the funny association of the so-called "wise men" with the "three stooges" (Larry, Mo, and Curly) to conversation with Amy-Jill Levine.

73. Contrast Mic 5:2—"But you O Bethlehem of Ephrathah, who are one of the *little clans of Judah,* from you shall come forth for me one who is to rule in Israel"—with Matt 2:6—"And you, Bethlehem, in the land of Judah, are *by no means least among the rulers of Judah;* for from you shall come a ruler."

74. I was prompted to reflect on this troubling mix of tragedy and comedy by the trenchant comments of Professor Frances Taylor Gench at the Biblical Colloquy at Union Theological Seminary, Richmond, VA.

75. On "female saviors" in Exodus, see Ilana Pardes, *Countertraditions in the Bible: A Feminist Approach* (Cambridge, MA: Harvard University Press, 1992), 81–83; J. Cheryl Exum, "'Mother In Israel': A Familiar Figure Reconsidered," in *Feminist Interpretation of the Bible* (ed. Letty M. Russell; Philadelphia: Westminster, 1985), 80–82. On the connection between these women and Joseph in Matthew, see Levine, "Matthew," 341.

76. See "Matthew and Masculinity" in *New Testament Masculinities* (ed. Stephen D. Moore and Janice Capel Anderson; Semeia Studies; Atlanta: SBL, 2003), 81: "On the one hand, therefore, that consummately masculine type, the Greco-Roman master of a house, looms exceedingly large in this Gospel [of Matthew], and his traditional hegemonic prerogatives are nowhere explicitly called into question. On the other hand, however, the repeated devaluation or disruption of

biological kinship ties, and hence of the male generation of heirs, undercuts the traditional power base of the *oikodespotēs* and threatens its eventual erosion—another instance of the profound contradictions in which masculinity in Matthew is enmeshed."

77. Amy-Jill Levine, "Women's Humor and Other Creative Juices," in *Are We Amused? Humour about Women in the Biblical Worlds* (ed. Athalya Brenner; New York: T & T Clark, 2003), 122.

78. Ibid, 121.

79. Amy Jill Levine, "Matthew's Advice to a Divided Readership," in *The Gospel of Matthew in Current Study: Studies in Memory of William G. Thompson, S.J.* (ed. David E. Aune; Grand Rapids: Eerdmans, 2001), 36.

80. Cited, with critique, in M. Eugene Boring, "The Gospel of Matthew," in *The New Interpreter's Bible* (vol. 3; Nashville, TN: Abingdon, 1995), 336n343; and in Levine, "Matthew's Advice," 31–32. The conjecture that Jesus conveys "a half-humorous tenderness of manner" comes from A. H. McNeile, *The Gospel According to Saint Matthew: The Greek Text with Introduction, Notes, and Indices* (London: Macmillan, 1915; repr. 1961), 231. The equally baseless supposition that Jesus speaks to the woman with a "twinkle in his eye" comes from R. T. France, *Matthew* (Tyndale New Testament Commentaries; Grand Rapids: Eerdmans, 1987), 247.

81. "But she came and *knelt* before him . . ." (Matt 15:25). Levine notes that the woman's kneeling posture does not necessarily connote worship: "rather, she stops his movement. He can either walk around her, as she literally holds her ground, or he can respond." "Matthew's Advice," 36–37.

82. Levine particularly relates the Canaanite woman's strategy of using Jesus' words to her own advantage with Ruth's manipulation of Boaz's language (cf. Ruth 2:12; 3:9). "Matthew's Advice," 38–39.

CHAPTER 3

Shall We Dance?:
Women Leading Men in Mark 5–7

She went before all the people in the dance, leading all the women, while all the men of Israel followed, bearing their arms and wearing garlands and singing hymns. (JDT 15:13)

T his is not the conventional victory celebration where the women come out of their homes singing, dancing, and shaking their tambourines to hail their returning, conquering male heroes ("Saul has killed his thousands, and David his ten thousands," 1 Sam 18:6–7). Quite the contrary: here a female heroine, together with "all the women," *lead* the victory dance, while the male soldiers *follow*, brandishing garlands and singing backup. Such a scene, strange though it be, provides a fitting climax to a story in which a clever, courageous woman single-handedly saves the day for her besieged people by infiltrating the enemy camp and exiting with the commander's severed head in her lunch bag. Entirely without male assistance (she does have a helpful maidservant), Judith earns the right to lead the parade and orchestrate the final anthem. Unlike her warring, singing, and dancing foresisters, Miriam and Deborah, Judith has no Moses or Barak encroaching on her spotlight. She is a renowned, remarkable woman—but also, if not contained, a dangerous figure in a patriarchal world. And so, as the Bethulian women had earlier been "sent home" while the townsmen were dispatched "to their various [military] posts" (Jdt 7:32), the triumphant Judith, after three months of celebrating, ultimately "returns home" and "remains on her estate . . . in her *husband's house*" as a chaste widow until the ripe old age of 105—becoming "more and more famous" as she is more and more domesticated (16:21–25).[1]

This precarious, ambiguous position of the wily, dancing woman who commands and conquers men resonates with, if not directly influences, the exotic tale of Herodias and the dancing daughter (traditionally known as Salome) in Mark 6:14–29.[2] The most salient parallels are unique in biblical tradition: a female duo (Judith/maid; Herodias/daughter) slyly manipulates male authorities (Holofernes; Herod) to effect the beheading of a powerful male adversary (Holofernes; John the Baptist) in a grisly—or should we say, gristly—culinary context (What's your pleasure: enemy head on a platter or in a pouch, dining in or take-out?). These women are not mirror images of each other, however; important differences and oppositions remain. For example, Judith dances to crown her victory, Salome to create hers (although Judith also uses her alluring body to attain her goal). But most salient in their canonical contexts, Judith the Jewess/Judean (as her name signifies) executes the heinous Assyrian general Holofernes who is threatening her people, while Herodias and daughter eliminate the pious Judean prophet John, who proclaims the imminent establishment of God's redemptive reign in Israel. One is a heroine, the other a villainess; the latter, the dark shadow of the former.

But biblical ideology—while rife with dualistic tendencies—also resists unilateral, black-and-white polarities. Recall Judith's portrait—a heroine, yes, in a desperate, exceptional situation—but otherwise a too-virile (masculinized) woman who must be tempered for consumption in ordinary, polite, male-dominated society (let's not lose our interpretive heads or headships over this; we can't have all our women going around playing super spy and headhunter, can we?).[3] On the other hand, if Judith and the dancing women of Bethuliah must be domesticated, then perhaps Herodias and her dancing daughter can be rehabilitated in some measure (nothing's more biblical than redemption). This is a banner case of perspective: it all depends on point of view. As Janice Capel Anderson observes, Mark's story is told from a male narrator's viewpoint focused chiefly through "King" Herod's words and thoughts.[4] Herod's wife and (step-)daughter are completely objectified. If given independent voice, Herodias might well offer a very different report about matters such as permitting a young daughter to provide the main entertainment at her husband's stag birthday party (the ancient equivalent of popping out of the cake) and her thorough vilification as "Mommie Dearest," to borrow Maureen Mara's telling image, while

Herod is given the benefit of the doubt as a hesitant, conscience-stricken partner in John's execution.[5]

In her 1994 presidential address to the Society of Biblical Literature, Phyllis Trible explored a similar reassessment of another infamous biblical villainess, Queen Jezebel.[6] Jezebel represents yet another forerunner to Herodias: a powerful wife who violently opposes the Lord's prophet (Elijah himself or the Elijah-styled John the Baptist)[7] and manipulates her husband-king (Ahab/Herod) to kill a righteous man (Naboth/John) who dared to say "no" to the king's desires.[8] Unlike Judith, who is usually viewed as an anti-type to Herodias, Jezebel provides a perfect moral match. Or does she? Trible observes that Jezebel "belongs to a genealogy of schemers, connivers, and murderers who populate the story of Israel. The list includes males and females, foreigners and natives: Abraham, Rebekah, Jacob, Rachel, Jael, Abigail, Joab, David, and on to Esther and [yes] Judith"—and, we could add, Herodias and Salome.[9] What is most revealing, however, is that Trible also includes *Elijah* among Jezebel's spiritual and ethical kin: "Elijah and Jezebel, beloved and hated. In life and in death they are not divided. Using power to get what they want, both the YHWH worshiper and the Baal worshiper promote their gods, scheme, and murder."[10] Of course, in the sacred scriptures of ancient Israel, the prophet of YHWH is right and the patroness of Baal wrong. But their haunting affinities persist. The juxtaposition of this "odd couple"[11] in the Bible, along with a host of other tricksters and troublemakers, good and evil, complicates our character judgments, subverts our ideological fundaments, and, in Trible's words, "may just upset our cherishing of polarity" in the guild of biblical scholarship.[12]

So from a more fluid, depolarized[13] perspective—imaged in Elisabeth Schüssler Fiorenza's hermeneutics as a "spiraling circle-dance" or "transformative dance of interpretation" inspired by dancing figures such as Miriam and Judith who model the first steps of an "ongoing, never closing, shifting movement of a feminist biblical interpretation for liberation"[14]—what do we do with Herodias and the dancing daughter in Mark 6? In addition to various intertextual associates such as Jezebel and Judith, which we have already considered, and also perhaps Jephthah's daughter (a rash oath provokes an unjust execution)[15] and Queen Esther (a banqueting *korasion* is offered "half the kingdom" and connives to have a malicious male official put to death),[16] what about inner-textual affiliates in the Markan narrative? Scholars often observe how the titillating, gruesome story surrounding John's beheading stands apart from the rest of Mark as a "novellistic digression"[17] and the only episode in which Jesus is not central.[18] In comparison with the other women in Mark, most of whom are disadvantaged, anonymous examples of "Christian" faith and service, Herodias stands out like a sore thumb as a powerful, named female representative of treachery and violence, the only "bad guy," as Anderson puts it, in the bunch.[19]

When critics move beyond surface distinctions to wrestle with possible narrative connections and reasons why Mark incorporated this story in his gospel, the focus typically falls not upon women, but upon the intertwined characterizations of Jesus, his disciples, and John the Baptist. Sandwiched between reports of Jesus' hometown rejection (6:6) and the mission of Jesus' twelve disciples (6:7–13, 30), the account of John's death portends the heightened persecution awaiting Jesus and his followers, a theme developed further in the triple passion predictions in chaps. 8–10, the apocalyptic discourse in 13:9–13, and the climactic scenes of the passion narrative in chaps. 14–15. Like John before him, Jesus is executed by political authorities and his body laid in a tomb—although, ironically, not by his closest disciples, as was the case with John (6:29; 14:50; 15:42–47). Elizabeth Struthers Malbon clearly sketches these parallels among John, Jesus, and the disciples in her extensive narrative-critical study of Mark's characters.[20] But she also exposes other connections and lays the groundwork for more complex character comparisons and contrasts. For one, she takes seriously the role of Herodias and daughter, albeit not to rehabilitate them in relation to other women. Malbon perceives that Herodias exploits her dependent daughter to compel Herod to carry out her murderous plot against John, just as the chief priests, scribes, and elders manipulate the impressionable crowds to demand that Pilate crucify Jesus. As such, Herodias and Salome seem to have little to do with other pairs of positive female characters in Mark, such as the "bold and faithful" hemorrhaging and Syrophoenician women in Mark 5 and 7, and the "self-denying, serving" widow and anointing woman in Mark 12 and 14. But Malbon also makes clear that the world of Markan characterization is not uniformly flat. Characters can change, surprise, and display various qualities, both favorable and problematic. Disciples, male and female, are best viewed as "fallible followers" of Jesus, a dynamic blend of loyalty (followers) and betrayal (fallible).[21] The brotherhood of the Twelve, while often lampooned in Mark, are not complete dullards; and women, while frequently presented as exemplars of faith and service, are not all virtuous (witness Herodias) or diametric opposites of the male disciples in their faithless and selfish moments. In fact, "enemies can become exemplary followers, but fallible followers can become enemies. Nothing is static. Nothing is absolute."[22] The bottom line resulting from Mark's "composite and complex image" of fallible followers is that "discipleship is both open-ended and demanding; followership is neither exclusive nor easy."[23] Similarly, Malbon reminds us, "interpretation, like followership, is never easy, and never perfect, and never ending."[24]

Although Malbon herself does not explore other dimensions of the Herodias and daughter figures, her understanding of Mark's dynamic juxtaposition of various characters encourages further investigation. Mary Rose D'Angelo suggests (but does not develop) an interesting connection between Herodias and the poor widow and anointing woman of Mark 12:41–44 and 14:3–9, respectively. All three function as foils for men: Herodias for the righteous John the Baptist, the widow for the rapacious scribes, and the anointing woman for the betraying Judas.[25] Of course, from the narrator's viewpoint, Herodias still stands apart from these other women as the only *negative* foil. I want to pursue Herodias's associations, both positive and negative, with another pair of women in closer proximity in Mark's narrative. Flanking the portrait of Herodias in 6:14–29, we find depictions of a hemorrhaging woman in 5:25–34 and a Syrophoenician woman in 7:24–30. Centered within the tight unit of Mark 4–8—which Malbon, again, has shown to be replete with rhetorical links[26]—these scenes form a kind of triptych of aggressive women, each connected with a daughter and each manipulating male power for her own aims. Joel Marcus calls attention to this grouping of Markan characters in his recent commentary:

> [T]he [hemorrhaging] woman . . . displays the same sort of bold, risk-taking attitude that will be shown by the Syrophoenician woman in 7:24–30. These two plucky women . . . form a divine counterpoint to the demonic impetuosity of Herodias and Salome in the intervening story in 6:17–28, and Mark seems to have deliberately juxtaposed the four female characters in order to bring out the similarities and contrasts among them.[27]

Although overdrawing, in my view, the polarity between the "divine" women seeking healing from Jesus and the "demonic" Herodias and choosing an awkward, if not patronizing, term to describe them (I don't think vigorous women prefer to be called "plucky" any more than "perky"), I think Marcus is on the right track.

The present study investigates the similarities and differences among the stories in Mark 5–7 where women lead men, focusing on three broad analytical categories: social-relational, physical-material, and biblical-intertextual; or, more simply, the one category of body or embodiedness in three expressions: the body politic (corporate body), the physical body (corporeal body), and a body of literature (literary corpus). The first area concentrates on relations pertaining to gender (women and men), kinship (parents and daughters), class (upper and lower), ethnicity (Jew and Gentile), and honor (patrons and clients). The second deals with physical-material issues concerning body zones (head and feet), body needs (blood and food), spatial movements (in and out), and financial resources (means and measures). The third continues the intertextual probe of scriptural stories surrounding Jephthah's daughter, Queen Jezebel of Israel, Esther of Persia, and the formidable Judith. I will begin with the central narrative featuring the blood-greedy Herodias and dancing daughter and then proceed to compare and contrast the framing portraits of the bleeding woman and dying daughter in Mark 5 and the pleading woman and demonized daughter in Mark 7.

The Blood-Greedy Woman and Dancing Daughter (Mark 6:14–29)[28]

From the outset, this story revolves around problematic issues of gender and kinship. As Mark tells it, the Herodian conflict with John concerned his challenging the legitimacy of Herod's marriage to "his brother Philip's wife," Herodias. John's objection presumes that Philip was still alive and that the new royal couple had arranged an unlawful (adulterous) divorce and remarriage (6:17–19).[29] The matching of masculine and feminine names—Herod/Herodias—underscores their common purpose and prominence in Galilean politics. The family drama is further complicated by the appearance of the daughter in 6:22, who is introduced either as "his [Herod's] daughter [also named] Herodias" or "the daughter of Herodias herself." Metzger frankly admits, "It is very difficult to decide which reading is the least unsatisfactory."[30] The first reading commands stronger external attestation but flies in the face of historical and contextual considerations: Antipas had no daughter named Herodias (he was granduncle and stepfather of Herodias's daughter, Salome); and 6:24, 28 portray the girl as "her mother's" daughter, not Herod's.

But if we let Mark's story stand on its own apart from the complex network of Herodian family history, there is nothing unusual about the "little girl" (*korasion*) being cast as the daughter of both her mother and father (who are married to each other) and bearing the name of both mother and father. From a feminist-rhetorical perspective, the close conjunction of father Herod, daughter Herodias, and mother Herodias suggests a tight family unit acting together—as one consolidated, androgynous Herodian power, thus sharing the blame for John's death and mitigating the tendencies in the narrative to let "King" Herod off the hook as one sympathetic to John.[31]

The birthday-banquet setting highlights other social features of the story. In terms of class, we are clearly dealing with an elite affair. A royal potentate who can afford to give away "half the kingdom" (Mark 6:23) recalls the extravagant wealth of Ahaseurus (Esth 1:1–8; 5:6) and other filthy rich rulers. Accordingly, Herod's birthday celebration is not a casual "open house" event for the Galilean masses but rather a lavish bash "for his courtiers and officers and for the leaders of Galilee" (Mark 6:21)—bigwigs only.[32] And probably for men only, in keeping with aristocratic banqueting customs, but this is not specified.[33] Although Queen and Princess Herodias are not initially in Herod's banquet hall, we are not told that they are sponsoring a separate women's brunch somewhere else in the palace, as Vashti did in the book of Esther. The ethnic flavor of Herod's festival is very Hellenistic—Greek and Roman nobles relished their birthday parties and symposia[34]—but Jewish elements also underlie the scene. The part-Jewish Herod Antipas rules over Galilean Jews and provokes the moral criticism of the Jewish prophet John, who speaks not only for pious Jews but also for peasants fed up with the profligate excesses of the Herodian court.[35]

Whether women are present or not, Herod's birthday party provides a classic setting for gaining and maintaining male honor. Herod reinforces his superior status by inviting his principal cronies and clients to the banquet, and they in turn honor his highness by attending and (presumably) paying homage. Unfortunately, Herod becomes caught in an honor trap of his own making, much as Jephthah did. "Solemnly [and stupidly] swearing" to cede up to half the realm to his daughter (6:23), he has no choice—"out of regard for his oaths and *for his guests*" (6:26)—but to comply with her request for John's head. The fact that such action "deeply grieved (*perilypos*)" Herod (6:26), who "feared John . . . protected him . . . and liked to listen to him" (6:20), is often viewed as a means of lessening Herod's guilt for John's death and increasing the two Herodian women's blame and shame. But the case is not as simple as that. Suffering emotional grief or sadness over a bad decision ("I'm really sorry to do this, but I have no choice") does not neutralize guilt. When later in Mark another wealthy man "[goes] away grieving (*lypoumenos*)" (10:22), unwilling to meet Jesus' stringent demands of discipleship, Jesus cuts him no slack: "how hard it will be for those who have wealth to enter the kingdom of God" (10:23). By contrast, when Jesus himself becomes "deeply grieved (*perilypos*)" over his impending death (14:34), he remains firmly committed to fulfilling God's will despite the distress it will bring. Whether he realizes it or not, Herod has a choice in the matter of John's fate—a choice to sacrifice his own personal honor to save a righteous man's life, a choice that ultimately leads to the greater honor of divine approval.[36] As for Herod being forced against his will and better judgment by a cunning wife and daughter to execute John, this is only partially true. Herodias does indeed seize the "opportune" (*eukairos,* 6:21) moment to provoke her husband into satisfying her blood vengeance against John. But she doesn't, as is sometimes thought, create the opportunity. She hatches no master sinister plot ("Now, honey, I want you to go in there and shake your stuff before dad and his buddies, get him all worked up so he promises you the world, and then ask him for that bastard Baptist's head"). The account does not indicate who summons or sends the girl into the party: it simply notes, "His daughter came in and danced" (6:22). It's highly unlikely she decides to pop in on her own, but she could just as easily be responding to her father's invitation as her mother's instruction.[37] The Esther connection could go either way: Ahaseurus called for Vashti; Esther came at Mordecai's prodding. In any event, once daughter Herodias arrives, dances, and pleases her father, *he* initiates the "make a wish" deal, whereupon she goes out to ask her mother's advice (6:22–24). It's only at this point that the light dawns for Mrs. Herod: now is the accepted time, now is the day of retaliation. But this scenario has been created by the king's rash behavior and, at the end of the day, John's beheading will result from the king's order.

Further insight into the roles played by the Herodian royal family in killing John comes from considering the physical body language of the story. We have already noted something of the in-and-out movements of the daughter. As Mark's story begins, the two Herodian females are outside the banquet hall in other quarters (unlike Matthew's account, which presumes their constant presence at the party[38]); whether they are formally sequestered with other women guests or just temporarily out of the room (taking a powder?), we are not told. In any case, the girl eventually "came *in* and danced," then "went *out*" again to consult her mother, "rushed back" *in* once more with the plea for John's head, and finally delivered the pate-on-a-plate, like a waitress, back to the queen (6:22, 24–25).[39] While it was customary for upper-class Greek women to dine separately and for the most part occupy domestic space partitioned from their husbands and fathers, the back-and-forth bustling of the little girl blurs these boundaries.[40] Again, the Herodians, male and female, appear more united than divided. On the other hand, we must notice that mother Herodias never shows up at (or returns to) the banquet in Mark: she does all her work offstage, behind the scenes, *outside.* This location demeans her as a subservient queen who must surreptitiously manipulate male authority to get what she wants, yet also diminishes her sole responsibility for John's execution. Unlike Jezebel, who personally ordered "killing off the prophets of the Lord," and Judith, who herself hacked off Holofernes' head with his own sword, Herodias must wait for Herod to act.[41]

The same *feet* that carry daughter Herodias in and out of Herod's banquet hall also orchestrate her dance that leads to the loss of John's *head*. The head and feet at the extremities of the human body evoke images of authority and sexuality. Bowing one's head at another's feet acknowledges the superior authority—or headship—of that figure. In a patriarchal culture, it is the male head—and the commanding voice issuing from it—that represents supreme authority, symbolized in the phallus crowned with its own distinctive head and mouth. The man's feet, as well, could also stand for his genital potency, as in the famous threshing-floor incident with Boaz and Ruth (Ruth 3:4–9). Thus John's decapitation represents a kind of humiliating emasculation, cutting off his influence over the people, throttling his powerful voice that dared to challenge the political headship of Herod over Galilee and his sexual union with Herodias. The fact that the "hand of a woman" plays a part in John's unmanning makes it all the more shameful.[42]

What role does female sexuality play in this scenario? Judith and Esther provide precedent for using their seductive bodies to accomplish their aims in a man's world, and the usual reading—perpetuated in art, literature, drama, and opera as well as in biblical scholarship—is that Salome (Herodias in Mark's account) uses her dancing feet and undulating body to similar erotic effect.[43] As such, she is cast in the company of whores, hetaerae, flute girls, and other courtesan-entertainers who frequented Hellenistic banquets and sometimes even requested a decapitation for their own macabre amusement. For example, the "brazen whore" reclining at a banquet on the breast of proconsul L. Quinctius tells her lover "that she had never seen anyone's head cut off with an axe, and she would very much like to." The besotted proconsul promptly complies and orders up a beheading for his bloodthirsty lady.[44] Of course, these various banquet call girls were not usually nice royal wives or young daughters[45]—that's the shocker in the Markan story, or maybe not, given the Herodian reputation for depravity and licentiousness. Shocking or not to Mark's audience, Kathleen Corley contends that the story portrays the two Herodiases, mother and daughter, as "madam and fledgling courtesan."[46]

But while the background fits this characterization, the details do not. Mark offers no description whatsoever of the little girl's appearance (beauty, make-up, jewelry, perfume, sandals, anklets, etc., as we learn about Esther and Judith)[47] or the nature of the dance (tap dance or lap dance? Shirley Temple or Charo?—we don't know).[48] All we do know is that the daughter's dance "*pleased (ēresen)* Herod and his guests" (Mark 6:22). The verb *areskō*, however, carries no necessary connotations of sexual pleasure or excitement. In the LXX it is used to express the king's delight with the beautiful *korasion* Esther (2:4, 9). But of its seventeen uses in the New Testament (mostly in Paul), only two carry any sexual overtones, and both of these appear in the chaste context of marriage (pleasing a husband or wife; 1 Cor 7:33–34). Half deal with the pious duty to please God or one's neighbor in the sense of obedience and service.[49] Thus it's not unreasonable to surmise that little Herodias pleased her father with an innocent little girl's dance, much as young daughters today bring smiles to their fathers at ballet recitals (that's my baby in the center with the perfect plié). Now to be sure, I give my budding ballerina a rose and take her for ice cream—no offers of half the kingdom (which wouldn't be much anyway). But proud fathers, even Herodian ones, can be quite generous.

If one persists in stressing the erotic mood of Mark's banquet scene, I would further point out that there is no reference to any touching, fondling, kissing, or sexual banter, as was typical of such occasions.[50] Now a modest Markan narrator might have withheld such explicit language for decency's sake (especially regarding a young daughter), but the fact remains that the story as we have it suggests no contact or conversation between Herod and his dancing daughter beyond the king's extravagant offer and the girl's gruesome request.[51] If you're looking for an erotically charged banquet scene in the Gospels, consider the anointing "loose" woman in Luke 7:35–50, who douses Jesus' feet with oil, kisses them repeatedly, and wraps her loosened tresses around them. None of that stuff happens in Mark 6:14–29.[52]

While the sex rating of the scene is for general audiences, the violence factor is another matter. The gory picture of John's severed head on a platter displays a horrifying, cannibalistic mixture of blood and food, sure to put anyone off her lunch (not to mention blatantly offending kosher sensibilities). And there is no way to deny or downplay the two females' role in this scenario. This is their distinctive contribution to the drama, and they provide it with relish: the daughter "rushes" back to the king, at her mother's behest, insisting that John's head be served up "at once"! (6:25)—a ghoulish twist to the traditional woman's function of food preparer and server. The jolting effect is similar to that which Livy describes concerning L. Quinctius's beheading of a prisoner for his lady-friend's sport: "It was a wild and gruesome deed. . . . At a meal, where it was customary to offer part of the food and drink to the gods and to call down blessings on one another, a human being was slaughtered like a sacrificial animal and the table sprinkled with his blood, all as a show for a brazen whore who was lying on the consul's breast."[53]

Instead of graciously sharing food with the gods and the needy, the proconsul senselessly spiced his table with human blood. The comparable action of the Herodian royal family in Mark contrasts sharply with the charitable feeding miracles of Jesus that follow in Mark 6:30–42 and 8:1–10;[54] but there's another dimension to this bloody mealtime gesture. Livy's use of "sacrificial" and "sprinkling" language to describe the travesty of the banquet beheading trades on cultic images of worship and thanksgiving, which the Christian Gospel of Mark translates into Eucharist. The Markan Jesus will "serve up his life as a ransom for many" (10:45) and command his followers to "eat . . . my body" and "drink . . . my blood of the covenant, which is poured out for many" (14:22–24). The Herodian offering of John's bloody head on a platter thus becomes a proleptic parody of Jesus' self-offering of his "sacred head now wounded" for the nourishment of many.[55]

Of course, in the Markan scheme, it is ultimately God, Jesus' *Abba*, who demands that Jesus drink this "cup" of death and offer himself for execution (14:36). A peculiar shadow alliance is thus struck between mother Herodias and father God as solicitors of human sacrifice. While God's motives are holy and redemptive and Herodias's heinous and vindictive, if allowed to give her side of the story, Herodias might offer a different perspective: she has the rabble-rousing Baptist killed in order to preserve her marriage and maintain order in the realm.[56] Better to eliminate one ringleader than to put down a mass revolt. In this case, cut off the head, and the body will live.

The Bleeding Woman and Dying Daughter (Mark 5:21–43)

While at first blush the Herodian court tale appears to have little to do with the healing stories in the previous chapter, closer examination reveals a number of suggestive echoes. The social setting is once again Jewish Galilee. Jesus and his disciples had previously been in the Gentile region of the Decapolis among herds of swine (5:11–20); but now they "cross again in the boat to the other side" (5:21)—that is, back to the western bank of the Galilean sea, to the heart of Herod Antipas's territory. The cast of characters is also similar in terms of gender, kinship relations, and class status: a leading male official (Herod/Jairus), his wife, and "little daughter" (*korasion*—unnamed, however, in 5:41–42), and a controversial prophet (John/Jesus). Jairus is a religious leader (synagogue president), not a Roman political appointee like Herod. But religion and politics were cozy bedfellows in first-century Galilee, and in

Mark's understanding, Jewish synagogue officials, scribes, and Pharisees typically form an opposition block against Jesus in concert with the Herodians (3:6).[57] Jairus and Herod are also both supported by friends at important ceremonies. The occasions are different, to be sure; but more than that, they are diametric opposites and thus ironically linked: whereas clients honor the Herodian family at the king's birthday party, mourners attend Jairus and his wife at their daughter's death-day vigil (5:38). But life and death curiously intermingle in both stories. Herod's celebration of his own life results in John's death, but Herod can't escape the haunting notion that John "has been raised" to life again in the person and work of Jesus (6:16). Jairus's daughter doesn't stay dead very long, but rises to renewed life when Jesus "takes her by the hand" and lifts her up (5:41). Mark reports: "immediately the girl got up and began to walk about" (5:42). Could this have included a dance step or two? That would certainly be fitting for such a joyous occasion, which also prompts a spontaneous banquet suggested in Jesus' final words: "give her something to eat" (5:43).

Granted that Jairus's and Herod's families overlap in Mark's narrative, what about this other character—the bleeding woman—who interrupts the Jairus story, invades Jesus' private space, and, in the minds of many interpreters, intrudes into a crowd where she would not have been welcome (5:25–34)? The portrait of this woman as intruder/outsider, outcast/pariah needs to be carefully nuanced and in many respects revised. As most scholars appreciate, her story is not an extraneous literary intrusion at all, but rather a skillfully designed intercalation with the story of Jairus's daughter (both accounts feature "twelve years," "daughter," and healing through touch). Likewise, the hemorrhaging woman is not quite the social intruder she's often thought to be. While destitute when she encounters Jesus, she is no stranger to wealth. For years she "had spent all that she had" on physicians' fees (5:26)—proportionally more than Herod's "half kingdom" and quantitatively much more than the poor widow's "two mites" (12:42). Only those with means could afford extended "professional" medical care.[58] Her social background is thus comparable to Jairus's wife and Herodias.

But she now appears to be a single, unattached woman—nobody's wife. This single status is sometimes taken as a sign of her marginal position in society: no man would have her because of her bleeding disorder (damaged goods). But apart from our limited knowledge of her condition (see below), the story reveals nothing about the woman's marital or sexual history. She could just as easily have been a wealthy widow (like Judith) who took twelve years to exhaust her resources, an ostracized divorcee, or a lifelong spinster. The only familial connection that emerges is Jesus' adopting her as his "daughter" (5:34). Again, this reference is often viewed as a marker of the woman's alienation from society: the loving Jesus welcomes her when no one else will. Positive evidence for Jesus' compassion, however, is clear enough in Mark without painting all of his contemporaries as callous misanthropists. The hemorrhaging woman was suffering terribly, and no one could help her; but that doesn't mean no one cared. No one among the crowd recoils from this woman or criticizes her in any way. Moreover, Jesus doesn't heal her and call her "daughter" *because* everyone else has rejected her. His ultimate acceptance of this woman springs not from extraordinary compassion, but from recognition of her active faith ("Daughter, your faith has made you well," 5:34).[59]

Considering this woman's action in the story prompts us to examine the condition and movement of her body. Most commentators assume that the woman suffers from irregular uterine bleeding that renders her permanently unclean and untouchable (again, a lonely social pariah) according to Mosaic law.[60] But Jewish scholars such as Shaye Cohen, Ross Kraemer, Amy-Jill Levine, and Paula Fredriksen have persuasively challenged this stereotype.[61] Mark's description of the woman's malady (scourge) as an irregular "flow/fountain of blood" (*en rhysei/pēgē haimotos*, 5:25, 29) fits the Levitical category of an abnormal, vaginal "discharge of blood" outside the monthly period (Lev 15:19–33).[62] Technically, she is not a menstruant (a perfectly normal, necessary condition), but a *zābâ*, or "oozer," in Cohen's terms.[63] And, according to a strict interpretation of the Levitical code, she abides in a state of impurity as long as her discharge persists. But so what? If she were impure, she would have a lot of company in Galilee, since most folks were ritually unclean for some reason or another most of the time. The main restrictions would have been against her entering the temple, having sex with her husband, or having someone touch her bed or something she's sat on (which was not illegal per se but simply contaminating to others, requiring a little extra washing and waiting before going to the sanctuary—hardly a fatal consequence [Lev 15:19–30]). The fact is, none of these limitations has any relevance to the woman's case in Mark 5. She's by the Sea of Galilee, nowhere near the temple; she seems to have no husband and is not trying to have sex with Jesus; and she's walking outside in public, not lying or sitting on her bed or chair and certainly not carrying them with her. She touches Jesus' garment, yes, but cloth contact outside of bedding and upholstery is not mentioned in Lev 15. Even if we assume that touching one's clothes is tantamount to touching one's body (and not everybody did),[64] the particular issue of physical contact is not raised with respect to the *zābâ*, (Lev 15:25–30) as it is to the regularly menstruating woman ("whoever touches her . . ." [Lev 15:19]) and the man who has a penile discharge ("all who touch the body . . ." [Lev 15:7]).

However we parse the Torah restrictions, the most telling point against a purity-oriented interpretation of the bleeding woman's story is that Mark says nothing about it.[65] Neither the Markan Jesus nor narrator pronounces the woman "clean"—as they do with the leper and "all foods"—or dispatch her to a priest for examination (1:40–44; 7:19). The matter never arises, and filling in Mark's silence with Pharisaic/rabbinic arguments is risky business because of the lateness of this material, its limited application to the Galilee of Jesus' day (much of it utopian, as was the Qumran literature), and its legal complexity (including forensic experts inspecting the quality of various bloodstains, not all of which were pollutants).[66] In sum, just as we found little warrant for judging Herodias and her daughter as immoral seductresses (dirty dancing), so we detect little interest in the hemorrhaging woman as an impure contaminator (dirty bleeding). She suffers from a physical infirmity requiring healing, not a ritual impurity demanding cleansing.

But whereas the bleeding woman does not inject Jesus with some toxic contagion, she does *extract* therapeutic power from his body. She initiates a kind of intercourse: her touching Jesus' garment triggers a potent discharge from his body into hers; his dynamic flow into her body remedies her defective flow. And, like the two Herodiases, this woman manipulates male power for her own purposes; and like Herod, Jesus' intentions (and Jairus's as well) are thwarted by a demanding woman.[67] As Jesus heads to Jairus's house to heal his dying child, Jesus apparently does not intend to heal anyone else along the way. The narrator and disciples both observe that a large crowd "presses in" on Jesus (5:24), but no indication is given that their reaching out to touch Jesus produces any miracles, as we find in 3:10 and 6:56. The focus is on Jairus's daughter, not on the crowds—until the hemorrhaging woman stops the proceedings (we might say she interrupts the *flow* of Jesus and his followers). Jesus knows that "power had gone forth from him" without his permission and so inquires, "Who touched my clothes?" (5:30). The concern is not with the act of touching (a bunch of folks are doing that) or polluting (no one's worried about that) but with a kind of *stealing*. I think there's an edge of irritation, even a sense of personal insult, reflected in Jesus' response: "Who dared take my power from me without asking? Let the thief show him/herself!" Thus exposed, the woman who had snuck up "behind" (5:27) Jesus in the crowd now falls down "before" him, not simply in praise and thanksgiving, but "in fear and trembling" (5:33). This is a tense moment. The woman is not at all certain how Jesus will react to her intrusion. But Jesus is on the spot too: everyone's watching to see what the healer will do now.

Jesus' honor crisis is not as obvious as Herod's, but it is implied. Jesus cannot allow himself to become a puppet for the power-mongering masses, yet his mission revolves around serving and giving himself to save many (cf. 10:43–45). On this occasion, the woman gives Jesus little choice but to affirm his wonder-working operation on her behalf, since she confronts Jesus before a large crowd of witnesses (including his closest disciples) as one who has already appropriated his miraculous power by faith. To rebuke her publicly or retract her healing because she obtained it through unauthorized means would undermine his reputation as a gracious benefactor.[68]

Amid the echoes between the story of Jesus and the hemorrhaging woman in Mark 5 and the episode involving Herod and his wife and daughter in Mark 6 are notable counterpoints. Ultimately Jesus commends the woman's faith for stopping her bleeding and making her "whole," quite the opposite of the Herodian women's scheme effecting John's bloody dismemberment. And, while initially questioning the woman's approach, Jesus comes around not only to endorse her healing and embrace her as "daughter," but also to identify with her suffering in a personal way. In his passion Jesus will experience the woman's (and others') "plague" or "scourge" (*mastix*) of affliction (5:29, 34): "they will mock him, and spit upon him, and flog/scourge (*mastigōsousin*) him, and kill him" (10:34).[69] In contrast to Herod, who spilt the blood of a righteous prophet, Jesus' own blood will be shed to ransom the enslaved and the oppressed.

The Pleading Woman and Demonized Daughter (Mark 7:24–30)

While this scene also features a woman and daughter pair, the web of gender and kinship relations surrounding them is somewhat distinct from what we've encountered thus far. This woman and her daughter are biologically related—like the two Herodiases and unlike the bleeding woman and twelve-year-old daughter—but there is no father in sight, whether biological (Jairus/Herod?), adoptive (Herod?), or metaphorical (Jesus). The only man in the picture is Jesus, and this is not his most paternal or compassionate moment.[70] Far from addressing the woman as "daughter" (or even seeming concerned about this woman's ill daughter), Jesus calls her a scavenging "dog" (7:27). If a domestic image is in view with the dog or puppy functioning as a household pet,[71] it is still not an altogether tender image, like the "little ewe lamb" in Nathan's parable who was "like a daughter" to the poor man and drank from his cup (2 Sam 12:1–3). While the term *kynarion* can mean "lapdog," that is not Jesus' intent here. It makes no sense to "throw" (*ballō*) table food to a dog sitting in one's lap (a scrap dog is closer to the mark than a lapdog, as the woman's response makes clear [7:28]). So Jesus does not seem to call the visiting woman "pet" in any endearing sense (the British equivalent of "honey" or "dear"). At best, he associates her with a stray mongrel that has wandered into the house and been allowed (grudgingly by the master) to hang around the premises.

The key question, in any case, is not what kind of dog Jesus has in mind (any dog is subhuman and of lesser value than "children"), but why does Jesus think of this woman in canine terms? Why call her a dog? First, is her gender a key factor here? In our culture there is no question that pejorative, even degrading uses of dog language are most often applied to women: "she looks like a dog"; "she's such a bitch"; the "doggie" position. Male comparisons are typically more positive: "you sly dog, you"; powerful athletes or executives are nicknamed "big dog" or "top dog." In the biblical world, however, negative canine images fit men as easily as women. A telling case is that of Jonathan's crippled son, Mephibosheth, who regarded himself as a pathetic "dead dog." The context, however, is King David's extraordinary kindness to this lone surviving descendant of Saul's house, granting him favor "to eat at my table always" (2 Sam 9:1–13). That is more hospitality than Jesus initially shows the woman in Mark 7. But, again, is this because of her gender? Not necessarily, since the noun for "little dog" (*kynarion*) is neuter, not gender specific, but it is striking in Mark that *paternal* suppliants seeking healing for sick children—Jairus for his daughter (5:21–24) and an unnamed father for his spirit-tormented son (9:20–27)—are treated with more respect by Jesus than this desperate mother.

Beyond her identity as woman and mother, she is also characterized in ethnic and, possibly, economic terms as a "Gentile/Greek (*Hellēnis*) of Syrophoenician origin" (7:26). Gerd Theissen argues that such a profile fits an upper-class urbanite from Tyre or Sidon profiting from the exploitation of peasant farmers in neighboring upper Galilee.[72] While Theissen demonstrates that rural Galilee did function not too happily in the first century as the "breadbasket" for the wealthy Greek/Phoenician city-states along the coast, there is no clue in Mark's story that the Syrophoenician woman was herself rich or oppressive—characteristics that Mark does not hesitate to associate with other figures (10:22–25; 12:41–44).[73] Moreover, it makes little sense in the present context that Jesus refuses to give this woman any bread because she has unfairly extorted bread from his people. For one thing, she's not asking for bread, but rather healing for her daughter; for another, there is no reference to her typical practices of procuring grain (maybe she paid a fair price; maybe she had her own garden—who knows?). Overall, the economic tenor of the story is parsimonious. Unlike Herod and Ahaseurus, who offered women half their fortune, Jesus seems loathe to give this woman anything; and her counter bargain does not include any attempt to purchase Jesus' services (as the bleeding woman had paid her doctors), but merely a plea for "crumbs" (7:28).

Whatever her economic condition, the woman's Gentile ethnic status is clear, leading to the prevailing view that Jesus spurns this unclean pagan "dog" because his mission is "first" and foremost to his own Jewish people.[74] But we must be cautious here, too. "Dog" is not automatically a cipher for "Gentile" in Jewish parlance. Paul, for example, derisively branded his conservative Jewish opponents at Philippi as rapacious "dogs" for wanting to circumcise (mutilate) believing Gentiles (Phil 3:2–4). "Dog" thus serves as an apt deviant label for any person or group, Jew or Gentile, who exploit others' "flesh" for their own benefit. Further, it is "not fair" (Mark 7:27) to label all first-century Jews as xenophobic Hellenist-haters. While some Jews (like the Qumran sect) excluded Gentiles from their company and covenant, many did not (witness in Acts the acceptance of Cornelius and other "God-fearers" in the synagogue). It is thus misguided to mitigate Jesus' harsh response to the Syrophoenician woman by shifting the blame to some naïve stereotype of Jewish parochialism.[75] If anything, it makes Jesus look worse: he's the one Jew who appears ethnocentric here; he models and reinforces the stereotype, which did not fit many other first-century Jews (Philo, Paul, and Stephen, to name three) and in fact does not fit the Markan Jesus. This Jesus has already reached out to the Gerasene demoniac in the pig-farming region of the Decapolis (if anyone fits the pattern of a "wild dog," it's this poor fellow [5:1–20]). Why, then, is the case of the Syrophoenician mother and her demon-possessed daughter any less deserving of Jesus' attention and exorcising powers? Right before encountering this woman, Jesus does distinguish between "pure" and "defiled" persons, but the latter are characterized not by ethnic status but by "evil intentions" and depraved actions—fornication, theft, murder, and the like (7:21–23)—none of which apply to the desperate mother! And the implication that "all foods are clean" (nothing that enters the mouth can defile, 7:14–20) suggests the possibility of open commensality between Jews and Gentiles.[76] So nothing pertaining to racial bigotry or ritual impurity in Mark's narrative prepares us for Jesus' stark repudiation of the Syrophoenician woman.

And yet there it is, and not delivered with any twinkle in the eye ("just kidding, honey") as some desperate commentators have suggested.[77] Within the story itself, the main hints regarding Jesus' attitude relate to his and the woman's physical movements. After ministering around the Sea of Galilee and debating with certain scribes and Pharisees, Jesus "set out and *went away into* (*apēlthen eis*) the region of Tyre," where he "*came into* (*eiselthōn eis*) a house and did not want anyone (*oudena*) to know he was there" (7:24). Whatever his motivation (rest? retreat? reflection?), Jesus crosses "into" (*eis*) Phoenician territory and "into" (*eis*) a private house with every intention of remaining incognito. "But immediately (*all' euthys*)"[78] the Syrophoenician woman hears that Jesus is in the area, enters the house where he is staying, and bows down at his feet (7:25). Jesus is in no mood to receive this uninvited visitor and dance to her beat. He is not in a party spirit, like Herod, happy to receive a female guest; he is not in a gracious mood, like Ahaseurus, willing to welcome a suppliant woman who comes unbidden; and he is not in a crowded open setting, where a woman's approach—though disruptive and irritating in the case of the *zābâ*—was not improper and could not be impugned without calculating the key factor of public opinion. While recent studies have cautioned against hard-and-fast presumptions of separate male and female space in the ancient world (segregation was not always the norm),[79] in the present situation, the Syrophoenician woman seems shamelessly to intrude into Jesus' private household domain. In Jesus' isolationist mode, any visitor, male or female, would be unwelcome, but a female intruder may well be considered more offensive, given common (though not absolute) partitions between male and female quarters.

But she approaches Jesus with deferential body language rather than with brazen impudence, bowing at his feet as she begs for mercy on behalf of her tormented daughter (7:25–26). This position recalls that of the hemorrhaging woman, except for the notable distinction that the Syrophoenician *starts* with bowing before Jesus instead of first grasping him from behind. One might expect Jesus to appreciate such open, straightforward submission, but in fact, with surprising lack of sympathy, he reconfigures the woman's words and actions. He speaks about children who need feeding, but not her child who needs healing; and he reimages her reverential kneeling/begging posture into a demeaning dog-like position—nose to the ground, scrounging for scraps.[80] Amazingly, the woman plays out her assigned role and turns it against Jesus:[81] "It's not just the streets and alleys where we dogs wait for the garbage to be thrown out. It's inside the house, too, under the table where we lap up the crumbs your well-fed children drop from their mouths. That's all I want for me and my daughter" (7:28, paraphrase). At this remarkable statement—"for this saying" (7:29)—Jesus changes his tone and announces her daughter's deliverance, which the woman confirms upon returning home (7:30).

A terrific ending, but a terrible beginning and middle for Jesus. Why would Mark present Jesus in such a bad light? Drawing on the work of Wendy Cotter, Amy-Jill Levine cites the intriguing parallel of Emperor Hadrian's encounter with a pleading woman, as reported in Dio Cassius's *Roman History*: "[W]hen a woman made a request of him [Hadrian], as he passed by on a journey, he at first said to her, 'I haven't time,' but afterwards, when she cried out, 'Cease, then, being the Emperor,' he turned about and granted her a hearing." Dio tells us that he selected this story to enhance Hadrian's reputation: "This is a kind of preface, of a summary nature, that I have given in regard to his character."[82] Having the humility and courage to learn from one's underlings, to change one's mind, to correct one's errant conduct, is a sign of true greatness (we might recall that even God "repented" at strategic moments in the Old Testament). Mark's Jesus will later teach his disciples, "whoever wants to be first must be . . . servant of all," and illustrate his point by taking a "little child" in his arms (9:35–37). He must first learn this lesson for himself under the surprising tutelage of a foreign, female visitor. To Jesus' credit, he's willing to learn and become the model servant.

Another dimension of the Syrophoenician woman's pivotal role in Jesus' development may be detected with reference to his feeding ministry. The combined elements of blood and food associated with John's head on a platter are split in the surrounding stories in Mark 5 and 7: the former accentuates bleeding (hemorrhaging woman), the latter features feeding. Although, as we have noted, Jesus' focus on feeding does not address the Syrophoenician's immediate concern, it does reflect a key aspect of Jesus' work in this section of Mark, which the woman uses to her advantage and for Jesus' instruction. The first episode following Herod's execution of John presents Jesus' feeding of the multitude—five thousand *men* (*andres*), all Galilean Jews, it seems, representing the people of Israel (twelve baskets = twelve tribes) (6:30–44). Is it accidental that Jesus' second feeding miracle, which comes soon after his transforming encounter with the Syrophoenician woman, is performed in the *Gentile* region of the Decapolis on behalf of four thousand *people* (*tetrakischilioi*, not necessarily restricted by gender), multiplying seven loaves into a feast yielding seven baskets of leftovers (70 = standard tally of "the nations" in Gen 10) (Mark 8:1–10)? The dogs are getting much more than crumbs now from Jesus. He has learned his lesson well.[83]

While the "feeding" aspect of the Syrophoenician woman's story is prominent, a secondary "bleeding" element may also lie beneath the surface in connection with the Old Testament story of Jezebel and Elijah, which we have already correlated with Mark's tale of Herodias and John. Like the woman in Mark 7, Jezebel was also a demanding Phoenician interloper in northern Israelite affairs; but unlike her humble counterpart, she came not submissively before the Jewish prophet but with every intention of forcing the people to bow down to her, her prophets, and her deity. As their attitudes differ, so do their ultimate fates and associations with dogs. While Mark's lowly Syrophoenician woman manipulates her assigned canine role with "dogged"[84] persistence to secure her daughter's healing, the mighty Phoenician princess and Queen of Israel cannot resist Elijah's word and Jehu's wrath, consigning her (and husband Ahab) to a gruesome end as the bloody fare for rapacious dogs (1 Kgs 21:17–24, "dogs will also lick up your blood"; 2 Kgs 9:30–37, "the dogs shall eat the flesh of Jezebel"). Here we may envisage a peculiar twist on Jesus' paradox, "the first shall be last and the last first": the first become food for wild, bloodthirsty dogs; the last, imaged as "dogs," receive food—children's food, no less—from the bounty of God's table.

Conclusion

Amid stark differences of ethnic identity, social position, political intent, and moral outcome, the cluster of stories in Mark 5–7 involving the hemorrhaging woman (5:25–34), the Herodian family (6:14–29), and the Syrophoenician woman (7:24–30) cohere around a common character/plot scheme: desperate mothers and/or daughters take matters into their own hands to compel reluctant male authorities to achieve their—the women's—goals and fulfill their desires. Working within a system where men are expected and empowered to lead, these remarkable women and/or girls make sure the men move in the direction they—the women—want things to go. In short, whatever the culturally scripted choreography, the women of Mark 5–7 take over the dance, and the men follow their lead.

An unnamed and unattached Jewish woman suffering from a chronic bleeding condition that has sapped her economic resources as well as her physical health dares to press through the crowd to touch Jesus' garment in such a forceful ("faith"-ful) way as to detonate a surge of healing energy into her body. Her desperate touch taps a dynamic flow from Jesus' body to stanch her debilitating flow. But it is also an unbidden (if not forbidden) touch. Jesus does not invite her to "come to me" or present himself to her (or anyone else in the crowd) as "open for business." He has other plans, a determined mission to go to Jairus's house and heal his dying daughter. Thus, the eruption of Jesus' healing power that the hemorrhaging woman sparks is a marked disruption of his holy purpose. If not uttered in stern anger, Jesus'

"Who touched me?" reflects more than a little irritation and frustration. He is not fully in control of his emotions or the situation (the woman has proven that with her surprising intervention). Mark's narrative allows a brief but critical moment for Jesus to gather his composure and compassion. It doesn't take long, but it doesn't happen instantaneously, either. It is only after the power-seizing woman shows herself and tells "the whole truth"— with "fear and trembling"—that Jesus acknowledges her as his "daughter" in the faith. Her respectful boldness elicits Jesus' word of affirmation, just as it had triggered his work of restoration.

A named and powerful Herodian queen suffering the indignity of John the Baptist's denunciation of her royal standing seizes the "opportune" moment, afforded by Herod's oath to her (their) dancing daughter, to quell the Baptist's critical voice once and for all. To hedge his bets and sooth his conscience, the king would have preferred not to kill John (at least not yet); likewise, he would have doubtless preferred giving the pleasant dancing girl a bevy of more customary material rewards. But Herod's desires, whatever they might have been, become subservient to those of Herodias (ironically, at his own honorific party). The responsibility for John's beheading remains Herod's: only he has the authority to pronounce the death sentence—a prerogative that he (and his Herodian forebears) had doubtless exercised with little compunction many times before. But this time, in the face of his (uncharacteristic) ambivalence, Herodias and her dancing daughter prompt the king to deal decisively and ruthlessly with a political enemy—in true Herodian fashion.

Finally, an unnamed and unaccompanied Syrophoenician mother suffering the distress of caring for her demon-possessed daughter persuades the Jewish healer Jesus to cure her child's infirmity. Yet again, the male authority has other plans that a determined woman redirects. Whereas, in the case of the hemorrhaging woman, Jesus was intent on reaching Jairus's house to heal his little girl, here Jesus has no desire to leave the house he's already in for any reason, including aiding the woman's ill daughter. But just as the bleeding woman stops Jesus in his tracks, the pleading mother jolts Jesus out of his inertia, spurring him to reach out (by word) and deliver her tormented child. And just as Herodias turns Herod's munificent promise against him, so the Syrophoenician woman exploits Jesus' restrictive proclamation in order to achieve her more inclusive aims. She holds him to his vow of loving service and increases its scope.

While the women in these three stories lead the male leaders, they do not topple the male hierarchy. Quite the contrary, the women simply compel the men to be true to their natures during an atypical moment of vacillation.

What is Herod doing pussyfooting around with John the Baptist and trying to "protect" him? And what is Jesus doing rushing past and refusing to help needy suppliants? Herod is violent and wicked; Jesus is compassionate and righteous. That is the way things are and the way things will be, if the women in Mark's narrative have anything to say about it.

But even as they preserve the dualistic moral and masculine establishment, the women's stories in Mark 5–7 open up potential cracks in the system. For all their neat compartmentalizing in separate chapters (the stories are not contiguous in Mark 5, 6, and 7) and separate locales (road, palace, home), the stories still "bleed" into one another in destabilizing, disorienting ways. The careful reader is especially left reeling over the seepage between the odd-coupled characters of Herod and Jesus. Is it possible that even a Herodian might change his (or her?) evil ways? Herod seems quicker to grant the prospect of renewed life and restored justice ("John, whom I beheaded, has been raised," 6:16) than Jesus' own followers will be at the end of the gospel. And Jesus comes perilously close to having blood on his hands by ignoring or resisting the approaches of the "pro-life" bleeding and Syrophoenician women. Malbon's astute observation about Markan characters (cited above) is thus reinforced: "Enemies can become exemplary followers, but fallible followers can become enemies. Nothing is static. Nothing is absolute." While neither Malbon nor I would strictly classify Jesus among those many "fallible" figures in Mark's narrative, Jesus' example as a developing, maturing figure—open to women's leadership and guidance—strengthens the fluidity (or depolarity, in Trible's terms) of all character judgments. Nothing—and no one—is as static or as absolute as we might think.

Notes

1. See Amy-Jill Levine, "Sacrifice and Salvation: Otherness and Domestication in the Book of Judith," in *Women in the Hebrew Bible: A Reader* (ed. Alice Bach; New York: Routledge, 1999), 372.

2. See Pheme Perkins, "The Gospel of Mark," in *The New Interpreter's Bible* (vol. 8; Nashville, TN: Abingdon, 1995), 598; and Janice Capel Anderson, "Feminist Criticism: The Dancing Daughter," in *Mark and Method: New Approaches in Biblical Studies* (ed. Janice Capel Anderson and Stephen D. Moore; Minneapolis: Fortress, 1992), 128–29.

3. The concern is similar to that which prompts the dismissal of the "rebellious" Queen Vashti from the Persian royal court: "For this deed of the queen [refusing to come when summoned] will be made known to all women, causing them to look with contempt on their husbands." Esth 1:17; cf. 1:10–22.

4. In Mark 6:14, 17, 18, 20, the narrator's viewpoint hangs on a string of four explanatory *gar* (for) clauses; see Anderson, "Feminist Criticism: The Dancing Daughter," 119; Robert M.

Fowler, *Let the Reader Understand: Reader-Response Criticism and the Gospel of Mark* (Minneapolis: Fortress, 1991), 92–98.

5. Mara's imaginative reconstruction of Mark 6:14–29 arose out of a seminar with Elisabeth Schüssler Fiorenza and is reproduced in the latter's *But She Said: Feminist Practices of Biblical Interpretation* (Boston: Beacon, 1992), 48–50.

6. Phyllis Trible, "Exegesis for Storytellers and Other Strangers," *Journal of Biblical Literature* 114 (1995): 3–19.

7. The association between Elijah and John as eschatological prophets is intimated in Mark 1:6 (similar attire) and 6:14–15; cf. further reflection on Elijah's vocation in 9:11–13.

8. See 1 Kgs 21. Among those who note the Jezebel/Herodias link, see Perkins, "Gospel of Mark," 598; Anderson, "Feminist Criticism: The Dancing Daughter," 129–30; Gail Corrington Streete, *The Strange Woman: Power and Sex in the Bible* (Louisville, KY: Westminster/John Knox, 1997), 150; Florence Morgan Gillman, *Herodias: At Home in That Fox's Den* (Interfaces; Collegeville, MN: Liturgical Press, 2003), 84–85.

9. Trible, "Exegesis," 10, 18n42; on the trickster motif in biblical literature, see Susan Niditch, *Underdogs and Tricksters: A Prelude to Biblical Folklore* (New Voices in Biblical Studies; New York: Harper & Row, 1987); Esther Fuchs, "Who Is Hiding the Truth? Deceptive Women and Biblical Androcentrism," in *Feminist Perspectives on Biblical Scholarship* (ed. Adela Yarbro Collins; Atlanta: Scholars Press, 1985), 137–44; Heather MacKay, "'Only a Remnant of Them Shall Be Saved': Women from the Hebrew Bible in New Testament Narratives," in *A Feminist Companion to the Hebrew Bible in the New Testament* (ed. Athalya Brenner; The Feminist Companion to the Bible 10; Sheffield, UK: Sheffield Academic Press, 1996), 54–57.

10. Trible, "Exegesis," 17.

11. Trible, "The Odd Couple: Elijah and Jezebel," in *Out of the Garden: Women Writers on the Bible* (ed. Christina Büchmann and Celina Spiegel; New York: Fawcett Columbine, 1994), 166–79.

12. Trible, "Exegesis," 19; she further explains: "Contrary to the unrelenting ideology of the Deuteronomists, the polarity of Elijah and Jezebel turns in upon itself. Opposites converge. Gender, class, ethnicity, religion, and land: dissimilarities produce similarities to untie the incompatible. . . . To understand their inseparability is to perceive the limits of polarized thinking and so alter the strictures of theological discourse. Though we may find the convergence repugnant, we can be sure that we are heirs to it, indeed that we participate in it" (p. 18).

13. Trible, "Exegesis," 19n44, mounts a challenge to eliminate, as much as possible, the whole notion of polarity as a fixed interpretive category: "Note that the issue is not polarized versus anti-polarized thinking: that scheme is but another polarity."

14. Schüssler Fiorenza, *But She Said*, 52; cf. pp. 9–10, 52–53; and her *Wisdom Ways: Introducing Feminist Biblical Interpretation* (Maryknoll, NY: Orbis, 2001), 7–19.

15. See Judg 11:29–40; Perkins, "Gospel of Mark," 598. There are also differences between the two dancing girls, most notably: Jephthah's daughter (unlike Herod's) is herself slated for execution; she dances with her friends as a last fling before offering herself up for sacrifice, in accordance with her father's rash vow (Judg 11:34–40).

16. On the close linguistic connections between the Esther and Markan stories, see Anderson, "Feminist Criticism: The Dancing Daughter," 128; Gillman, *Herodias*, 85–87. Again, there are patent contrasts as well as comparisons, most obviously: Esther plays the role of a redemptive heroine, not a destructive villainess.

17. Martin Hengel, *Studies in the Gospel of Mark* (Philadelphia: Fortress, 1985), 35. Others have noted the eccentric, "bizarre" character of this anecdote within the New Testament. Cf. the comment of Graham N. Stanton: "With the possible exception of the rather bizarre story of the death of John the Baptist (Mark 6:14–29 = Matt 14:1–12), the gospels do not use the stock in trade of the ancient biographer, anecdotes which are intended merely to satisfy curiosity or to entertain the reader." Stanton, *The Gospels and Jesus* (Oxford Bible Series; New York: Oxford University Press, 1989), 19.

18. Mary Ann Tolbert, "Mark," in *Women's Bible Commentary* (ed. Carol A. Newsom and Sharon H. Ringe; 2nd ed.; Louisville, KY: Westminster/John Knox, 1998), 359.

19. Anderson, "Feminist Criticism: The Dancing Daughter," 130.

20. Elizabeth Struthers Malbon, *In the Company of Jesus: Characters in Mark's Gospel* (Louisville, KY: Westminster/John Knox, 2000), 28–29; 206–9.

21. Ibid., 41–69.

22. Ibid., 209; cf. pp.198–209.

23. Ibid., 45.

24. Ibid., 69.

25. Mary Rose D'Angelo, "(Re)Presentations of Women in the Gospels: John and Mark," in *Women and Christian Origins* (ed. Ross Shepard Kraemer and Mary Rose D'Angelo; New York: Oxford University Press, 1999), 143.

26. Malbon, "Echoes and Foreshadowings in Mark 4–8," *JBL* 112 (1993), 211–30; *In the Company of Jesus*, 21–40.

27. Joel Marcus, *Mark 1–8* (Anchor Bible 27; New York: Doubleday, 2000), 367. Cf. p. 466: "In the overall Markan context it [the story of the Syrophoenician woman] forms an inclusion with the narrative of the woman with the hemmorhage in 5:21–43. The latter is, like the heroine of our story, an anonymous, plucky, ritually unclean woman who 'hears about Jesus' and receives healing from him, and is coupled with a younger girl (Jairus' daughter, the Syrophoenician's daughter) who is healed. These two female combinations surround a more sinister mother/daughter combination, Herodias and her daughter (6:14–29). It is hard to believe that this arrangement is accidental." Again, I'm not sure "plucky" is the best word to describe these women, and I will argue below that their stories have little or nothing to do with "ritual uncleanness." But I agree with Marcus that the clustering of mother/daughter tales in Mark 5–7 is a significant and purposeful narrative arrangement.

28. See Tolbert, "Mark," 359: "Since Herodias had no direct means to accomplish her aim against her husband's wishes, she had to bide her time until an opportune moment arrived and then take on the ancient female role of the trickster to satisfy her blood greed."

29. Obviously, this taking a (half-)brother's wife—while the brother is still alive!—is not a case of lawful, levirate marriage in Jewish tradition. Herod Antipas's marital status was further complicated by a previous divorce from an Arabian princess. See Josephus, *Jewish Antiquities* 18.109–40; and the discussion of Herodian family politics in Gillman, *Herodias*, 1–32; and Steve Mason, *Josephus and the New Testament* (Peabody, MA: Hendrickson, 1992), 92–94.

30. Bruce M. Metzger, *A Textual Commentary on the Greek New Testament* (2nd ed.; Stuttgart: Deutsche Bibelgesellschaft, 1994), 77.

31. This apologetic nod on Herod's behalf is most evident in his purported "grief" over having to kill John in order to keep his oath (Mark 6:26). Yet, Jennifer A. Glancy also stresses the importance of Herod's self-confession of executing the Baptist in Mark 6:16 ("'John, whom *I* beheaded'"): "[T]he framework of the story insists on Herod's responsibility, guilt that he assumes when he recalls that *he* had John decapitated." Glancy, "Unveiling Masculinity: The Construction of Gender in Mark 6:17–29," *Biblical Interpretation* 2 (1994): 43; cf. p. 38.

32. The Greek terms suggest "power-elites (*megistanoi*), chiliarchs (*chiliarchoi*), and leaders (*prōtoi*) of Galilee (Mark 6:21b). This list leads us to conclude that those attending Herod's party are his clients and retainers, since he is not only the head of the government but also the most powerful patron of the region. . . . All of these stand over against the general population: the peasants. These elites have some combination of superior honor, power, office, influence, networks, and wealth." K. C. Hanson and Douglas E. Oakman, *Palestine in the Time of Jesus: Social Structures and Social Conflicts* (Minneapolis: Augsburg Fortress, 1998), 84.

33. Streete, *Strange Woman*, 149, avers: "There is neither a suggestion nor an assumption that Herodias's daughter dances before an exclusively male audience, one such as Vashti in Esther refused to appear before, or that the dance was erotic in nature, only that it was pleasing to Herod." While I agree that interpreters have too facilely assumed the erotic thrust of the

daughter's dance (see below), I still think Mark's sketch of the elite banquet audience suggests a primarily male group.

34. See Hanson and Oakman, *Palestine,* 84–85; Kathleen E. Corley, *Private Women, Public Meals: Social Conflict in the Synoptic Tradition* (Peabody, MA: Hendrickson, 1993), 93–95.

35. On the social and political background of Mark 6:14–29, see Gerd Theissen, *The Gospels in Context: Social and Political History in the Synoptic Tradition* (Edinburgh, UK: T & T Clark, 1992), 81–96.

36. A clear contrast emerges between the self-serving, power-preserving action of King Herod in this story and the self-giving, redemptive work of Servant Jesus in Mark 10:42–45; see Corley, *Private Women,* 94; Sean Freyne, *Galilee, Jesus, and the Gospels: Literary Approaches and Historical Investigations* (Philadelphia: Fortress, 1988), 36–37.

37. Glancy, "Unveiling Masculinity," 40–41.

38. See Matt 14:6–11; Corley, *Private Women,* 158–60.

39. It is not perfectly clear in Mark 6:27–28 where the daughter first receives the bloody platter. She could be either back in her mother's quarters or still in the banquet hall. If the latter (which seems the more natural reading), she must transport the grisly "gift" from one place to another, as did Judith's maid with the head of Holofernes (Jdt 13:9–15).

40. Customs varied in the ancient Mediterranean world concerning the propriety of men and women eating together. Generally speaking, Greek culture favored separate space for the sexes and Roman allowed for more commingling. See the helpful discussion in Carolyn Osiek and David L. Balch, *Families in the New Testament World: Households and House Churches* (The Family, Religion, and Culture; Louisville, KY: Westminster/John Knox, 1997), 5–35; Corley, *Private Women,* 24–79. Corley (p. 29) cites a representative text from one Cornelius Nepos in the late first century BCE: "Many actions are seemly according to our code which the Greeks look upon as shameful. For instance, what Roman would blush to take his wife to a dinner party? What matron does not frequent the front rooms of her dwelling and show herself in public? But it is very different in Greece, for there a woman is not admitted to a dinner party unless relatives only are present, and she keeps to the more retired part of the house called 'the woman's apartment', to which no man has access who is not near of kin."

Theissen, *Gospels in Context,* 92, notes a similar distinction between ancient Macedonians and Persians, citing a passage from Herodotus:

> After dinner, while the wine was still going round, one of the Persians said: "At important dinners like this, my Macedonian friend, it is our custom in Persia to get our wives and mistresses to come and sit with us in the dining-room. You have welcomed us kindly, provided us with an excellent dinner, and offered earth and water to our King Darius, come then—won't you do as we do?" "Gentlemen," Amyntas replied, "what you mention is by no means the custom in Macedonia; with us, men and women are kept separate." (*Histories* 5.18)

41. Mark 6:19 stresses that Herodias "could not" (*ouk ēdynato*) act on her own in this matter, without Herod's consent.

42. On the shameful potential of the "hand of a woman" doing a man's job and taking a man's life, see Judg 4:9 (portending the conquest of Sisera by Deborah and Jael); Jdt 13:15 (celebrating Judith's beheading of Holofernes).

43. See a sampling of various artistic representations of Herod's banquet and John's beheading in Anderson, "Feminist Criticism: The Dancing Daughter," 115–18; and Glancy, "Unveiling Masculinity," 43–45.

44. The story from Livy, *Epit.* 39.43.2–4, is cited in Theissen, *Gospels in Context,* 93.

45. The impropriety of an official's daughter serving as the evening's entertainment for lusty male guests is illustrated in Cicero's account of the social visit of Gaius Verres, governor of Sicily, to the home of Philodamus, a respected local magistrate and father of a virgin daughter.

As soon as Rubrius [one of Verres's cronies] thought the ice was sufficiently broken, he said, "Tell me, Philodamus, why not send for your daughter to come in and see us?" The respectable and already elderly father received the rascal's suggestion with astonished silence. As Rubrius persisted, he replied in order to say something, that it was not the Greek custom for women to be present at a men's dinner party. At this someone in another part of the room called out, "But really, this is intolerable: let the woman be sent for!" At the same moment, Rubrius told his slaves to shut the front door and stand on guard at the entrance. Philodamus, seeing that their purpose was the violation of his daughter, called his slaves and told them not to trouble about himself, but to save his daughter. (Cicero, *Against Verres* II.1.26.66–67)

See the text and discussion in Corley, *Private Women*, 36–38; Theissen, *Gospels in Context*, 91.

46. Corley, *Private Women*, 95. See also Joanna Dewey, "The Gospel of Mark," in *A Feminist Commentary* (vol. 2 of *Searching the Scriptures*; ed. Elisabeth Schüssler Fiorenza; New York: Crossroad, 1994), 483: "In antiquity . . . it is not her [the daughter's] age but her highborn status as Herodias's daughter that makes her presence and dance shocking. Herodias and her daughter are clearly labeled as disreputable women."

47. Esth 1:9–12; Jdt 10:3–4; 15:12–13; see also Ruth 3:3.

48. Streete, *Strange Woman*, 151. There is simply no basis in Mark's text for assuming, as Dan O. Via Jr. does, that "the girl dances so seductively" and "is apparently quite ready to exploit her charms publicly, and if she is here represented as pre-pubescent, there is something incongruous in the highly sexual nature of her dancing." Via, *The Ethics of Mark's Gospel—In the Middle of Time* (Philadelphia: Fortress, 1985), 108. The choreography envisioned here is Via's, not Mark's.

49. Rom 15:1–3; 1 Cor 10:33; Gal 1:10; 1 Thess 2:4, 15; 4:1.

50. In Herodotus's account of the visit of Persian nobleman to the court of the Macedonian King Amyntas, the Persians can't understand why women might attend them at the banquet table without also offering sexual favors: "Amyntas sent for the women, and they came in and sat down in a row opposite the Persians, who, finding them very charming, remarked to Amyntas that such an arrangement was by no means a good one: it would surely have been better for the women not to have come at all if, instead of sitting beside them, they merely intended to sit opposite. It was a painful thing only to be allowed to look at them. Amyntas could not avoid taking the hint; he told the women to move over and sit with the guests, and as soon as they did so, the Persians, who were very drunk, began to touch their breasts, and even, in some cases, to try to kiss them." Herodotus, *Histories* 5.18, cited in Theissen, *Gospels in Context*, 92.

51. While I agree with Glancy ("Unveiling Masculinity," 38–49) that the history of interpreting the scene surrounding Salome's dance has been dominated by male voyeurism and fantasizing about women's seductive (and destructive) movement, I do not see "the construction of femininity as 'to-be-looked-at-ness'" (p. 42) as primary within Mark's story. Mark gives us very little to "look at" regarding Herodias or her daughter, certainly nothing on the stark level of the Baptist's head on a platter, which is surely the image most likely to linger in (haunt) the reader's mind.

52. See chap. 5 in this book for a full analysis of the "loose" woman in Luke 7:36–50. Dewey's assumption that the story in Mark 6:14–29 carries "sexual overtones" and hints of "lewd behavior" goes beyond the details the narrative supplies. "Gospel of Mark," 483.

53. Livy, *Epit.* 39.43.2–4, cited in Theissen, *Gospels in Context*, 93.

54. See Corley, *Private Women*, 93–94: "Mark wants to be sure that the reader sees a contrast between the kind of feasting Jesus practices in chap. 2 and that of another 'King of the Jews,' Herod. This story serves the literary function of providing an 'anti-type' of Jesus' meals in the Gospels, especially the feeding of the five thousand which immediately follows (6:30–44). . . . Thus the meals of Jesus and Herod serve as bold contrasts."

55. See Anderson, "Feminist Criticism: The Dancing Daughter," 133: "John, become food, is a type of Jesus, who will soon give his body to be eaten. . . . Jesus' own body is offered as nourishment—like that of a mother. So, too is John's. Jesus and John are female. They are sources of food who bleed and feed just as women bleed and feed."

56. See Glancy, "Unveiling Masculinity," 49–50: "She [Herodias] is not seeking revenge, but acting to secure her own position. Her action may *seem* like a castration—of the Baptist, of Herod, of masculinity—yet it is not. The Baptist, whose criticism of Herod's marriage had political implications, is executed for equally political reasons." I take the political point but see no reason to exclude the revenge factor. Political maneuvering is often combined with a payback motive against threatening opponents.

57. On the characterization of Jewish leaders in Mark, see Malbon, *In the Company of Jesus,* 131–65.

58. For an assessment of the health-care system in Mediterranean antiquity, comparing and contrasting "professional" physicians (who failed this woman and took all her money) and popular "folk healers" (like Jesus), see Bruce J. Malina and Richard L. Rohrbaugh, *Social-Science Commentary on the Synoptic Gospels* (Minneapolis: Fortress, 1992), 209–11; and John J. Pilch, "Sickness and Healing in Luke-Acts," in *The Social World of Luke-Acts: Models for Interpretation* (ed. Jerome H. Neyrey; Peabody, MA: Hendrickson, 1991), 192–200.

59. Through her active faith, the woman demonstrates her conformity with God's will and thus secures her place in Jesus' extended "family," according to Mark 3:31–35.

60. See, e.g., Marla J. Selvidge, "Mark 5:25–34 and Leviticus 15:19–20: A Reaction to Restrictive Purity Regulations," *JBL* 103 (1984): 619–23; Ben Witherington III, "Women, New Testament," *Anchor Bible Dictionary,* vol. 6 (ed. D. N. Freedman; 6 vols.; New York: Doubleday 1992), 958.

61. Shaye J. D. Cohen, "Menstruants and the Sacred in Judaism and Christianity," in *Women's History and Ancient History* (ed. Sarah B. Pomeroy; Chapel Hill: University of North Carolina Press, 1991), 278–79; Ross Shepard Kraemer, "Women's Judaism(s) at the Beginning of Christianity," in Kraemer and D'Angelo, eds., *Women and Christian Origins,* 65–66; Paula Fredriksen, *Jesus of Nazareth, King of the Jews: A Jewish Life and the Emergence of Christianity* (New York: Knopf, 1999), 197–207; Amy-Jill Levine, "Discharging Responsibility: Matthean Jesus, Biblical Law, and Hemorrhaging Woman," in *Treasures New and Old: Contributions to Matthean Studies* (ed. David R. Bauer and Mark Allan Powell; Society of Biblical Literature Symposium Series 1; Atlanta: Scholars Press, 1996), 379–97.

62. Matthew uses more general language ("hemorrhaging [*haimorroousa*]," 9:20) to describe the woman's condition, allowing for a wider variety of bleeding disorders than Mark's account.

63. Cohen, "Menstruants," 274–81.

64. For purposes of prohibiting menstruating women from participating in the Christian Eucharist, an early Christian student of Origen, Dionysius of Alexandria, makes the point that the hemorrhaging woman in the Gospels touched only the edge of Jesus' outer garment, not his body ("hem" not "him"): "For I think that they [menstruants], being faithful and pious, would not dare in such a condition either to approach the holy table or to touch the body and blood of Christ. For even the woman who had the twelve-year discharge and was eager for a cure touched not him but only his fringe." *Patrologia Graeca* 10:1281, cited in Cohen, "Menstruants," 288; cf. discussion, pp. 287–90.

65. See Mary Rose D'Angelo, "(Re)Presentations of Women in the Gospels: John and Mark," 140–41.

66. See the helpful discussion in Tal Ilan, *Jewish Women in Greco-Roman Palestine* (Peabody, MA: Hendrickson, 1995), 100–105, regarding the rigorous and complex process of detecting menstrual blood—and distinguishing it from other types of blood and emissions—in early rabbinic law.

67. Drawing on the work of Antoinette Clark Wire, D'Angelo ("[Re]Presentations of Women in the Gospels: John and Mark," 141) categorizes Mark's account of the hemorrhaging

woman as a "demand story" with a particular "focus on an obstacle: a rebuke or rebuff from the healer or an intensification of the difficulties of the cure, like a crowd that obstructs access."

68. In "Mark's Hero of the Twelfth-Year Miracles: The Healing of the Woman with the Hemorrhage and the Raising of Jairus's Daughter (Mark 5:21–43)," in *A Feminist Companion to Mark* (ed. Amy-Jill Levine; Sheffield, UK: Sheffield Academic Press, 2001), 57–60, Wendy Cotter focuses on a somewhat different aspect of this story's honor-shame implications. She locates the bleeding woman's potentially shameful behavior not in stealing (as I have suggested) but in her touching a strange man in public, in violation of modesty standards for the ideal Greco-Roman woman. I do not regard the woman's physical contact with Jesus as the main locus of controversy (since many others—presumably including women—are touching Jesus as well [5:31; cf. 3:10; 6:56]), but I am intrigued by Cotter's assessment of Jesus' concern to protect the woman's honor as well as his own:

> With the woman physically at his feet, feeling ashamed of her boldness, Jesus calls her "Daughter," protecting her honor by giving their encounter the safest relationship for touch. . . .
>   Jesus protects the woman's honor by affirming her bold action as an expression of deep faith. This removes her shame and accords her respect. In my view, this story functions to signal the reader that the hero around whom the community is gathered is astonishingly free from the need for public honors, and also from the need to dominate women. (pp. 59–60)

69. The term *mastix* is also used in Mark 3:10 in relation to Jesus' healing ministry: "For he had cured many, so that all who had diseases (*mastigas*) pressed upon him to touch him." See Selvidge, "Mark 5:24–35," 622n20.

70. Cf. the provocative comment from Sharon H. Ringe in her groundbreaking article, "A Gentile Woman's Story," in *Feminist Interpretation of the Bible* (ed. Letty M. Russell; Philadelphia: Westminster, 1985), 69: "The very strangeness and offensiveness of the story's portrayal of Jesus may suggest that the core of the story was indeed remembered as an incident in Jesus' life when even he was caught with his compassion down."

71. A diminutive form of *kyōn*, the term *kynarion*, used in Mark 7:27, may mean a "housedog or lap-dog in contrast to a dog of the street or farm . . . but [is] also used with no diminutive force at all." Walter Bauer, William F. Arndt, F. Wilbur Gingrich, and Frederick W. Danker, *A Greek-English Lexicon of the New Testament and Other Early Christian Literature* (2nd ed.; Chicago: University of Chicago Press, 1979), 457.

72. Theissen, *Gospels in Context*, 61–80. Theissen's sociopolitical reading of Mark 7:24–31 is supported by Sharon Ringe in her most recent reflections on the story: "A Gentile Woman's Story, Revisited: Rereading Mark 7:24–31," in Levine, ed., *Feminist Companion to Mark*, 83–100.

73. Theissen, *Gospels in Context*, 71–72, observes that the word denoting the child's "bed" in Mark 7:30 is *klinē*, a somewhat more "elevated" term than the "vulgar" *krabbaton* (cot, mattress). But this is not much to go on (Theissen himself admits this is a "very modest indication that the Syro-phoenician woman was relatively affluent"); beyond learning that some sort of bed was provided for the sick daughter, we know nothing about the size or status of the woman's home (*oikos*).

74. See, e.g., David Rhoads, "Jesus and the Syrophoenician Woman in Mark: A Narrative-Critical Study," *Journal of the American Academy of Religion* 62 (1994): 343–75.

75. See Amy-Jill Levine, "Matthew's Advice to a Divided Readership," in *The Gospel of Matthew in Current Study: Studies in Memory of William G. Thompson, S.J.* (ed. David E. Aune; Grand Rapids: Eerdmans, 2001), 25–26, 39–41; D'Angelo, "(Re)Presentations of Women in the Gospels: John and Mark," 139–40.

76. By virtue of their indiscriminate carnivorous habits, dogs were regarded as "unclean" animals, according to Exod 22:31 (see P. Pokorný, "From a Puppy to the Child: Some Problems

of Contemporary Biblical Exegesis Demonstrated from Mark 7:24–30/Matt 15:21–8," *New Testament Studies* 41 [1995], 324). But since the Markan Jesus appears to neutralize kosher restrictions and since the woman he calls a "dog" exhibits no signs of moral corruption, it does not seem that purity issues contaminate the story in 7:24–30 at all.

77. See n. 80 in chap. 2 of this book.

78. Mark uses the strong adversative "but" (*alla*) together with "immediately" (*euthys*) to create a strong impression of contrast and intrusion.

79. See n. 40 above.

80. Cf. Rhoads, "Jesus and the Syrophoenician Woman," 351: "She comes, kneels, and begs. The posture of the woman in begging for a healing is integral to Jesus' depiction of her as a scavenger dog."

81. Ringe, "A Gentile Woman's Story Revisited," 90–91; Levine, "Matthew's Advice," 38–39.

82. Dio Cassius, *Roman History* 69.6.3; Levine, "Matthew's Advice," 37–38.

83. See Pokorný, "From a Puppy to the Child," 329–37: "The readers (hearers) must have realized that the verb 'feed' [*chortazein,* 7:27] occurs also in the stories about miraculous feeding of the crowd (6:42; 8:4, 8), and that 'take bread' is a key phrase in the Institution of the Lord's Supper in Mark 14:22–5" (pp. 330–31). "And the woman asking for remnants (crumbs) from the children's table according to Mark undoubtedly asks for this fullness of left-overs from the miraculous feeding" (p. 334). Corley, *Private Women,* 95–102, appreciates the link between the Syrophoenician woman's story and the flanking feeding miracles as "foreshadowing" or "prefiguring" "the admittance of Gentiles to the Christian table"; within the contours of Mark's narrative, however, she views "the ministry of Jesus . . . as being primarily to Israel" (p. 101).

84. I draw this notion of the Syrophoenician woman's "doggedness," that is, her undeterred boldness to get what she needs, from F. Gerald Downing, "The Woman from Syrophoenicia and her Doggedness: Mark 7:24–31 (Matthew 15:21–28)," in *Women in the Biblical Tradition* (Studies in Women and Religion 31; ed. George J. Brooke; Lewiston, NY: Edwin Mellen), 129–49. Downing draws some suggestive parallels with characterizations of Cynic philosophers (who by name and reputation were known for their "canine" [*kyōn*] tenacity and effrontery), but the story in Mark 7:24–31 does not provide enough information to confirm that "this is an encounter with a woman Cynic" (p. 140).

CHAPTER 4

"You Just Don't Understand!" (or Do You?): Jesus, Women, and Conversation in the Fourth Gospel

As well as providing female scholars a welcome forum for their own critical viewpoints, the recent burgeoning of feminist biblical interpretation has also opened up fresh opportunities for dialogue with male scholars who are willing to listen to—and learn from—feminist female colleagues (see chapter 1). Yet such intercourse between male and female critics does not always proceed smoothly or amicably. Not all feminist women scholars have much interest in (or hope of) enlightening their male counterparts, and not that many men make the effort to absorb the work of feminist thinkers. Even assuming congenial dispositions on both sides of the gender divide, we confront the sociolinguistic phenomenon exposed by Deborah Tannen that, for all our supposed sensitivity, correctness, and professionalism, we modern women and men—including those with Ph.D.'s—often talk past each other in our respective "genderlects."[1] However compatible our ethnic, economic, and educational heritages, we still face stiff challenges of "cross-cultural communication" when we try to comprehend members of the opposite sex. Hence, the all-too-familiar rejoinder: "You just don't understand."[2]

Perhaps we in the biblical studies guild can make further progress if we focus not simply on women's roles or on men's treatment of women in various contexts, but on conversation patterns *between* women and men in biblical narratives. In other words, as male and female scholars, let's attempt to talk about how women and men talk in the Bible. By exploring dialogues between male and female characters, we may understand better the subtleties of gender relations in biblical society and, perhaps, communicate more effectively as interpreters.

Little has been done in analyzing conversation styles between women and men in the Bible—and for good reason. Biblical narratives are largely action adventures with few extended dialogues, especially between men and women. What few cross-gendered conversations appear are literary creations—not transcripts of "real life" exchanges—most likely by male authors. If men typically voice their own androcentric concerns when speaking to women and misinterpret, if not ignore, women's speech, how can male writers help but provide biased, distorted accounts of male-female discourse? Won't women characters simply sound either like men or like what men think women sound like?

While the Hebrew Bible offers a wider sample of narratives and perhaps even traces of female authorship,[3] the four Gospels and Acts supply a much more limited database (especially considering the synoptic overlap) almost certainly composed by men. Acts features a series of extended monologues by Spirit-inspired men and, despite its hype about female prophets in 2:17–18, gives them no voice.[4] The Gospels privilege the dynamic, authoritative voice of the man Jesus above all others and, even given their emphasis on his extraordinary compassion and inclusivity, provide few examples of positive conversations between Jesus and women.

Although Mark's Jesus ministers to various women (1:30–31; 5:21–43) and commends certain women's behavior (12:41–44; 14:3–9), the only occasion in which a woman verbally initiates contact with Jesus—a Syrophoenician woman implores Jesus to heal her daughter (7:24–30)—is not his most tender moment.[5] As we discovered in the previous chapter, despite her deferential (bowing) and desperate (begging) plea, Jesus rebuffs this woman and insinuates that she is a "cur" unworthy of his provision. To the woman's credit, she doesn't take "no" for an answer, and to Jesus' credit, he eventually accedes to her demand and heals her child. Ultimately they talk through their differences and arrive at a mutually satisfying solution. But the happy ending does not erase the dialogue's serious tension.

Matthew, in addition to adapting the story of the Syrophoenician woman (e.g., identifying her as a "Canaanite"),[6] edits other Markan material to introduce another solicitous mother who speaks to Jesus. Again, this is Matthew's sole additional example of a woman's addressing Jesus, and, again, Jesus resists her plea. The mother of James and John kneels before Jesus and requests that he honor her sons with privileged posts in his coming kingdom (20:20–21). Admittedly, this ambitious concern for her adult sons' advancement is not as worthy of Jesus' attention as the Syrophoenician/Canaanite woman's desperate desire for her little daughter's healing. Still, it is striking that Jesus not only rejects Mrs. Zebedee's request, but effectively ignores her as well. He speaks only to James and John (20:22): jockeying for honor is men's business.

Luke makes no mention of either the Syrophoenician woman or James and John's mother but does introduce a unique scene featuring some sharp words from Jesus' mother. Upon finally discovering her missing son disputing with the teachers in the temple, Mary—far from commending Jesus' piety or precociousness—blurts out in frustration: "Child, why have you treated us like this? Look, your father and I have been searching for you in great anxiety" (2:48).[7] And Jesus—offering no apology for his actions or concern for his mother's distress—coolly replies: "Why were you searching for me? Did you not know that I must be in my Father's house?" (2:49). "Did you not know?"—in other words, "Don't you understand?" That's the rub: mother and son are talking past each other. While the narrator places the burden on Mary's (and Joseph's) confusion—"they did not understand what [Jesus] said to them" (2:50)—the problem is one of mutual misunderstanding.[8]

Sparks also fly in the curt exchange between Martha and Jesus concerning sister Mary's conduct. When Martha complains about Mary's leaving her "to do all the work," Jesus chides Martha and defends Mary's devotion to his word. Tellingly, he commends Mary's "better choice" of sitting and listening *in silence* over Martha's serving and speaking (10:38–42).

Women address Jesus in two other brief Lukan scenes, although these are not conversations per se. In each case, Jesus responds with a memorable statement to the women's utterances, and that is the end of it. Yet each reply again constitutes a correction of women's viewpoints: first, after an anonymous woman enthusiastically praises Jesus' mother—"Blessed is the womb that bore you and the breasts that nursed you"—Jesus shoots back without as much as a "thank you": "Blessed *rather* are those who hear the word of God and obey it" (11:27–28); second, on the road to the cross, Jesus redirects the focus of female mourners: "Daughters of Jerusalem, do not weep for me, but weep for yourselves and for your children. For the days are surely coming when they will say, 'Blessed are the barren, and the wombs that never bore, and the breasts that never nursed'" (23:27–29). While in both cases Jesus spurns these vocal women less than he uses them as a foil for a loftier theological point, his language scarcely affirms their interests or, for that matter, their bodies (wombs and breasts).

Although not an incident involving Jesus personally, he does tell a tale in Luke about another very vocal woman, an exploited widow, who persistently pleads her case before a callous judge and eventually receives justice (18:1–8). Jesus' sympathies clearly lie with this woman, but his presentation of her ordeal again demonstrates the serious communication gap between men and women. The male judge never gets the widow's point or appreciates her crisis: he just wants her to shut up.

All of these synoptic examples of women speaking with men (particularly Jesus) attest to conflict, to a breakdown in understanding. But these cases are few in number and relatively brief. In the distinctive narrative world of the Fourth Gospel, however—where Jesus not only expounds his views in lengthy discourses but also engages various individuals in extended dialogues—he carries on several conversations with key women. While the longest exchange is with a Samaritan woman at a well, Jesus also has important discussions with his mother at a wedding, his friends Martha and Mary at a funeral, and his follower Mary Magdalene in a garden. Once again, all of these conversations feature a level of misunderstanding that must be negotiated. Our concern is to investigate why and at what points communication breaks down between Jesus and these women and how these social barriers are reinforced and/or overcome. Although the dialogues are thoroughly Johannine in style, the fact that they display tension between male and female speech suggests a certain "artistic verisimilitude."[9] If Jesus and women always perfectly understood one another in the Fourth Gospel, we would be dealing with fantasy or nonsense.[10]

This exploration of both connection and conflict in Jesus' conversation with women resists simple constructs of male-female relations in John as either ideally egalitarian or hopelessly hierarchical. As Colleen Conway concludes, "gender matters in John" as a complex, self-conscious phenomenon; that is, distinctions between men and women play an explicit role in the narrative, not least with respect to cross-gendered dialogue ("they were astonished that *he* was speaking with *a woman*," 4:27). Accordingly, flat notions of either blissful "equality," on the one end, or polarized "dualism," on the other, fail to do justice to the fact that "gender representations and relations function in ambiguous and multifaceted ways in this gospel, just as they do in life."[11]

[T]annalyzing the Discourse

In a host of writings, both professional and popular, over the past two decades, Deborah Tannen has established herself as a leading authority on gender-related modes of communication.[12] Although neither a biblical scholar nor a literary critic,[13] she offers sociolinguistic analyses of conversational tendencies among men and women that provide suggestive frameworks for interpreting the dialogues between the Johannine Jesus and his women interlocutors. Two fundamental perspectives govern Tannen's work: 1) variable, contextually relative factors; and 2) stereotypical, commonly shared assumptions.

The first perspective isolates three key elements in a culturally sensitive analysis of conversation: "The interpretation of a given utterance, and the likely response to it, depends on the *setting,* on individuals' *status and their relationship to each other,* and also on the *linguistic conventions* that are ritualized in the cultural context."[14] Each factor is potentially significant in interpreting the Johannine dialogues. The settings of wedding, well, funeral, and garden provide the stages upon which different verbal dramas are enacted; a simple "peace be with you," for example, while appropriate at both weddings and funerals, would carry different tones and nuances in each situation. The status positions that Jesus occupies as son, Jew, friend, and (presumed) gardener—not to mention his authority as prophet, Messiah, teacher, and Lord—necessarily affect how Jesus and the women speak to one another. And linguistic conventions accepted in first-century Jewish and Greco-Roman contexts might vary considerably from those governing contemporary American society. For example, the first word Jesus utters to a woman in the Fourth Gospel is "Woman" (*gynai,* 2:4), addressed to his mother; while most Americans would interpret this maternal reference as impolite, if not impudent, we should not presume it had the same connotation in John's world.

Although Tannen's most popular work explores conversational patterns among men and women in middle-class America, she has also investigated minority and other cultural groups, both foreign and domestic—particularly Jews and Greeks. Such studies pose important challenges to "negative stereotyping" based on misunderstanding of communication norms. For example, New York Jews (Tannen's own heritage) are often branded as loud, pushy, domineering speakers.[15] Outside observers typically find such conduct unacceptable, especially for women (Jewish or not), whose patterns of interrupting and overlapping others' speech evoke the deviant tag of "noisily clucking hens."[16] Such blinkered reactions, however, ignore the "ambiguous" and "polysemous" nature of communication. Not all apparent interruptions intend to cut off or put down the original speaker; one can interrupt or "overlap" to show agreement or encouragement. As Tannen stresses, "research has shown that New Yorkers of Jewish background often use overlap—that is, simultaneous talk—in a cooperative way; many members of this group talk simultaneously in some settings without intending to interrupt."[17] Similarly, while aggressive, argumentative speech is often considered rude and uncivilized, "Greek conversation provides an example of a cultural style that places more positive value, for both women and men, on dynamic opposition."

Similarly, studies have shown that for other ethnic groups, such as Eastern European Jews, "friendly argument is a means of being sociable," "a pleasurable sign of intimacy."[18]

Thus Tannen underscores the potential "relativity of linguistic strategies" employed by speakers, not least among female and male discussants. Interpreting the significance of a range of rhetorical moves—for example, interrupting, objecting, shifting the topic, shouting to make a point versus shutting down in silence, circumlocution versus direct engagement— requires both sensitivity to diverse cultural norms and openness to subtle and supple complexities of linguistic exchange.[19]

Counterbalancing this emphasis on cultural relativity is Tannen's other main perspective: the recognition that communication within any given culture follows widely accepted, predictable rules, codes, and patterns. While not stifling human creativity, such norms provide a common arena within which individual performance may be evaluated. As Tannen observes, many of these linguistic guidelines are gender specific: male discourse typically serves interests of competition and status enhancement, while female speech forges bonds of connection and interpersonal intimacy. Given different social expectations inculcated from infancy, men and women encounter the world in distinctive ways. On one side, men characteristically

> engag[e] the world . . . as an individual in a hierarchical social order in which he [is] either one-up or one-down. In this world, conversations are negotiations in which people try to achieve and maintain the upper hand if they can, and protect themselves from others' attempts to put them down and push them around. Life, then, is a contest, a struggle to preserve independence and avoid failure.

On the other side, many women

> approach the world . . . as an individual in a network of connections. In this world, conversations are negotiations for closeness in which people try to seek and give confirmation and support, and to reach consensus. They try to protect themselves from others' attempts to push them away. Life, then is a community, a struggle to preserve intimacy and avoid isolation. Though there are hierarchies in this world too, they are hierarchies more of friendship than of power and accomplishment.[20]

Vertical, asymmetrical negotiations for advancement versus horizontal, symmetrical negotiations for closeness; protection from being pushed around versus protection from being pushed away; preserving independence versus preserving intimacy; and avoiding failure versus avoiding isolation—such polarities mark the repertoires of male and female discourse and set the stage for inevitable conflict and confusion. Appreciating the fluidity of language styles, Tannen acknowledges that not all women or men readily conform to generic modes of speech. But individual exceptions do not neutralize the pervasive influence of stereotypical expectations. Following Erving Goffman, Tannen carefully associates sex-linked conversational patterns "with members of the *class* of females or males . . . rather [than] with each individual who is a member of that class."[21]

While Tannen's basic distinctions among female and male language styles seem appropriate to many, if not most, contemporary cultures, her balancing emphasis on cultural relativity along with a sense of historical development cautions against facilely applying her insights to conversation patterns in John's milieu. Still, it is remarkable how Tannen's understanding of what motivates male speech—competition, status elevation, opposition, self-assertion—squares with the agonistic, honor-shame model of Mediterranean male conduct adapted from cultural anthropology by some biblical scholars.[22] Although these scholars run the risk of retrojecting modern phenomena into ancient societies, their work is sufficiently buttressed by first-century evidence (chiefly literary) to merit attention. Across both testaments, biblical literature is replete with male struggles for attaining honor by dominating both women and other males in a belligerent banter of challenge and riposte.[23]

Applied to women, however, the honor-shame model is less compatible with Tannen's framework. The former stresses women's passive role as guardians of proper shame, interpreted in terms of modesty, chastity, and sexual exclusivity (shame*less*ness is thus embodied in female wantonness and promiscuity). Women in this construction are pawns in men's games of conquest and acquisition; they must remain in the protective custody of their fathers and husbands, secluded from the public sphere of masculine competition in which they seductively threaten male honor and in turn risk losing their own decorous shame.[24] Missing in this isolationist, shame-oriented model is Tannen's appraisal of women's drives to make connections, preserve intimacy, protect and reinforce community, *avoid* isolation.[25]

Alongside well-known examples of women's sexual exploitation and isolation in the service of men's lust for honor and power,[26] the Old Testament features other women who speak in the interests of intimacy and connectedness—to both men and other women—as Tannen would expect. Ruth's classic "Where you go, I will go" speech (Ruth 1:17–18) is as moving a declaration of solidarity and determination to maintain intimacy as any in biblical literature. While Ruth's world remains thoroughly patriarchal—the whole point is her redemption through marrying a kinsman and bearing his son—Ruth and Naomi, women closely knit in their struggle for survival, take the initiative in creating and nurturing the new familial unit (Boaz is just along for the ride).[27]

Ultimately, Ruth's main claim to fame is her role as great-grandmother to Israel's most honored and virile ruler, King David. Among the women in David's life, however, another stands out for her remarkable "verbal power" to maintain peace and forestall bloody revenge (1 Sam 25).[28] Before becoming David's wife, Abigail had been married to the churlish Nabal, who had snubbed David's request for hospitality and thus incurred his wrath. Into this typical scenario of boorish battles for male honor[29] steps the "clever and beautiful" Abigail (25:3), who "ride[s] out from the closed security of her home to face the storms of her husband's enemy."[30] Her goal, achieved through verbal persuasion as well as with more customary womanly provision of food and drink, is "to halt the destructive action of a male."[31] While thoroughly affirming David's authority, Abigail still manages to deter his murderous plan—and thus preserve peace—by appealing to his good conscience as the Lord's servant (25:23–31). In short, she uses *her voice* to defuse male conflict and preserve community.[32]

Additional models of rhetorically skilled, female peacemakers are represented by the two "wise women" of 2 Samuel: one from Tekoa (14:1–24), the other from Abel (20:14–22). The first, at Joab's behest, plays out a fabricated family drama before King David. Capturing the king's interest, the Tekoite woman presses her real point, namely, David's obligation to "bring his banished one home again"—his son, Absalom, exiled for killing Amnon (cf. 13:23–39). Reconciliation takes precedence over revenge. The second "wise woman," speaking against Joab rather than as his agent, beseeches him to spare the city of Abel. Her message is both forceful and touching: "I am one of those who are *peaceable* and faithful in Israel; you seek to destroy a city that is a *mother in Israel*; why will you swallow up the *heritage of the LORD?*" (20:19). She appeals to her own gentle loyalty (peaceable) and sense of covenantal community ("heritage of the LORD"), punctuated by a moving maternal image: how dare Joab think of harming a nurturing "mother in Israel"![33] Taken aback by the woman's challenge ("Far be it from me, far be it ...," 20:20), Joab announces that his grudge is not against the city (despite the fact that he is razing its walls) but against the rebel Sheba hiding inside. He then promises to "withdraw from the city" if Sheba is turned over to him, which the woman arranges (20:21–22).

These cases clearly highlight the restorative, redemptive aim of female speech against the virulent, vindictive grain of male conduct. Why did Joab hire a woman to enact a parable to compel David's reconciliation with Absalom when he could have told the parable himself or employed the prophet Nathan, an effective storyteller two chapters earlier (12:1–7)? The ruthless Joab would have been hard pressed to pull off the role of peace-maker, and Nathan's parabolic prowess focused on one man's violent con-quest of another's female property. The job of healing a family rift and restoring a banished son seemed best suited to female concerns and conver-sational style expressed by a wise woman and mother. Similarly, while com-parisons may be made between the woman of Abel and Abner's successful negotiations with the marauding Joab (cf. 2 Sam 2:24–28),[34] Abner's plea was a last-ditch tactic of self-preservation preceded by customary male horn butting: "Abner said to Joab, 'Let the young men come forward and have a *contest* before us'" (2:14). Biblical men are never far from honor-seeking competition. If intimacy and diplomacy are required, better find a woman.

We conclude this brief survey of verbal women in the Old Testament with the signature case of the Shulammite in the Song of Songs. No biblical woman speaks more extensively, more authentically, or more intimately; she amplifies with vivid and personal language her theme of mutual love: "My beloved is mine and I am his" (2:16; 6:3; 7:10).[35] Moreover, far from being sequestered, this woman boldly seeks and meets her lover in public venues (banquet houses and open fields). As Dianne Bergant observes, "behavior such as this does not follow the exacting pattern of female seclusion. Despite this, such deviance is in no way criticized by the characters within the Song or by its final editor."[36] Nor is her lover simply a passive and silent respon-dent. He acts and speaks as well (although not quite as much as she), but not in a domineering or contentious fashion; at every stage of love's pursuit, he echoes his beloved's intense desire for intimacy. Together, the two lovers, female and male, dramatically disrupt honor-shame conventions. As Bergant avers, "A close reading of the poems reveals social relationships that are anomalous, if the honor/shame model is the norm."[37]

This example of male-female conversation—exhibiting idyllic[38] love, mutuality, and intimacy—reminds us that stereotypes can be resisted; bibli-cal women and men can find an almost egalitarian way to talk without con-flict and confusion. But the other examples (Ruth, Abigail, the wise women) reveal that the pattern is indeed "anomalous": most of the time women, when allowed to speak, fill in the harmony parts, while the men belt out the lead in an effort to overpower all other voices. In Tannen's terms, women seek to connect; men seek to conquer. Women yearn for intimacy; men strive for independence.

We now come to explore the usefulness of these sociolinguistic strategies in accounting both for the misunderstanding that garbles the conversation between Jesus and women in the Fourth Gospel and for the bridging of this communication gap to reach better understanding. Alongside investigating the influence of setting, status relations, and linguistic conventions, we will probe the extent to which the Johannine Jesus and various female interlocutors support and/or subvert linguistic stereotypes.[39]

Jesus and His Mother at a Wedding

The first of four dialogues between Jesus and women in John, consisting of a single terse exchange between Jesus and his mother (2:3–5), establishes important precedents for interpreting the other three. The opening verse, fixing the setting as a wedding celebration in Cana, provides suggestive cultural and geographical clues to deciphering the ensuing conversation. Weddings were special events where protocol was paramount; everything must function properly to avoid embarrassment for the host families.[40] And Cana's proximity to Jesus' hometown of Nazareth (cf. 1:45), coupled with his mother's prominent presence in the story, intimate that Jesus' family were either relatives or close friends of the bride or groom's family. In any case, Jesus' mother seems personally and socially invested in the success of the proceedings. Finally, weddings were optimal occasions for reflection on both male honor—the importance of acquiring a "capable wife" and child bearer who would enhance her husband's reputation (cf. Prov 31:10–31)—and female-male intimacy, à la that extolled in the Song of Songs, which may have been composed for nuptial ceremonies.

The conversation that concerns us, however, is not between bride and groom, but between mother and son, a pairing linked by its own special web of status relations. In addition to representing an interesting hierarchical inversion in which the male must honor the female—"Honor thy father and mother"—the mother-son bond was (and is) among the closest kinship bonds in the Middle East: the son owed his earliest and closest nurturing to his mother, and the mother boasted in producing and rearing a male heir. But as tight as this tie could be, it was also typically fraught with conflict as the son matured and developed his own identity in a man's world.[41] I have already pointed out Luke's account of the adolescent Jesus asserting his independence from his mother in order to be about his "Father's business." In the present Johannine scene, we find the adult Jesus, who has already commenced his itinerant public mission (1:35–51), interacting with his mother.

The conversation unfolds in three stages: 1) the mother's opening gambit (2:3); 2) Jesus' direct reply (2:4); and 3) the mother's response to Jesus' words, addressed not to him but to the servants (2:5). At each stage, as Beverly Roberts Gaventa stresses, the statements remain open to multiple interpretations for both characters and readers,[42] and they thereby sustain dramatic tension as well as recall Tannen's point concerning the ambiguous and polysemous proclivity of cross-gendered communication. The content of the mother's initial report to Jesus—"They have no wine"—is easy enough to grasp; her *intent* is less clear. Is she simply relaying inventory information? (Perhaps Jesus had requested a drink, prompting his mother to say, "Sorry, son, it's all gone.") Or is she indirectly inviting Jesus to solve the problem with her (to run short of wine at a wedding feast was a serious social gaffe) or, more presumptuously, insisting that Jesus himself remedy the crisis?[43] The likely sensitivity of Jesus' mother to the embarrassment of insufficient wine—alongside women's cultural conditioning to elicit male support initially through indirect speech ("nagging" comes later, after men repeatedly ignore more subtle quests for attention)[44]—suggest that the mother is indeed calling for Jesus to take some kind of action.

That is certainly how Jesus interprets her remark. He assumes she is making demands on his time ("my hour") and energy, and in some sense he resists, if not resents, the imposition. The question is how forcefully Jesus responds. Does his reply amount to a "gruff refusal" of his mother's wishes[45] in which he is "abrupt and draws a sharp line" between himself and her,[46] or is it a milder case of conveying a certain "aloofness" from maternal control?[47] The language is, as noted above, ambiguous: "Woman, what concern is that to you and to me? My hour has not yet come" (2.4). The more literal—"What to me and to you, woman?" (*Ti emoi kai soi, gynai*)—too readily translates into a crude lingo, something like "What's it to you, lady?" Certainly this is no way to talk to mom, and in fact this rough paraphrase does not adequately capture Jesus' meaning. In a touching farewell scene at the cross, Jesus again addresses his mother as "Woman," without a hint of derision (19:25).[48] Still, "woman" is an unusual, stilted way to refer to one's mother in the ancient as well as in the modern world. Jesus also calls the Samaritan and Mary Magdalene "Woman" (4:21; 20:15), linguistically linking them with his mother.[49] But to what purpose? Is Jesus intending to relativize his biological mother's importance in favor of broader, "fictive" kinship ties, or is he suggesting something of the strong affection he feels toward these other women, akin to that which knits him to his mother? The Fourth Gospel's penchant for double meanings allows for both aims.

In probing the possible nuances of Jesus' reply, we must admit with Schnackenburg that the limits of written discourse do not always allow access to the tone of reported speech.[50] Thus aural descriptions of Jesus' response as "gruff" or "sharp" cannot be verified. But whatever his tone, Jesus clearly conveys that he will not be dictated to by his mother. Whereas she might have "reported" the wine shortage to build "rapport" with Jesus— that is, sharing a problem for mutual discussion—Jesus takes it as a threat to his honor and independence.[51] And so he parries her perceived challenge with a riposte, asserting that his life will run according to *his* schedule ("*my* hour"), not his mother's. And, in Johannine terms, Jesus' "hour" is the standard time appointed by his heavenly Father.[52] What we have, then, in John 2 is similar to Luke 2: Jesus must be about his Father's business, concerned with his Father's interests, *not his mother's*.

But unlike Mary in Luke, Jesus' mother in John is neither taken by surprise at his answer nor compelled to mull over the matter in her heart. Without skipping a beat, she orders the servants, "Do whatever he tells you" (2:5). This statement achieves two purposes. On the one hand, it discloses the mother's recognition of Jesus' independence and the importance of following his wishes; she is thus a model disciple.[53] On the other hand, her message to the servants provides an indirect opening for Jesus to settle the crisis on his own terms—which is precisely what he does! (2:7–11). Thus, the mother and Jesus (not to mention the thirsty guests) both get what they want and become partners in averting a family fiasco. Yet while Jesus displays unmistakable authority and power, his mother gets the credit for seeking and preserving intimacy with her son.

As a token of persisting harmony, the narrator observes that, after the wedding, Jesus "went down to Capernaum with his mother, his brothers, and his disciples; and they remained there a few days" (2:12). This is quite the opposite of the Capernaum incident in Mark, which depicts sharp division between Jesus and his followers on the one side, and his mother and siblings on the other (Mark 3:20–21, 31–35). While the Johannine Jesus "came unto his own, and his own people did not accept him" (1:12), this pattern of rejection does not pervade his immediate family. Later we learn that "not even his brothers believed in him" (7:5), but such doubt never extends to his mother. She remains faithful to the end, even to Jesus' death on the cross (19:25–27).[54]

Jesus and a Samaritan Woman at a Well

We proceed from the briefest exchange between Jesus and a woman in John to the most extensive: Jesus' well-known encounter with the Samaritan woman at Jacob's well (4:1–42). I make no attempt here to exhaust the scene's rich interpretive possibilities.[55] Our focus remains on setting, status relations, and strategies of connection/opposition affecting male-female discourse.

From a wedding in Cana of Galilee the setting shifts to a well in Sychar of Samaria (4:4–6). These disconnected venues actually share some common ground, because a well—Jacob's well at that—where a man and woman meet evokes images of biblical betrothal scenes.[56] For example, at a well, Abraham's servant arranged for Isaac's marriage with Rebekah (Gen 24:10–61), Jacob kissed and wept for joy over Rachel (Gen 29:1–14), and Moses first impressed Zipporah (Exod 2:15–22). When women and men gather around a well, something tends to happen! No wonder Jesus' disciples, upon finding him in this situation, "were astonished that he was speaking with a woman" (4:27). The shocker is not so much Jesus' speaking with a woman or even his speaking with a woman in public, but rather his speaking with a woman in public *at a well!*[57] This did not quite fit the disciples' conception of their master as a celibate bachelor.

The timing of the encounter at "about noon" (4:6) has often signaled to interpreters the outcast status of the woman: why else draw water at the hottest part of the day except to avoid other women? But other explanations are equally plausible, such as the literary contrast with Nicodemus's recent coming to Jesus "by night" (3:1)[58] or the sociohistorical observation that the Samaritan's workload might have required multiple trips to the well.[59]

Whether or not her midday arrival reveals anything about the woman's position in society, the conversation with Jesus quickly focuses on status relations. Jesus makes the first move, a bold and personal move soliciting the woman for a drink to pass through his lips and into his body. The man initiates an intimate connection with the woman, strongly reminiscent of Abraham servant's "opening line" to Rebekah: "Give me a drink" (John 4:7)/"Please let me sip a little water from your jar" (Gen 24:17).[60] Unlike the eager Rebekah, however, the Samaritan woman is taken aback on two points of social propriety by Jesus' request: "How is it that you, a *Jew*, ask a drink of me, a *woman* of Samaria?" (4:9). The first point concerns ethnicity. Whereas Rebekah dealt with a kinsman's representative, this Samaritan confronts "a Jew," with whom she would normally "not share things in common" (4:9).[61] While she still might welcome a connection, it needs to be an appropriate one. The second point focuses on gender. Jesus' interlocutor is very much aware that she is not simply a Samaritan, but "a *woman* (*gynē*) of Samaria." Likewise, she is well acquainted both with traditions surrounding Jacob's well (cf. 4:12, 19–20, 25) and with the habits of men (4:18). Jesus' line of talk at this location is a little too close for comfort. Still, the woman is not so spooked that she drops her jug and runs away (that comes later, 4:28); she hangs in there as a worthy conversation partner for Jesus.

While the discussion takes a number of intriguing twists, it adheres in large measure around the theme of right "knowing." In addition to explicit phrases like "if you knew" (*ei ēdeis,* 4:10) and "what we know" (*ho oidamen,* 4:22), the issue of "who knows what about whom" colors the entire scene. This cognitive focus is particularly relevant to our concerns in three respects. First, knowing and not knowing is another way of saying understanding and misunderstanding, the critical components of evaluating female-male conversation. Second, the old adage, "knowledge is power," raises issues of hierarchy and honor-building; if "I know something you don't know" or "I know something about you that you wish I didn't know," I can lord it over you, use it to my advantage: it puts me in a "one-up" position, a favorite male goal.[62] Finally and conversely, knowledge about someone, considerately deployed, can also forge intimate connections consistent with female goals: comments like, "I know how you feel," "I know where you're coming from"—if spoken with sincerity—create community and solidarity.

Three main topics occupy the discussion: water, wedlock, and worship or, alternatively, hydraulics,[63] husbands, and holy places. The conversation about water flows between the banks of literal H_2O on the one side, and "living water . . . gushing up to eternal life" (4:10, 14) on the other. Jesus especially emphasizes this polarity between figurative and literal, heavenly and earthly, material and spiritual water (4:10, 13–14). According to the usual reading, the Samaritan woman's principal problem is that she fails to grasp this hierarchy due to her preoccupation with the quotidian realm of buckets and wells. But, as Stephen Moore deftly demonstrates, this hierarchical, androcentric reading (even by feminist critics!) is not the only or even the best reading on Johannine terms.[64] Jesus does, in typically male fashion, promote a hierarchical dualism. The dichotomy between literal and living water, between mere liquid and true life, is a fundamental tenet he knows but the woman doesn't ("If you knew . . . ," 4:10). Yet throughout the Fourth Gospel, Jesus has been revealed as the dynamic *bridge* between heaven and earth, spirit and matter: he is the "Word made flesh" (1:14), which is to say, the Word made water (and blood, bones, etc.). The incarnate Jesus signals the collapse of a dualistic universe, the intimate connection among the totality of God's creation. Why, then, does he talk the way he does to the

Samaritan woman, dividing, as it were, what God had joined within his divine-human nature? From a deconstructive perspective, Jesus' speech belies his character in a strange, reversed kind of hypocrisy. As Moore puts it:

> Mistaking his place on the table of elements, he speaks to the Samaritan woman ... as though he were a mixture composed of separable elements, as though the living water could be clearly distinguished from spring water ... the figurative from the literal, the spiritual from the material, and the heavenly from the earthly. What Jesus *says* is contradicted by what he *is*.[65]

The Samaritan woman, however, does not so neatly swallow Jesus' point about different waters: "The distinction between the material and the spiritual was no sooner made by Jesus than it was muddied by the woman."[66] But her challenge to Jesus is not from some banal preoccupation with the daily chores of drawing water. She knows well enough about drinking and bathing water, but she also knows about "deeper" water ("the well is deep"), "ancestral water"[67] that miraculously connects her and her people with the great forefather Jacob/Israel "who gave *us* the well" (4:11–12). Her confusion is not that Jesus brings up the subject of living water about which she knows nothing, but rather that he claims to supply such eternal sustenance apart from the fountain of God's covenant with Jacob/Israel, sacramentalized in Jacob's well. She has yet to learn that the Johannine Jesus is indeed "greater than our ancestor Jacob, who gave us the well" and greater than the water in the well. He satisfies humanity's deepest thirst, but he does so in *corporeal-material* form as the incarnate Word, born both of water and of spirit (cf. 3:5). Although it takes her a while to make the connection to Jesus, the Samaritan woman at this stage speaks more "correctly" than he does about the essential interconnectedness binding God's people together, then and now, and the various facets of God's creation, both material and spiritual. In Tannen's terms, the Samaritan woman attempts to preserve community and connection, while the male Jesus maintains hierarchy and competition. In Moore's terms,

> [T]hat other hierarchical structure within which Jesus and the Samaritan woman conversed has also suffered some water damage. I refer, of course, to the hierarchy of male over female. If what Jesus has said to the Samaritan woman is indeed contradicted by what he is, and if what Jesus is has indeed been affirmed by what she has said, then the female student has outstripped her male teacher, even though he himself was the subject

of their seminar. She has insisted, in effect, that earthly and heavenly, flesh and Spirit, figurative and literal, are symbiotically related categories: each drinks endlessly of the other, and so each is endlessly contaminated by the other. To draw a clear line between them, as Jesus attempts to do, is about as effective as drawing a line on water.[68]

Abruptly Jesus shifts the discussion to the woman's marital status. The new topic permits him to display his remarkable knowledge, and it also suits the well setting where intimate thoughts about marriage are in the air (or, rather, in the water). Although ostensibly inviting the woman to return with her husband, Jesus actually sets her up for confessing "I have no husband," which then allows him to disclose her history of five previous spouses as well as her current cohabitation with a man who "is not your husband" (4:16–18). As Mary Rose D'Angelo observes, this exchange has generated astonishing "exegetical extravaganzas,"[69] concocting various scenarios about the woman's pathetic philandering or promiscuous past ("five-time loser"/ "tramp")[70] or, in a thoroughly allegorical reading, interpreting her "husbands" as the alien gods of the five nations ancient Assyria relocated in Samaria.[71] A kinder and simpler reading is preferred. Jesus makes no moral judgments about this woman, and neither should we. Her unfortunate run of husbands could easily owe to widowhood and legal remarriage to successive brothers-in-law (the Sadducees posed the presumably plausible case of a *seven*-time widow in similar circumstances [Mark 12:18–23 par.]). Having outlasted all her brothers-in-law, perhaps she currently lives with a more distant relative unable or unwilling to marry her.[72] We don't know, and Jesus couldn't care less about the implications of the woman's marital status (there is no "go and sin no more," as with the adulterous woman in 8:11), except possibly to justify his approaching her at the well (she's single [technically] and he's single—so there's nothing improper about intimate conversation between them there).

Most significantly, the Samaritan woman is not remotely put off by Jesus' disclosure. In fact, it is at this moment that she first lets down her guard and responds with some enthusiasm: "Sir, I perceive you are a prophet" (4:19). As it turns out, Jesus is not some stranger accosting her at Jacob's well; rather, he is God's messenger who knows not only his theology, but who also knows *her* intimately and accepts her as a worthy interlocutor. When she heads back to town, her excited report features this "man who told me everything I have ever done" (4:29). While this awareness leads her to the brink of a messianic confession ("he cannot be the Messiah, can he?" [4.29]) with global ramifications ("we know that this is truly the Savior of the world" [4.42]), it remains rooted in a very *personal connection* that Jesus makes with her. He knows "everything *I* have ever done." Here Jesus breaks the stereotype; here the man uses his knowledge not to dominate but to communicate, not to erect an empire but to create a bond with an engaging woman.

As for the final topic—the right place to worship—now the woman ironically presses the points of hierarchy and distinction: Gerizim or Jerusalem, your place or mine? (4:20). Jesus responds in corrective fashion, by referring to "Woman" and "the hour" as he did when setting his mother straight at Cana (4:21). And he plays his true-knowledge trump card again in order to best the woman and her people: "You [Samaritans] worship what you do not know; we worship what we know, for salvation is from the Jews" (4:22). Having thus satisfied his competitive impulse, Jesus proceeds to abolish distinctions among sacred sites, to level Gerizim and Zion by proclaiming that true worship is open to any who approach "the Father in spirit and truth" (4:23). He continues to drive a wedge between the spiritual and the material, but toward a more inclusive end: Jesus invites the Samaritan woman and her people to worship the true God with him and fellow Jews not at this hill or that, but in their hearts. The eventual embracing of Jesus as Savior by "many Samaritans" testifies to his verbal power ("we have *heard* for ourselves, and we know") to make connections among divided peoples (4:39–42). Again Jesus both exhibits and explodes stereotypical patterns of male discourse.

Jesus, Martha, and Mary at a Funeral

Continuing our journey south through Israel as well as forward through John's narrative, we proceed from Cana of Galilee, through Sychar of Samaria, to arrive at Bethany of Judea, just outside Jerusalem. We also shift from lively talk about weddings and marriages to mourning. At Bethany Jesus encounters the sisters Martha and Mary in a funeral setting, lamenting the loss of their beloved brother Lazarus, already four days cold in the tomb when Jesus appears. Although striking an opposite tone from wedding celebrations, funerals evoke similar expectations of social propriety and familial-community support: they are occasions for uniting relatives and friends and enacting ritual practices. Appropriately, in terms of status relations, Jesus joins the sisters as an "in-group" associate, a cherished friend of the family.[73] He "love[s] Martha and her sister and Lazarus" (11:5; cf. v. 3) and calls Lazarus "our friend" (11:11). Such language is highly prized in the Fourth Gospel, reserved only for community intimates such as Jesus' disciples (cf. 15:9–17).

This context of friendship illuminates the key problem surrounding the conversations between Jesus and Lazarus's two sisters. Jesus is four days late in coming to comfort his grieving friends, and not because he was ignorant of Lazarus's condition. Martha and Mary had sent word that their brother was seriously ill (11:3), whereupon Jesus *chose* to stay two days longer where he was before making the trek to Bethany (11:5). Some friend! Of course, the ever-in-control Johannine Jesus had his reasons for the delay, three in fact: he had informed his disciples that Lazarus's "illness was not unto death" (11:4); that he was going to Judea to "awaken" Lazarus who had "fallen asleep" (11:11–13); and that he was actually "glad" he would not be present to prevent Lazarus's death "for your [the disciples'] sake," since now they would be able to witness Jesus' resurrection power (11:14–15).

Good for Jesus and good for the disciples: a wonderful educational opportunity! But not so good for Martha and Mary, who spend four days mourning their loss. However much Jesus might be strengthening his other followers' faith, it is difficult to interpret his procrastination in coming to Bethany as the least bit beneficial to Martha and Mary—to say nothing of Lazarus. Both sisters flatly express their disappointment in Jesus, although, true to form (cf. Luke 10:38–42), Martha confronts Jesus first, out on the road, "while Mary stayed at home" (11:20). Notably, the sisters register identical complaints: "Lord, if you had been here, my brother would not have died" (11:21, 32). In one sense, this statement "charges Jesus with failure"[74] and challenges his honor.[75] From Martha and Mary's perspective, Jesus had defaulted on his obligations as both Lord and friend. In another sense, however, the sisters speak out of a deep yearning for presence versus absence, intimacy versus distance, community preservation versus disintegration: "Lord, if you had been *here* (rather than away), our brother would still be *here* (instead of gone) and everybody would still be together." We might further add (beyond the text): "Lord, if at least you had come sooner to help us grieve, it might have lightened our load a little."

What does Jesus have to say for himself? Although the two sisters pose the same objections, Jesus' response is different in each case: the first focuses on his power and position; the second on his pathos and passion. After voicing her annoyance at Jesus' delay, Martha appends the more congenial affirmation that "even now" God will grant Jesus whatever he desires (11:22). Jesus seizes this more positive opening and proceeds to consider Lazarus's death from what Thomas Brodie aptly describes as "a very elevated point of view."[76] He centers on Lazarus's impending resurrection from the dead (not just "on the last day") guaranteed by Jesus' lofty self-identification ("I AM," *egō eimi*) as "the resurrection and the life" (11:23–25). Brushing off Martha's complaint, Jesus assumes a dominant, exalted position in the conversation as he steadily leads Martha from subdued disappointment to a "crescendo of believing"[77] (11:26–27).

Martha then heads back into the house to inform her sister that Jesus "is here [finally!] and is calling for you" (11:28). A shift in Jesus' attitude is suggested as he reaches out to console Mary; but his sympathy is still muted somewhat by the narrative's focalization of his "calling" for Mary through Martha's speech, not his own.

Mary jumps up, dashes to meet Jesus, and registers her own complaint (11:32). In contrast to Martha, however, she adds nothing to her statement except a torrent of tears. She is "weeping" (*klaiousan*, 11:33)—wailing in typical mourner's fashion—along with other "Jews" who accompany her. At least some friends share her bereavement; conspicuously, Jesus has *not* been among them. But now, encountering this sorrowful exhibition, the normally calm, collected Johannine Jesus himself erupts with intense emotion.[78] He becomes "greatly disturbed/angry in spirit" (*enebrimēsato tō pneumati*), "deeply moved/troubled in himself" (*etaraxen heauton*), and bursts into tears ("Jesus wept [*edakrysen*]") (11:33, 35).[79]

This gut-wrenching "crescendo of lamentation" in response to Mary's mourning marks quite a change from Jesus' elevated theologizing with Martha.[80] But how should we interpret his emotional display? Commentators (mostly male) have tended to shy away from "soft"[81] or "sentimental"[82] readings on linguistic grounds.[83] The verb *dakryō* describing Jesus' "weeping" in 11:35 is less intense than *klaiō*, which denotes the mourners' crying (the nuance is something like "shedding tears" vs. "demonstrative wailing"); and the verb *embrimaomai*, rendered "greatly disturbed" by the NRSV in 11:33 (and again in v. 38), carries strong connotations of "snorting with anger."[84] Thus, according to some scholars, while Jesus is clearly upset and irritated, he is not grieving with Mary and her companions; rather, he resents their outpouring of sorrow as an affront to his honor,[85] an imposition on his power,[86] and a deplorable symptom of their faithless despair.[87]

But I see no reason to interpret Jesus' feelings as antagonistic rather than sympathetic. First, concerning Jesus' "weeping," the amount of tears shed is beside the point. Grief is not measured in buckets. Although Jesus' "weeping" (*edakrysen*) may be less dramatic than Mary's "wailing" (*klaiousan*), it still represents a genuine response of sympathy. He weeps *because* she weeps ("when/as he saw her weeping," 11:33). Second, regarding his anger, he never vents it personally against any mourner, which we would expect if he felt insulted, threatened, or disappointed by their demonstration. In fact, he says nothing to them apart from, "Where have you laid him [Lazarus]?" (11:34).

What, then, is Jesus mad at? It's difficult to say, since anger and grief often swirl together in a painful complex of emotion. Maybe Jesus rages against the ravages of death and the toll it exacts from surviving loved ones. Or maybe, just maybe, he is angry in some sense *at himself* ("disturbed *in spirit*" [*enebrimēsato tō pneumatic*]; "troubled *in/at*[?] *himself*" [*etaraxen heauton*]), angry that he let it go this far, that he left his friends in agony. What had seemed like a good idea and what he defended to Martha now—in the face of overwhelming sorrow—no longer seems so salutary. The knowledge that he is about to raise Lazarus cannot blunt the piercing awareness of the horrible loss suffered by Lazarus's family and friends. Martha's final words recall the grisly details: "Lord, already there is a stench because he has been dead four days" (11:39). Martha, Mary—*and Jesus*—will remember not only Lazarus's miraculous resurrection, but also the putrid fumes of his decomposition. The same sympathetic nostrils "snort in anger," sniffle with weeping, and smell the stench of death.

While some might judge this interpretation as overly sentimental, I suggest that it reflects a legitimate feminist interest in preserving intimacy. Initially flaunting his sovereignty with Martha, Jesus ultimately connects with Mary on a more personal level, understands her deepest feelings, and truly communicates his sympathy—not with words, but with tears. He still displays his remarkable power (calling Lazarus from the grave), but not at the expense of his emotional connection with Mary and her sister. For proof of their persisting bond, we look no further than the dinner in 12:1–8, where Mary intimately and profligately anoints Jesus' feet and he defends her actions in no uncertain terms.[88]

Jesus and Mary Magdalene in a Garden

The final conversation between Jesus and a woman in the Fourth Gospel takes place in a provocative setting with multiple links to other Johannine scenes. As the first two encounters between Jesus and women revolve around wedding/marriage images, so the last two feature funeral/death backdrops. Mary Magdalene seeks and eventually finds Jesus in a site that is both graveyard and garden. It is where the crucified body of Jesus has been entombed, prompting her weeping (*klaiousa*, 20:11) in a manner reminiscent of Mary of Bethany's grieving over her deceased brother. But the cemetery is also a "garden" (*kēpos*, 19:41–42), recalling, most immediately, the private place where Jesus retreated with his disciples and was arrested (18:1–11; *kēpos*, 18:1, 26) and, more broadly, the classic spot for male-female intimacy, including the primeval couple Adam and Eve (Gen 2:15–25) and the passionate lovers in the Song of Songs (4:12–5:1; 6:2–3; 8:13).[89] The garden is thus a place of intense yearning both for loved ones *absent* (in dead, impotent bodies) and *present* (in live, sensuous bodies), a place of both decay and delight, of "passion" both in its specialized association with Jesus' death and in its more secular connection to erotic desire. As we shall see, Mary Magdalene will experience both dimensions in her relationship with Jesus.

A duality also marks the status relations between Mary and Jesus. When Mary first mistakes the risen Jesus for the gardener (20:14–15), the encounter is impersonal and functional: she hopes he can help her locate Jesus' "missing" body. When the climactic moment of recognition occurs, the relationship transposes into a deeply personal and passionate key: Mary reaches out to hold her beloved *Teacher* (*Rabbouni*) and *Lord* (*kyrios*), and Jesus deals with her as a messenger and disciple, indeed, as an "apostle to the apostles"[90] (20:16–18).

The conversation unfolds in three segments: the first and last reflect both distance and connection; the central exchange stresses intimacy.

1.   **Jesus:** Why are you weeping? Whom are you looking for? (two interrogatives)

       Mary: Sir, if you have carried him away, tell me where you have laid him, and I will take him away (20:15).

2.   **Jesus:** Mary!

       Mary: Rabbouni! (20:16).

3.   **Jesus:** Do not hold on to me, because I have not yet ascended to the Father. But go to my brothers and say to them, "I am ascending to my Father and your Father, to my God and your God." (two imperatives)

       Mary: I have seen the Lord (20:17–18).

When the risen Jesus appears to Mary Magdalene, she is frantic with worry over his empty tomb. "They" have taken his life from her; how dare "they" take his corpse as well! She vocalizes her own and the other women's frustration first to Simon Peter and the anonymous beloved disciple: "*we* do not know where they have laid him" (20:2). She then repeats this report to two mysterious messengers (*angelous*, 20:12) sitting where Jesus had lain, focusing exclusively on her own distress—"*I* do not know where they have laid him"[91]—and "weeping" as she speaks (20:11–13). When Jesus emerges on the emotional scene, Mary does not recognize him for some undisclosed reason (she is too upset to see straight? He is disguised or looks different in some way?). And Jesus curiously does not make himself known straightaway to Mary, but starts in with the impersonal address, "Woman," which he used previously with both his mother and the Samaritan woman in the context of challenge and debate. In the same vein, he proceeds to quiz Mary.

The tone and intent of his queries are ambiguous. On one level, they are almost insultingly redundant: Jesus knows exactly why Mary is weeping and whom she is seeking. Is he just toying with her, then, or is there some nobler purpose behind his probes? Is he chiding her unbelief in the resurrection, which does seem pretty ridiculous with the living Jesus standing right there? Jesus had said earlier (to the male disciples): "Very truly, I tell you, you will weep and mourn . . . ; you will have pain, but your pain will turn into joy. . . . So you have pain now; but *I will see you again,* and your hearts will rejoice, and no one will take your joy from you" (16:20, 22). This is that moment of joy: "I am here, Mary, so *why are you still weeping?*"[92] But Jesus' question may also be more sympathetic, more solicitous, more like his weeping with Mary of Bethany: "Mary (Magdalene), tell me what's causing you such pain; let me share it with you; let's talk about it."

Jesus' second question—"Whom are you looking for?"—can also be taken in two ways. Is it a patronizing rebuke—"Silly girl, quit your blubbering; I'm standing right here for goodness' sake!"—or a luring invitation to open her eyes to the truth—"I know you're looking for me and I've come to you, can't you see?" The latter option is more compelling, not only because it is more congenial, but also because of the close parallel with Jesus' calling his first disciples: "When Jesus turned and saw them following, he said to them, '*What are you looking for?*' They said to him, '*Rabbi*'" (1:38).[93] Still, a degree of teasing ambiguity in Jesus' discourse with Mary Magdalene is undeniable.

Mary's "Rabbouni" response will come soon enough, matching Jesus' first disciples, but not yet. She is in no mood to play twenty questions with this caretaker fellow. Rehearsing her agony over the missing body yet again, she pushes the matter further by asking the "gardener" to help her find "him." Her goal is not to finger the body snatcher, but to find the body: "Tell me where you have laid him, and *I will take him away*" (20:15). She seeks connection, contact—what limited contact she can have after death—with her beloved. She can scarcely bear that he is gone. The "gardener" could be more helpful, if he just would!

In fact, now he does solve the mystery. Jesus stops questioning her and utters one simple, piercing exclamation: her name, "*Mariam!*" There is now no doubt about Jesus' tone: as the loving, protective Good Shepherd, he knows and "calls his own sheep *by name*," and they "follow him because they know his voice" (10:3–4). That special voice speaking her very own name: whatever his appearance or her apprehension, this can only be her beloved Jesus. And so she responds in faithful recognition with her own appellation, uttered "in Hebrew [Aramaic]": "*Rabbouni!*" "There is a level of intimacy implied by the recourse to an original language in both the naming and the response,"[94] and *Rabbouni* "is a personal address or form of endearment of the word for 'rabbi' [cf. 1:38], teacher or master."[95] While the master-pupil hierarchy is maintained, the emphasis falls on mutual love and fellowship. More than a mere disciple or servant, Mary has effectively been called, as were the disciples in the upper room, Jesus' *friend* (15:15). Carla Ricci poignantly captures this intimate moment, laying special stress not merely on the close teacher-disciple bond, but on the vital relationship between male and female reflections of God's image:

> There is in this moment a meaningful and indescribable synthesis of their existing relations and communications; in hearing herself called, the woman finds at the same time the voice she knows, the voice of the other, and now here of the Other, and finds herself, her perception and understanding of her own depths. The relationship, this contemporaneous double meeting with the other and with herself, in which otherness and identity are both present, this unity that includes duality, could be comprehensively such only in the manifestation of the Risen Christ to a woman, in harmony with the creation by God of a human being, the *adam*, with two visages: man and woman.[96]

But this intimate moment of communication, wondrous as it is, quickly gives way to another pair of ambiguous utterances on Jesus' part, this time in imperative rather than interrogative mode: "Do not hold on to me . . . But go to my brothers . . ." (20:17). Apparently, upon recognizing Jesus, Mary reaches out to embrace him and perhaps even succeeds (the present imperative with *mē* can imply "do not *keep* holding on to me" or "*stop* clinging to me").[97] Understandably, Mary wants to reinforce her personal talk with sensual touch, recalling the Shulammite who rose in the middle of the night to seek her lover and hold him tight:

> I will seek him whom my soul loves.
> *I sought him but found him not.*
> The sentinels found me, as they went about in the city.
> *"Have you seen him whom my soul loves?"*

Scarcely had I passed them, when I found him whom my soul loves.
I held him and would not let him go . . . (Song 3:2–4).[98]

But Jesus will have none of it: he resists Mary's advances in a strikingly
abrupt emotional swing. As Elisabeth Moltmann-Wendel emphasizes:

Up to that point everything is understandable, obvious and clear. But
then comes the remark which is strange, cold, and rejecting, and which
destroys all the feelings of returning happiness: "Don't touch me!" . . .
We cannot eliminate the shock which this remark necessarily causes.
This is no longer the tender, friendly Jesus. It is no longer possible to
touch or anoint his body. He cannot be brought back and held fast. Mary
Magdalene may no longer spontaneously throw her arms around him.
The continuity which women seek is broken.[99]

Moreover, Jesus reinstates a strict vertical hierarchy: he essentially tells Mary
that he is destined to be exalted forever above her in heaven (ascension), not
entwined closely with her on earth.

Nevertheless, Jesus counterbalances this drastic distancing with personal, familial language and a community-building commission to Mary. He
commands her (still in authoritative mode) to "go to *my brothers* [not disciples or apostles] and say to them, 'I am ascending to *my Father and your
Father* [not *the* Father, as previously], to *my God and your God.*'"[100] Jesus
makes clear to Mary Magdalene, even as he physically pushes her away, that
their spiritual bond in the family of faith remains—like that of Naomi and
Ruth—as intimate as ever: her Father is his Father; her God is his God.
Beyond this, Jesus spurns Mary's clinging not to reject her, but to redirect her
attention to nurturing the community of the living Lord on earth, to which
she is the prime (first) witness and apostle. As Moltmann-Wendel keenly
senses the sharpness in Jesus' resistance of Mary's embrace, she appreciates
an ongoing strain of communal compassion as well:

The voice is still near and familiar, and in this voice Jesus is still the same.
With this voice he gives her a task which does not do away with the distance now between them, but makes it comprehensible: his God is also
the God of them all. His Father is also the Father of them all. The apparently unbearable change becomes bearable. Mary Magdalene must go
and speak of this new distance and nearness. Her pain and her terror go
with her. Things are no longer as they were. *But a task and a new community depend on her.*[101]

Conclusion

Without intending to flatten these four rich dialogues between the Johannine Jesus and various women in different settings, we still may appreciate certain sociolinguistic patterns that hold these conversations together. For the most part, the women follow Tannen's stereotypical model of speaking in order to create and maintain intimacy, community, solidarity, and mutual dependence. The mother of Jesus indirectly—and thus as inoffensively as possible—seeks her son's cooperation in preserving the dignity of a family wedding threatened by a shortage of wine; when Jesus balks at his mother's presumed imposition, she deftly negotiates a deal between Jesus and the servants to solve the crisis and mollify Jesus' quest for independence at the same time. The Samaritan woman presses Jesus to maintain vital continuity with relatives, past and present, and with realms, physical and spiritual; "our ancestor" Jacob is not to be trivialized, and neither is the water in his cavernous well that has satisfied the thirst of God's people for generations. Sisters Martha and Mary lament both their deceased brother's absence from the family unit and their beloved Jesus' absence from the funeral party; above all, they desire their family and friends to be *here* with them, surrounding them, loving them, and being loved. And so, too, with Mary Magdalene: absence is agony; her every word exudes her obsession to find the missing body of Jesus, to be with him again, to make what contact she can to dilute the pain of his separation in death.

The major exceptions to these women's connection-driven conversation emerge in the Samaritan's wary distinctions between her ethnic and religious heritage and that of the Jerusalem-centered Jesus and in Mary Magdalene's attempted manipulation of the supposed gardener to serve her own interests. In both cases, initial status relations between the women and Jesus are more distant and impersonal than with Jesus' mother or the sisters from Bethany: Samaritan/Jew and body seeker/caretaker move far outside the close network of family and friends.

Jesus is a "rounder," more complex figure than the women, but he is also more unstable, vacillating in each dialogue between asserting his authority and power and protecting his honor and independence, on the one hand, and reaching out in intimacy and empathy and preserving community and solidarity, on the other hand. Thus he teeters between conventional male and female conversational styles, usually opening the discussion in the masculine, hierarchical mode of opposition and then ending with a more feminine, mutual tone of connection. Corresponding to this stylistic shift is a move in the dialogue from misunderstanding to understanding, conflict to consensus.

Jesus first objects to his mother's presumed demands on his time and attention, but ultimately he complies with her desire to salvage the family's festivities and happily communes with her in Capernaum for "a few days" afterward. Similarly, Jesus initially defends his tardy arrival at Lazarus's funeral from his lofty pedestal as the life-giving "I AM," but eventually comes down to empathize with the emotional turmoil of the sisters and the other mourners and, again, continues to socialize with the restored family of Bethany days later (now defending Mary's concern to preserve intimacy rather than trumpeting his own sovereignty; see 12:1–8). Finally, the risen Jesus approaches the distressed Mary Magdalene first with ambiguous questions, both distancing and inviting in their effect, before he makes a clear connection by calling her name.

In the conclusion to this garden scene, however, the pattern breaks down somewhat, as the soon-to-ascend Jesus reinstates a mixed message of separation and solidarity by sending Mary Magdalene away. The final note in John's gospel stresses Jesus' glorious position as God's Son above all people on earth as well as his continuing spiritual alignment with them. Another exception to Jesus' usual progress from opposition to connection surfaces in his opening statement to the Samaritan woman, which attempts to draw her nearer rather than to push her away. As the conversation ensues, the mix of hierarchical and interpersonal comments reappears, but first, given the ethnic and religious gap that separates him from this anonymous woman (unlike the kinship and friendship ties that bind him to the other women), Jesus must establish the basis for some kind of relationship with her.

For those accustomed to viewing Johannine Christology only in the highest, most authoritative, unequivocal, and dispassionate terms, this assessment of Jesus' volatile masculine and feminine discourse styles may come as something of a surprise. But what do we expect from "the Word made flesh"? Perhaps we would like the incarnate blend of human and divine, material and spiritual, masculine and feminine, oppositional and connectional elements to be better balanced, but maybe in our modern mania for perfect unity, the ragged edges and rough bumps of human communication—even for the Son of God and especially in dialogue with women—are among those things we "just don't understand" sufficiently.

Notes

1. D. Tannen, *You Just Don't Understand: Women and Men in Conversation* (New York: William Morrow, 1990), 42.

2. D. Tannen, *Gender and Discourse* (New York: Oxford University Press, 1996), 3–17; *You Just Don't Understand.*

3. Suggested examples include the songs of Miriam (Exod 15:20–21) and Deborah (Judg 5), the Song of Songs (Solomon), and Huldah's contribution to Deuteronomy (see 2 Kgs 22:14–20).

4. See chap. 6 in this book.

5. The hemorrhaging woman initiates physical contact with Jesus and eventually "told him the whole truth," but no actual dialogue is narrated (5:25–34).

6. Matt 15:21–28. Matthew softens Mark's account by stressing that the *disciples* urge Jesus to send the woman away. Still, Matthew retains Jesus' harsh statement associating the woman with a scavenging dog.

7. A strong sense of wrongdoing and betrayal is evident here, similar to that expressed by foreign kings in Genesis upon discovering Abraham and Isaac's deception concerning their wives ("What have you done to us?" Gen 20:9; cf. 12:10–20; 20:1–18; 26:1–11). See R. Pesch, "'Kind, warum hast du so an uns getan?' (Lk 2,48)," *BZ* 12 (1968): 245–48.

8. See the discussion of the altercation between the adolescent Jesus and his parents in F. Scott Spencer, *What Did Jesus Do? Gospel Profiles of Jesus' Personal Conduct* ((Harrisburg, PA: Trinity Press International, 2003), 33–36.

9. R. T. Lakoff and D. Tannen, "Conversational Strategy and Metastrategy in a Pragmatic Theory: The Example of *Scenes from a Marriage*," in Tannen, *Gender and Discourse*, 137–73.

10. Women are not the only ones who misunderstand the Johannine Jesus (e.g., Nicodemus, Thomas, and Pilate), but it is striking that *all* the conversations with women center around a key point of confusion.

11. Colleen Conway, "Gender Matters in John," in *A Feminist Companion to John* (ed. Amy-Jill Levine; vol. 2; Feminist Companion to the New Testament and Early Christian Writings 5; London: Sheffield Academic Press, 2003), 79–103. The cited material comes from pp. 79–81, 103.

12. Tannen's academic writings include *Talking Voices: Repetition, Dialogue, and Imagery in Conversational Discourse* (Cambridge, UK: Cambridge University Press, 1989); D. Tannen, ed., *Gender and Conversational Interaction* (New York: Oxford University Press, 1993); *Gender and Discourse* (1996). On a more popular level, see Tannen's *That's Not What I Meant! How Conversation Style Makes or Breaks Relations with Others* (New York: William Morrow, 1986); *You Just Don't Understand* (1990); *Talking from 9 to 5: How Women's and Men's Conversational Styles Affect Who Gets Heard, Who Gets Credit, and What Gets Done at Work* (New York: William Morrow, 1994); *The Argument Culture: Moving from Debate to Dialogue* (New York: Random House, 1998).

13. Although she has analyzed conversational patterns in the writings of a modern Greek novelist, Lilika Nakos, in *Lilika Nakos* (Boston: G. K. Hall, 1983) and of the Swedish playwright Ingmar Bergman in "Conversational Strategy."

14. Tannen, *Gender and Discourse*, 34 (emphasis mine; cf. p. 46).

15. E.g., Tannen cites Lawrence Durrell's letter to Henry Miller, describing a Jewish colleague: "He is undependable, erratic, has bad judgment, loud-mouthed, pushing, vulgar, thoroughly Jewish . . ." *You Just Don't Understand*, 206; *Gender and Discourse*, 71–72.

16. Tannen, *Gender and Discourse*, 72.

17. Ibid., 178–79.

18. Ibid., 44–45.

19. Ibid., chap. 1: "The Relativity of Linguistic Strategies: Rethinking Power and Solidarity in Gender and Dominance," 19–52; revised from *Gender and Conversational Interaction,* 165–88.

20. Tannen, *You Just Don't Understand,* 24–25.

21. Tannen, *Gender and Discourse,* 195–221; and *Talking from 9 to 5,* 15. Tannen builds on Goffman's careful distinction between "sex-*class*-linked" and "sex-linked" behavior. Cf. Erving Goffman, "The Arrangement Between the Sexes," *Theory and Society* 4 (1977): 301–31.

22. Drawing on the work of J. G. Peristiany, J. Pitt-Rivers, and D. D. Gilmore, among others, see Bruce J. Malina, *The New Testament World: Insights from Cultural Anthropology* (rev. ed.; Louisville, KY: Westminster/John Knox, 1993), 28–62; Jerome H. Neyrey, *Honor and Shame in the Gospel of Matthew* (Louisville, KY: Westminster/John Knox, 1998); Victor H. Matthews and Don C. Benjamin, eds., *Honor and Shame in the World of the Bible, Semeia* 68 (1994); David A. deSilva, *The Hope of Glory: Honor Discourse and New Testament Interpretation* (Collegeville, MN: Liturgical Press, 1999); and *Honor, Patronage, Kinship and Purity: Unlocking New Testament Culture* (Downers Grove, IL.: InterVarsity, 2000).

23. Cf. Bruce Malina and Jerome H. Neyrey, "Honor and Shame in Luke-Acts: Pivotal Values of the Mediterranean World," in *The Social World of Luke-Acts: Models for Interpretation* (ed. Jerome H. Neyrey; Peabody, MA: Hendrickson, 1991), 25–65.

24. Cf. David. D. Gilmore, "Introduction: The Shame of Dishonor," in *Honor and Shame and the Unity of the Mediterranean* (ed. David D. Gilmore; Washington, DC: American Anthropological Association, 1987), 2–21; Malina and Neyrey, "Honor and Shame," 41–44.

25. While recognizing the importance of honor and shame values in the biblical world, Carolyn Osiek and David L. Balch, *Families in the New Testament World: Households and House Churches* (The Family, Religion, and Culture; Louisville, KY: Westminster/John Knox, 1997), 36–47, warn against drawing a rigid, universal boundary between the public arena of male honor and the private sphere of female shame. In particular, they emphasize distinctive gender patterns among elites and peasants in the Roman West and the Greek East. Adeline Fehribach exemplifies a cautious use of honor-shame scripts in understanding women's roles in the Fourth Gospel in her *The Women in the Life of the Bridegroom: A Feminist Historical-Literary Analysis of the Female Characters in the Fourth Gospel* (Collegeville, MN: Liturgical Press, 1998), 13–15. For a sharper critique of the honor-shame model in New Testament studies by biblical scholars, see F. G. Downing, "'Honor' among Exegetes," *Catholic Biblical Quarterly* 61 (1999): 53–73; and Marianne Sawicki, *Crossing Galilee: Architectures of Contact in the Occupied Land of Jesus* (Harrisburg, PA: Trinity Press International, 2000), 75–80; and by anthropologists, see J. K. Chance, "The Anthropology of Honor and Shame: Culture, Values, and Practice," *Semeia* 68 (1994): 139–51; and G. M. Kressel, "An Anthropologist's Response to the Use of Social Science Models in Biblical Studies," *Semeia* 68 (1994): 153–61.

26. See Phyllis Trible, *Texts of Terror: Literary-Feminist Readings of Biblical Narratives* (Philadelphia: Fortress, 1984); Danna Nolan Fewell and David M. Gunn, *Gender, Power, and Promise* (Nashville, TN: Abingdon, 1993); Gail Corrington Streete, *The Strange Woman: Power and Sex in the Bible* (Louisville, KY: Westminster/John Knox, 1997); Renita J. Weems, *Battered Love: Marriage, Sex, and Violence in the Hebrew Prophets* (Overtures to Biblical Theology; Minneapolis: Fortress, 1995).

27. See Phyllis Trible, "A Human Comedy," in her *God and the Rhetoric of Sexuality* (OBT; Philadelphia: Fortress, 1978), 166–99. For "points of intersection between the book of Ruth and the Fourth Gospel," see Sharon H. Ringe, *Wisdom's Friends: Community and Christology in the Fourth Gospel* (Louisville, KY: Westminster/John Knox, 1999), 73–74.

28. See Alice Bach, "The Pleasure of Her Text," in *The Pleasure of Her Text: Feminist Readings of Biblical and Historical Texts* (ed. Alice Bach; Philadelphia: Trinity Press International, 1990), 27.

29. Cf. G. Stansell, "Honor and Shame in the David Narratives," *Semeia* 68 (1996): 61–65.

30. Bach, "Pleasure of Her Text," 28.

31. Ibid., 32.

32. Beyond Abigail's conciliatory role among competing males, Bach suggests that she may have also promoted peace among David's rival wives (e.g., Michal and Bathsheba) "in their actual lives" (behind the life of the narrative). Bach roots her speculation in Carol Gilligan's work on women's psychology, which bears an obvious similarity to Tannen's sociology: "Gilligan has concluded from her female informants that women embrace an ethic of responsibility, nurturance, and interdependence, which differs from the male ethic of autonomous individual entitlement" ("Pleasure of Her Text," 42n13; cf. pp. 29–30; Carol Gilligan, *In a Different Voice: Psychological Theory and Women's Development* (Cambridge, MA: Harvard University Press, 1982).

33. Cf. the woman of Tekoa, who also plays the part of a threatened mother. On maternal imagery in these two "wise women" stories, see Claudia V. Camp, "The Wise Women of 2 Samuel: A Role Model for Women in Early Israel?" in *Women in the Hebrew Bible: A Reader* (ed. Alice Bach; New York: Routledge, 1999), 201–4.

34. Ibid., 199–201.

35. "Song of Songs is the only biblical book in which a female voice predominates. In fact, the protagonist's voice in Song of Songs is the only unmediated female voice in all of Scripture." Renita J. Weems, "The Song of Songs," in *The New Interpreter's Bible* (vol. 5; Nashville, TN: Abingdon, 1997), 363; see also Marcia Falk, *Love Lyrics from the Bible: The Song of Songs. A New Translation* (New York: HarperCollins, 1991), xiii–xxii.

36. Cf. 2:3–4, 16; 3:3–4; 5:2–6; 6:3, 11; 7:12; 8:2, 5; Dianne Bergant, "'My Beloved is Mine and I Am His' (Song 2:16): The Song of Songs and Honor and Shame," *Semeia* 68 (1994): 35.

37. Bergant, "My Beloved," 37.

38. For a reading of Song of Songs as redolent of the idyllic love between the archetypal woman and man in the garden of Eden, see Phyllis Trible, "Love's Lyrics Redeemed," in *God and the Rhetoric of Sexuality*, 144–65.

39. Adeline Fehribach, *Women in the Life of the Bridegroom,* 1–21, observes an imbalance in most recent analyses—by both male and female scholars—of women in the Fourth Gospel: these studies have tended to be quite positive (pro-feminist), largely ignoring a feminist-critical "hermeneutic of suspicion." Although taking a distinctive approach focusing on conversation patterns, I follow Fehribach's lead in attempting to negotiate both favorable and problematic aspects of male-female relations in John.

40. Cf. Bruce J. Malina and Richard L. Rohrbaugh, *Social-Science Commentary on the Gospel of John* (Minneapolis: Fortress, 1998), 70–72; Ringe, *Wisdom's Friends,* 79.

41. Malina and Rohrbaugh, *Social-Science Commentary on the Gospel of John,* 272–73; Bruce J. Malina, "Mary—Mediterranean Woman: Mother and Son," *Biblical Theology Bulletin* 20 (1990): 54–64; Osiek and Balch, *Families in the New Testament World,* 42–43.

42. Beverly Roberts Gaventa, *Mary: Glimpses of the Mother of Jesus* (Personalities of the New Testament; Minneapolis: Fortress, 1995), 81–89.

43. Ernst Haenchen suggests "the reader also anticipates that Jesus will proceed to perform a miracle in response to this indirect request." *John 1: A Commentary on the Gospel of John, Chapters 1–6* (Hermeneia; Philadelphia: Fortress, 1984), 175. But since Jesus has worked no miracle thus far in the narrative (this will be the "first sign"), we should not assume that his mother is demanding a mighty display of Jesus' power.

44. On women's predilection for indirect speech, see Tannen, *Gender and Discourse,* 32–34, 177–93; and *You Just Don't Understand,* 171–74, 224–27.

45. "Jesus gruffly refuses and follows his 'No!' with the puzzling words: 'My hour has not yet come.'" Haenchen, *John 1,* 176.

46. C. K. Barrett, *The Gospel According to St. John: An Introduction with Commentary and Notes on the Greek Text* (2nd ed.; Philadelphia: Westminster, 1978), 191.

47. R. Schnackenburg, *The Gospel According to John* (3 vols.; New York: Crossroad, 1987), 1:327–28.

48. Adele Reinhartz notes that, apart from "Woman," the only other figure whom the Johannine Jesus addresses in a vocative form is God as "Father" (11:41; 12:28; 17:1, 5, 11, 24–25)—a term of obvious honor and intimacy. "The Gospel of John," in *A Feminist Commentary* (vol. 2 of *Searching the Scriptures;* ed. Elisabeth Schüssler Fiorenza; New York: Crossroad, 1994), 568–70.)

49. Cf. Gaventa, *Mary,* 84–86.

50. Schnackenburg, *Gospel According to John,* 1:328; cf. pp. 323–25.

51. Tannen discusses the conversational tension between women's desire to build *rapport* and men's concern to *report* the facts in "'Put Down That Paper and Talk to Me!': Rapport-talk and Report-talk," chap. 3 of *You Just Don't Understand,* 74–95; cf. also Tannen, *Gender and Discourse,* 209–11.

52. On the importance of synchronizing all of Jesus' work in John (culminating in Jesus' death) with the divinely appointed "hour," see 4:23, 52–53; 7:30; 8:20; 12:23, 27; 13:1; 16:25, 32; 17:1; 19:27.

53. Cf. Raymond E. Brown, *The Community of the Beloved Disciple: The Life, Loves, and Hates of an Individual Church in New Testament Times* (London: Geoffrey Chapman, 1979), 195–98; Reinhartz, "Gospel of John," 569, goes beyond "disciple" language to suggest the mother of Jesus' function as an "apostle": "It could be that this woman . . . who knows of Jesus' powers and instructs others to obey him, is to be seen as an apostolic figure."

54. She is not, however, at the empty tomb. The honor of first encountering the risen Jesus goes to another "woman," Mary Magdalene (20:14–18). For further discussion of the role of Jesus' mother in the Fourth Gospel, see Spencer, *What Did Jesus Do?,* 38–43.

55. See the extended studies of Teresa Okure, *The Johannine Approach to Mission: A Contextual Study of John 4:1–42* (WUNT, 2nd series, 32; Tübingen: J. C. B. Mohr [Paul Siebeck]), 1988; Gail R. O'Day, *Revelation in the Fourth Gospel: Narrative Mode and Theological Claim* (Philadelphia: Fortress, 1986), 49–92; J. E. Botha, *Jesus and the Samaritan Woman: A Speech Act Reading of John 4:1–42* (NovTSup 65; Leiden: Brill, 1991).

56. Cf. Robert Alter, *The Art of Biblical Narrative* (New York: Basic Books, 1981), 47–62; L. Eslinger, "The Wooing of the Woman at the Well: Jesus, the Reader and Reader-Response Criticism," in *The Gospel of John as Literature: An Anthology of Twentieth-Century Perspectives* (ed. Mark W. G. Stibbe; Leiden: Brill, 1993), 166–68.

57. The commonplace assumption that any public conversation between first-century Jewish men and women was scandalous, regardless of the circumstances, has been exposed by feminist historians as a gross exaggeration of the evidence. The conventional view derives largely from later rabbinic sources that warn against *excessive* (not all) talk between the sexes (e.g., "don't talk *too much* with women," *Pirke Avot* 1:5) and reflect an *idealistic* (not descriptive) opinion of certain rabbis regarding the bounds of intercourse principally with married women. The social reality of public discourse between men and ordinary (nonelite), single women was much more complex. See the careful studies of Kraemer, "Jewish Women and Christian Origins" and "Jewish Women and Women's Judaism(s)," in *Women and Christian Origins* (ed. Ross Shepard Kraemer and Mary Rose D'Angelo; New York: Oxford University Press, 1999), 35–79; Kraemer, *Her Share of the Blessings: Women's Religions among Pagans, Jews, and Christians in the Greco-Roman World* (New York: Oxford University Press, 1992), 93–127; and Tal Ilan, *Jewish Women in Greco-Roman Palestine* (Peabody, MA: Hendrickson, 1995), 126–29, 176–204.

58. Conway, "Gender Matters in John," 82; Mary Rose D'Angelo, "(Re)Presentations of Women in the Gospels: John and Mark," in *Women and Christian Origins* (ed. Ross Shepard Kraemer and Mary Rose D'Angelo; New York: Oxford University Press, 1999), 133.

59. Luise Schottroff, "The Samaritan Woman and the Notion of Sexuality in the Fourth Gospel," in *"What is John?"* (vol. 2 of *Literary and Social Readings of the Fourth Gospel;* ed. Fernando F. Segovia; Atlanta: SBL, 1998), 165–66. Francis J. Moloney suggests that the noon/well setting has nothing to do with the woman's status, but simply makes "good sense" as an appropriate

time and place for the traveling Jesus to stop for refreshment. *The Gospel of John* (Sacra Pagina 4; Collegeville, MN: Liturgical Press, 1998), 116.

60. Schottroff, "Samaritan Woman," 166–67.

61. The encounters at a well in Gen 24 and John 4 may also be distinguished on socioeconomic grounds: Abraham's servant brings ten camels and "all kinds of choice gifts" for Isaac's bride (Gen 24:10); Jesus comes alone to Jacob's well without so much as a bucket (John 4:11).

62. On the typical game of "one-upsmanship" played by men and the opposite framing of women in a "one-down" position, see Tannen, *You Just Don't Understand,* 224–26, 273–75.

63. Cf. Stephen D. Moore, *Poststructuralism and the New Testament: Derrida and Foucault at the Foot of the Cross* (Minneapolis: Fortress, 1994), 52–54.

64. Ibid., 43–64.

65. Ibid., 59 (emphasis his).

66. Ibid., 59.

67. Okure, *Johannine Approach,* 89, 99–100; cf. Moore, *Poststructuralism and the New Testament,* 60–61.

68. Moore, *Poststructuralism and the New Testament,* 62.

69. D'Angelo, "(Re)presentations of Women in the Gospels: John and Mark," 134.

70. Paul Duke, *Irony in the Fourth Gospel* (Atlanta: John Knox, 1985), 102–3.

71. Cf. 2 Kgs 17:24–41; Sandra M. Schneiders, *The Revelatory Text: Interpreting the New Testament as Sacred Scripture* (New York: HarperCollins, 1991), 180–99; "Feminist Hermeneutics," in *Hearing the New Testament: Strategies for Interpretation* (ed. Joel B. Green; Grand Rapids: Eerdmans, 1995), 356–69.

72. Schottroff's suggestion in "Samaritan Woman," 164–65, that the Samaritan was currently being exploited in "a non-marital sexual and work relationship with a man that did not even provide . . . the relative security of a marriage contract" is possible, but not provable. The text supplies no details about the couple's sexual or work arrangements.

73. Malina and Rohrbaugh, *Social-Science Commentary on the Gospel of John,* 193–97.

74. Elisabeth Moltmann-Wendel, *The Women around Jesus* (New York: Crossroad, 1997), 24.

75. Malina and Rohrbaugh, *Social-Science Commentary on the Gospel of John,* 200.

76. Thomas L. Brodie, *The Gospel According to John: A Literary and Theological Commentary* (New York: Oxford University Press, 1993), 385.

77. Ibid., 395; cf. pp. 383–98.

78. On the basis of Jesus' voluntary and stolid approach to death reflected in texts like John 18:18; 12:27; 19:11, 30, Conway ("Gender Matters in John," 101) concludes that the Johannine Jesus consistently fits the ideal mold of dispassionate, self-controlled masculinity in Greco-Roman society. However, I see the emotional portrait of Jesus at Lazarus's funeral partially running against the conventional masculine grain. For more on the passionate Jesus (albeit in Luke) in tension with Hellenistic notions of masculinity, see chap. 5 in this book.

79. On grammatical grounds, Barrett suggests the reading Jesus "burst into tears." *Gospel According to St. John,* 400.

80. Brodie, *Gospel According to John,* 394–95.

81. Cf. Moloney, *Gospel of John,* 341: "There is no need to resort to a softening of the context suggesting that Jesus is moved by his sympathy for his sufferers."

82. Note here the remarks of a female commentator, Gail R. O'Day: "It is again important that the tears [of Jesus] not be sentimentalized." "The Gospel of John," in *The New Interpreter's Bible* (vol. 9; Nashville, TN: Abingdon, 1995), 691; cf. pp. 690–91).

83. Recall Tannen's emphasis on linguistic conventions. There has also been an unfortunate anti-Judaic tendency to downplay Jesus' sympathy because it corresponds with "the Jews'" evaluation, "See how he loved him!" (11.36). See, e.g., Moloney, *Gospel of John,* 330–31; George R. Beasley-Murray, *John* (Word Biblical Commentary 36; Waco, TX: Word Books, 1987), 194.

84. On these semantic distinctions, see C. H. Talbert, *Reading John: A Literary and Theological Commentary on the Fourth Gospel and the Johannine Epistles* (New York: Crossroad, 1994), 174–75; Schnackenburg, *The Gospel According to St. John*, 2:335–36; Barrett, *Gospel According to St. John*, 398–400.

85. Malina and Rohrbaugh, *Social-Science Commentary on the Gospel of John*, 200.

86. "Jesus perceives that the presence and grief of the sisters and of the Jews are almost forcing a miracle upon him, and as in 2:4 the request for miraculous activity evokes a firm, almost rough, answer; here, in circumstances of increased tension, it arouses his wrath." Barrett, *Gospel According to St. John*, 399.

87. See the section on 11:28–44 in Beasley-Murray's commentary entitled "The Wrath of the Revealer in the Presence of Unbelief," in *John*, 192–99; cf. O'Day, "Gospel of John," 690–91; Ben Witherington III, *John's Wisdom: A Commentary on the Fourth Gospel* (Louisville, KY: Westminster/John Knox, 1995), 203–4.

88. I do not discuss this incident in detail because, while it features memorable body language, it reports no verbal discourse between Mary and Jesus.

89. In "(Re)Presentations of Women in the Gospels: John and Mark," 136, D'Angelo suggests that this scene "achieves these [erotic] effects by casting Mary in the role of the woman lover from Song of Songs 1:12." Cf. Trible, *God and the Rhetoric of Sexuality*, 152–62. A perversion of the sanctity and intimacy of the garden is evident in the rape scene in Sus 15–27.

90. Mary Rose D'Angelo points out the "longstanding traditional interpretation of John 20:18 that awarded her [Mary Magdalene] the title *apostola apostolorum*, 'apostle of apostles', that is, 'apostle sent to apostles' or even 'supreme apostle.'" "Reconstructing 'Real' Women from Gospel Literature: The Case of Mary Magdalene," in Kraemer and D'Angelo, eds., *Women and Christian Origins*, 106. Cf. Brown, *Community of the Beloved Disciple*, 190.

91. On the "we"/"I" distinction, see O'Day, "Gospel of John," 840–42; and Mark W. G. Stibbe, *John* (Readings: A New Biblical Commentary; Sheffield, UK: Sheffield Academic Press, 1993), 202–3.

92. O'Day, "Gospel of John," 841.

93. Ibid., 842. In a less congenial parallel, however, Jesus sardonically asks Judas and the arresting party in the garden, "Whom are you looking for?" (18:4, 7).

94. Moloney, *Gospel of John*, 528.

95. O'Day, "Gospel of John," 842.

96. Carla Ricci, *Mary Magdalene and Many Others: Women Who Followed Jesus* (Minneapolis: Fortress, 1994), 143.

97. See the excellent critical survey of feminist scholarship on this text in Harold W. Attridge, "Don't Be Touching Me: Recent Feminist Scholarship on Mary Magdalene," in *A Feminist Companion to John* (ed. Amy-Jill Levine; vol 2; FCNT 5; London: Sheffield Academic Press, 2003), 140–66.

98. See Stibbe, *John*, 205; D'Angelo, "Reconstructing 'Real' Women," 120; Moloney, *Gospel of John*, 528; Conway, "Gender Matters in John," 92.

99. Moltmann-Wendel, *Women around Jesus*, 71 (emphasis mine).

100. Cf. O'Day, "Gospel of John," 843.

101. Moltmann-Wendel, *Women around Jesus*, 72 (emphasis mine).

CHAPTER 5

Passions and Passion:
The "Loose" Lady, Woman Wisdom,
and the Lukan Jesus

With a penchant for sensational conversion stories, interpreters, both popular and professional, of the anonymous woman who washes Jesus' feet in Luke 7:36–50 commonly accentuate her promiscuous past as a prostitute from which Jesus gallantly rescues her. Betrayed by her unpinned, free-flowing locks that she brazenly entwines around Jesus' bare extremities, she emerges as a quintessentially "loose" lady whom Jesus mercifully reins in. Although it makes for a tantalizing tale of rehabilitation rivaling that of the Apostle Paul, the supporting evidence for the "sinful" woman's wretched past of prostitution falls considerably short of the clear testimony in Acts and Paul's letters concerning his former life of persecution. The Lukan narrator and Simon the Pharisee concur in labeling the woman a "sinner" (*hamartōlos*, Luke 7:37, 39), but what type of sinner she represents is never specified.

Simon's reaction suggests that he perceives her as a prodigious sinner of some notoriety, a point that Jesus seems to confirm with his reference to her "many sins" (7:47). But such a reputation need not automatically or exclusively signify prostitution. The first character tagged a "sinner" in Luke is Simon Peter (5:8),[1] and as far as I know, no one has ever intimated that he was anybody's gigolo or boy toy, despite the fact that he was out and about during the wee hours of the night (do we really think he spent all that time fishing?). Of course, Peter was a "man-sinner" (*anēr hamartōlos*) rather than a "woman-sinner" (*gynē hamartōlos*), and thus much less subject, if not exempt, from stereotypes of sexual deviancy. But still, even in the woman's case, must we simply assume the sinner/prostitute equation without adding up all the evidence? Do we assume that all wicked women are whores until proven innocent?

I will have more to say below about the character and conduct of the woman in Luke 7, but for now, I wish only to register a basic methodological point that this supposedly "loose" woman has suffered from some rather "loose" interpretation. That is, however loose she may or may not have been *sexually,* she and her story have been treated in rather loose fashion *contextually* by various readers. For example, source, form, and redaction critics have tended to pull every loose thread they can find in an effort to decipher how Luke has patched this account together from various traditions, both oral and written.[2] There are, of course, three other anointing-woman stories to play with in the Gospels—one each in Matthew, Mark, and John—providing an infinite variety of combinations for the putative "original" version and subsequent emendations. Which came first? Mary of Bethany or an unnamed woman of the city anointing Jesus' head or feet? And was the host of the affair Simon the leper or Simon the Pharisee (or some leprous-Pharisee hybrid)? In my judgment, the differences between Luke's story and its supposed counterparts are too numerous and distinctive to be harmonized or tracked in some logical editorial sequence (for instance, how or why might one transform a leper into a Pharisee?). Better, it seems, to appreciate fully the integrity of Luke's portrait of the anointing woman in 7:36–50, to root our understanding of her reputation and actions in the details of the story at hand rather than to "loosen" her from her immediate context.

Likewise, I would argue, when we begin to search for relevant intertextual links outside the immediate story, we must pay special attention to the surrounding material in Luke's narrative[3] and to pertinent precedents in Jewish Wisdom literature. Following the assessment of Luke 7:36–50 as a "conflated story" has been the related perception of the incident as only loosely tied to its Lukan setting. Joseph Fitzmyer, for example, regards this episode as "unrelated to the three preceding passages" and comments further that "it is not easy to discern the reason why it has been added just at this point." The most he concedes are "superficial connections" with the preceding controversy surrounding Jesus' "eating and drinking" habits and "perhaps" somewhat stronger resonance with recent references to the Pharisees' quibbling over Jesus' impious fraternization with sinners.[4] A growing number of other critics, however, detect more integral ties among the scenes in Luke 7. The story of Jesus' encounter with the sinful woman provides an apt climactic illustration of his outreach to "sinners" and other unfortunates, detailed throughout chap. 7, which provokes "offense" (7:23) on the part of certain Pharisees and scribes. And in terms of basic plot elements, the final story picks up on actions of "eating," "seeing," "weeping," "loving," and "believing," featured earlier in the chapter, as well as common characters, such as "Pharisee," "woman," "sinner," and "prophet."

The quest for Old Testament paradigms and patterns has become a staple of contemporary Lukan scholarship, based on Luke's evident absorption in scriptural language and imagery throughout his two-volume work.[5] There has been little agreement, however, as to which Old Testament texts, if any, should inform our reading of the anointing-woman story in Luke 7. Dorothy Lee argues that narrative portraits of the "heroine harlot" (Tamar, Rahab, and the "good" prostitute/mother in the famous Solomon case) provide the best models for interpreting the Gospels' presentations of female "sinners," including the foot-washing woman in Luke and the Samaritan woman at the well and the woman caught in adultery in John.[6] Thomas Brodie seizes on another Old Testament template in making his rather eccentric case that Luke 7:36–50 represents a deliberate, elaborate "internalization" and "imitation" of the paired Elisha stories involving the indebted widow and the bereaved Shunammite woman in 2 Kgs 4.[7] And, finally, D. A. S. Ravens suggests that Luke was inspired by Isa 52:7 to depict the sinful woman's gesture as "the beautifying preparation of Jesus' feet, for he is the one who will soon announce the good news of God's kinship to Jerusalem."[8]

Without engaging in a full critique of these studies, I suggest that they ignore the most obvious and potentially fruitful fund of biblical comparative material: the wisdom traditions in Proverbs and related literature. In Luke 7:35—the verse that immediately precedes and sets the stage for the story of the anointing woman's dealings with Jesus—Jesus announces in defense of his provocative practices of dining and table-fellowship that "*wisdom* is vindicated by all her children." The ensuing episode, then, vividly illustrates precisely how Jesus is justified as Woman Wisdom's offspring and envoy in his encounter with a woman "sinner" while reclining at a Pharisee's table. Even a cursory reading of the book of Proverbs reveals the importance of a young man's following the true path of Lady Wisdom in all his actions pertaining to eating, drinking, and consorting with sinners, women, and other dangerous liaisons. Exactly how Jesus stacks up as Wisdom's pupil at the banquet in Simon's house remains to be examined.

This study endeavors to anchor or "tie down" the interpretation of the story of the supposedly "loose" woman within the networks of 1) the inner-text of Luke 7:36–50 itself, treated as a coherent, self-contained literary unit; 2) the inter-text of Israel's sacred wisdom traditions; and 3) the co-text of the wider Lukan story, especially the passion and resurrection narratives in Luke 22–24, which reprise key elements of the anointing-woman scene.[9]

Inner-text: What Kind of Woman Is This?

First, we concentrate on the main point of conflict within Luke 7:36–50, which Simon voices inwardly, concerning "what kind of woman is this" (7:39) who has crashed the party and is caressing Jesus' feet. We have already flagged certain problems pertaining to the woman's identity, particularly in relation to her presumed background of harlotry. The fact that Simon's prejudicial judgments against her are never spelled out in the story, but rather kept "to himself" (7:39), should caution us further against over-interpreting his thoughts and feelings. Jesus may well be a clairvoyant prophet, but we are not so privileged. We have to read between the lines, and we have to do so carefully.

What we do know through multiple witnesses, cited above, is the woman's notoriety as a "sinner" (7:37). She is thus labeled as a female deviant from conventional standards of righteousness or holiness as understood by certain Pharisees and other law-observant Jews.[10] To help us unpack more specific deviant characteristics under this broad "sinner" banner, we employ several categories of "gender norms," sketched by sociologist Edwin Schur, which are typically used to track women's aberrant behavior. Schur delineates five key identity markers: 1) presentation of self, 2) marriage, maternity, 3) sexuality, 4) occupational choice, and 5) "deviance norms."[11]

The last two shed little light on our subject and may be quickly dismissed. We simply do not know the woman's occupation. Elsewhere Luke happily identifies women's work—table-waiting, purple dealing, tent making, and so on—but that is not his interest here; and Luke is not naïve or squeamish about designating women in the sex trade. He knows the word *pornē* and is not afraid to use it—on the lips of Jesus, no less—reflecting the Pharisees' stock disapproval of such folk in the parable of the prodigal son (15:30). If Simon the Pharisee in Luke 7 had thought that the woman fawning over Jesus in his home was a prostitute, Luke could have easily said as much without resorting to the euphemism of "sinner."

Schur's final category pertaining to "deviance norms" focuses on types of conduct that are peculiarly abnormal for women as women, but more typical of male deviants. In other words, this kind of deviance targets wayward women who act like bad *boys*—female bank robbers, for example (Bonnie working alongside Clyde), or drug madams rather than drug lords. In our Lukan story, the woman in question is not usurping some customarily masculine role. Female slaves often performed basic banqueting courtesies of washing and perfuming invited guests in the ancient world. It is the manner, not the manliness, with which the woman in Luke 7 carries out her duties that raises eyebrows.[12]

The precise nature of her deviance in Simon's eyes may be more profitably probed in conjunction with Schur's initial three categories.

Self-Presentation

The first category of self-presentation Schur subdivides into expressions of emotion, nonverbal communication, appearance, and speech/interaction.[13] Although the Lukan narrative provides no description of the woman's appearance and puts no words in her mouth, it vividly details her emotional state and various forms of nonverbal engagement with Jesus. For one thing, she "weeps" continuously (*klaiousa,* present tense participle, 7:38) and profusely, pumping enough water from her eyes to "bathe" Jesus' feet all by herself (Simon has offered no basin of his own). The verb *brechō* often signifies "rain" (Matt 5:45; Luke 17:29; Jas 5:17; Rev 11:6), thus suggesting that the woman "rains" or "floods" Jesus with her tears. Such an outburst might be appropriate for a woman at a funeral, but not at a feast. From the viewpoint of Simon the host, she may be playing out the deviant stereotype of the "hysterical woman," easily dismissed and thoroughly out of place in sophisticated male company.[14]

The woman's eccentric behavior in Simon's house may be further demonstrated by various facets of nonverbal communication or body language that Schur exemplifies as inappropriate: "gestures, postures, use of space, touching," and the like. We may isolate two critical zones that Simon may have thought the woman silently but surely invaded or trespassed in shameless fashion: first and most broadly, the banquet or party of Simon the host, a devout Pharisee; and second and more intimately, the body or person of Jesus the guest, a reputed prophet and teacher.

In terms of the banquet, we must appreciate, generally, the standard protocol of a restricted guest list—this was an exclusive, invitation-only affair, not a public festival or soup kitchen—and, more particularly, the heightened Pharisaic concern for holiness in matters of commensality intended to replicate ideals of temple purity in table-fellowship.[15] We can be sure that Simon planned his dinner carefully, including the participants (cf. 14:7–24). The story in Luke 7 opens with a clear comment that a Pharisee (whom we later learn is Simon) had "*asked* Jesus to eat with him,"[16] whereupon Jesus came "into the Pharisee's house and took his place at table" (7:36)—invitation duly extended and accepted; table properly set and arranged. The very next verse abruptly (*idou,* "behold") introduces the woman, described only as a city sinner, who comes into the Pharisee's home on her own initiative and makes her way not up to the table, but close behind the feet of a reclining guest. Unnamed throughout the story, she scarcely made Simon's honored guest list. She comes uninvited and unwelcome from Simon's point of view (a known male "sinner" would have been no less intrusive).[17] She appears to be one of those marginal city crawlers, street people, if you will, who certainly would have included prostitutes, but also other deviant denizens of the city's "streets and lanes," such as "the poor, the crippled, the blind, and the lame"—both female and male—featured later in Jesus' parable of the great banquet, uttered at another Pharisaic dinner party (14:13, 21). Needless to say, such folk, totally unable to reciprocate hospitality or to enhance the host's reputation, were not welcome party guests.[18] However typical and tolerated it might have been at ancient Eastern Mediterranean banquets (symposia) for anyone to wander in off the streets and line the walls as curious spectators,[19] a known sinner at a Pharisaic fellowship meal was probably not so commonplace, certainly not one who, far from being a wallflower, obtrusively imposes herself on a table guest. By the same token, however popular attentive courtesans might have been at other parties, they would likely not have been headlining entertainers at Pharisaic feasts.[20] (In any case, the woman in our story does not fit the courtesan bill: she provides no witty conversation or other amusements—she's weeping, remember). In short, the urban sinner-woman is a deviant, brazen outsider at Simon's table.

Her intimate handling of Jesus' body confirms this stigma. The narrator's report of Simon's inner thoughts reveals the woman's "touching" display as especially suspect (7:39). Not only has she pushed herself too close to the table, she has pressed herself—literally—onto one of the honored guests at the table. Proper guarding of bodily borders—putting "clean" food into the mouth, for example, with "clean" hands and utensils—was an important symbolic dimension of ceremonial meals observed by the Pharisees (and others), mirroring a wider concern to protect the nation, the body politic, God's people, from "foreign" invaders.[21] A prophet and teacher, as Jesus purports to be, must—like a priest—meticulously monitor the state of his body as God's holy vessel. Of course, he can scarcely avoid defiling contact with polluted things and people (sinners), and the Torah makes full provision for cleansing and renewal (impurity was not the unpardonable "sin" it is sometimes made out to be). But still, the pious prophet and teacher should not brashly court sinful companions nor act so indulgently or nonchalantly, as Jesus appears to, about receiving a sinner's unsolicited and unrestrained touch in a public ceremonial setting designed to promote the highest standards of holiness. In Simon's mind, the sinner-woman's deviance becomes Jesus' (guilt by association) through his cavalier indulgence of her bodily advances.

Marital and Maternal Identity

In addition to various modes of self-presentation, the marital and maternal identities of women represent key factors in determining their "place" within conventional society. Ideals of wife and mother, suitably devoted to husband and children, have prevailed across cultures for millennia. Even today, deviant labels of "spinster," "old maid," "unwed mother," "unfit mother," and the like still stick fast and cut very deep. In the case of the anointing woman in Luke 7, nothing is said concerning her marital or maternal status, but such silence may be revealing in itself. She does not grieve over a diseased or deceased child, like the widow earlier in the chapter (7:11–14); she appears as no one's wife, like Joanna in the next chapter (8:3); nor is she characterized as a dependent youth under her father's care, like Jairus's daughter at the end of the chapter (8:40–42, 49–56).

In the absence of these standard relations, the anointing woman appears dangerously independent, unattached, on the "loose," free to roam about city streets and into private homes and to latch onto any unsuspecting male she chooses.

Sexual (Mis)Conduct

Admittedly, we are getting close again to describing a prostitute, which takes us into Schur's third category of norms dealing with sexuality. But the labeling/deviance process need not trade in literal fact; the mere appearance of evil will do well enough. Sadly, many women through the ages have been branded unjustly as shameless "sluts," "hussies," and "whores" simply because these are the most convenient and damning tags that moral judges have ready at hand to attach to unattached, maverick women who live their lives, by choice or necessity, outside of male control. From Simon's perspective, the woman at Jesus' feet is no doubt too "loose" for comfort, too loose, that is, from traditional family structures. He may have also thought, by extension, that she had been especially loose morally, that her sins were chiefly sexual. But we cannot be certain from the evidence at hand that she had actually lived up to such a reputation.

This does not mean, however, that the woman's sexuality is negligible in the Lukan story, which, in fact, showcases a titillating, erotic scene, at least "PG-13," if not heading toward an "R" rating. Back to Simon's distress over the woman's "touching" Jesus (7:39), the verb describing such action can connote, in the middle voice used here (*haptomai*), explicitly sexual touching leading to and including intercourse, as in Paul the Pharisee's (and/or certain

Corinthians') notorious maxim: "It is well for a man not to touch (*hap-testhai*) a woman" (1 Cor 7:1).[22] Modifying the statement slightly, Simon may well be responding internally to the scene he witnesses: "It is well for a holy man not to allow himself to be touched—*in that way*—by a woman, a sinner-woman at that!"

Yet Jesus does allow himself to be touched repeatedly on his feet by the woman's tears, lips, and hair—combined in what one writer aptly character-izes as a "messy mixture" with the ointment of myrrh.[23] Delicious ambiguity surrounds each item, leaving the scene bristling with double entendre. The object of the woman's affection—Jesus' *feet*—mentioned no fewer than seven times in the story, may accent her humble gratitude for Jesus' compas-sion and willing submission to his authority. But on the other hand (or foot, maybe we should say), a woman's attention to a man's feet could betray euphemistically more phallic interests, as with Ruth's (in)famous uncovering of Boaz's feet on the threshing floor near Bethlehem. The "dirtiness" of man's lowest, "least honorable" extremities can cut two ways: dirty as in "dusty" or dirty as in "lusty" (as in a "dirty" joke).[24]

With her deluge of tears, the woman may be expressing deep sorrow over her past life of sin, but such intense display of emotion may also convey a wellspring of love and (com)passion for Jesus; in any case, the tearful flow represents a lavish personal gift to Jesus from the woman's own inner recesses, her bodily "waters." A polite kiss of greeting on the hand or cheek, accompanied by a refreshing application of household olive oil to the guest's head, constituted common practices of hospitality in the ancient world,[25] as Jesus confirms in his chiding of Simon's failure to provide such amenities (7:44–46). But prolonged, persistent kissing of the feet and dousing them with expensive perfume goes well beyond the call of duty and perhaps the code of propriety.

And then there's this business of the woman's unpinning her hair and wrapping its tresses around Jesus' feet. Is this just a resourceful matter of making do in the absence of a towel? Or is this disheveling of hair another exhibition of over-flagrant mourning, concomitant with the woman's weep-ing and with the rending of garments in Levitical custom (Lev 10:6; 13:45; 21:10)? Or yet again, is this more of a sensuous display—the unbound, free-flowing, tousled look of lovemaking—more appropriate to the private mari-tal bedroom than the public fraternal banquet?[26] While the analogy drawn by one commentator between a woman's letting her hair down in ancient Palestine and going topless in modern America may be a tad extreme,[27] it does capture the potential immodesty of the former act, especially when (as in the Lukan scene) a woman loosens her locks, entwines them around a man's appendages, and employs them in a refreshing body "massage" (the verb for "dry" or "wipe" is a compound of *massō*, meaning "to handle or touch as in a massage").[28] Taken individually, any of the sinner-woman's gestures toward Jesus might fit within "normal" parameters of behavior. But taken together, her extended personal wetting, kissing, perfuming, and hair wiping of Jesus' feet comprise excessive, deviant "public display of affection" (PDA) by almost anyone's standards, ancient or modern.

That being said, we still need not label the woman a whore or regard her actions as lewd. To state the obvious, all demonstrably affectionate women are not harlots; all female sexuality is not prostitution; and all erotica is not pornography. Simon may have been appalled at what he perceived to be the woman's whorish behavior and even extrapolated that she had regularly approached other men in such a wanton fashion—but that is not a necessary conclusion from the evidence at hand. Deviance is in the eye of the beholder.[29] Jesus, for his part, takes a very different view of the proceedings, thoroughly "neutralizing" Simon's deviant labeling of the woman.[30] Jesus never labels the woman anything except "this woman," whom he invites Simon to see in a fresh light (7:44). While agreeing that she has committed many sins (who hasn't?), Jesus never brands the woman with the "dominant status"[31] of a "sinner" of any stripe nor exhorts her to "go and sin no more," as he did in the case of the woman caught in adultery (John 8:11). Point by point—from 1) providing water and towel for dusty feet, to 2) extending the customary kiss of salutation, to 3) supplying suitable ointment—Jesus contrasts the woman's extravagant hospitality with Simon's utterly deficient response: no water, no kiss, no oil (Luke 7:44–46). The tables are turned on Simon; if anyone should be ashamed here, it should be the ungracious host. This sinful woman, far from being a deviant in Jesus' eyes, thoroughly out-strips Simon as a model of faith, love, and wholeness.

Inter-text: What Kind of Wisdom Is This?

Whether or not Jesus wins this honor-shame contest and is somehow vindi-cated in Simon's eyes remains open in the narrative. Simon's final verdict is never recorded. But from Luke's point of view, Jesus' honor is never in doubt. His interaction with the anointing woman in Simon's house vali-dates his filial tie to the very Wisdom of God (7:35). As parents derive due honor from the honorable deportment of their children, so Mother Wis-dom is "vindicated" by the righteous conduct of Jesus;[32] and in turn, Jesus is "vindicated" as the legitimate progeny, protégé, and proclaimer of Divine Wisdom, or in the language of the Wisdom of Solomon, a "holy soul" whom Woman Wisdom has permeated and inspired as "friend of God" and "holy prophet" (7:27; 11:1).[33]

However, for anyone familiar with Israel's sacred wisdom traditions—as Simon the Pharisee would have been—it is not immediately obvious how the scene around Simon's dinner table showcases Jesus as a model wisdom citizen. Indeed, on the surface at least, the evidence tilts in the opposite direction. Any consort with "sinners" of any kind posed a potentially lethal snare for the aspiring wise young man—to be avoided at all costs. Eating with sinners was no exception, as Sirach plainly states: "Let the righteous be your dinner companions" (9:16). Beyond this consistent general warning against fraternizing with sinners emerged a particular obsession with escaping the traps of "loose" or "strange" women, epitomized by adulteresses and prostitutes. Notice the characteristic language used in Proverbs and Sirach, with an ear tuned to resonances with the story in Luke 7:

> Then a woman comes toward him, decked out like a prostitute. . . . She is loud and wayward; her feet do not stay at home; now in the street, now in the squares, and at every corner she lies in wait. She seizes him and kisses him and with impudent face she says to him. . . . I have come out to meet you, to seek you eagerly, and I have found you! I have decked my couch with coverings. . . . I have perfumed my bed with myrrh, aloes, and cinnamon. Come, let us take our fill of love until morning; let us delight ourselves with love. . . . With much seductive speech she persuades him; with her smooth talk she compels him. Right away he follows her, and goes like an ox to the slaughter. (Prov 7:10–22)

※

> Do not go near a loose woman, or you will fall into her snares. . . . Do not look around in the streets of a city, or wander about in its deserted sections. Turn away your eyes from a shapely woman, and do not gaze at beauty belonging to another; many have been seduced by a woman's beauty, and by it passion is kindled like a fire. Never dine with another man's wife, or revel with her at wine; or your heart may turn aside to her, and in blood you may be plunged into destruction. (Sir 9:3–9)

Several elements seem to fit the scene in Luke 7: an aggressive woman wandering in off the city streets, seizing the man Jesus, kissing him, and, while not seeking to lure him back to *her* scented couch, she brings her myrrh to his couch where he reclines for dinner; furthermore, while she is neither anybody's wife (as far as we know) nor an invited participant in the banquet, Jesus tolerates, if not welcomes, the affectionate advances of a woman who, at any rate, is *not his wife*, while he is eating and drinking. All of this courts disaster for the would-be sage and teacher from the perspective of traditional proverbial wisdom. With such sapiential scenarios etched in his conscience, Simon's shock over Jesus' indulgence of the sinful woman is understandable.

But there is more to the wisdom picture than first meets the eye. While biblical wisdom is certainly prudent, it is not prudish. It does not reduce all female sexuality either to functional reproduction or to gratuitous seduction. With divine blessing, a man is encouraged to pursue and revel in physical intimacy with the wife of his youth, being always satisfied by her breasts and "intoxicated" by her love (Prov 5:18–19). In the Song of Songs, the female partner of the wise Solomon figure initiates lovemaking as much as the man in an altogether positive celebration of sexual pleasure. The opening verses, spoken by the woman, set the tone for the entire book: "Let him kiss me with kisses of his mouth! For your love is better than wine, your anointing oils are fragrant, your name is perfume poured out" (Song 1:2–3). The erotic elements of "kisses," "love," "wine" (appropriate to a feast), and "anointing oils" all find a counterpart in the Lukan story of Jesus' liaison with the anointing woman, as do other images scattered throughout the Canticles of joyous banqueting, perfuming with myrrh (4:14; 5:5), seeking out a lover in the city streets (3:1–4), foot bathing, and flowing locks of dripping wet hair (5:2–3).[34] The threat in this book comes *not* from the sexually active woman, but from those friends who might interrupt or disturb her lovemaking prematurely (2:7; 3:5; 8:4) or from callous city guards who brutally strip and shame her, attempting to thwart her passionate pursuits and treating her—unjustly—like a despicable prostitute (5:7).

Perhaps even more revealing of biblical wisdom's positive affirmation of female sexuality, albeit on a metaphorical level, is the use of erotic language to describe the mission of Woman Wisdom herself. As Gale Yee has demonstrated, Prov 1–9 uses remarkably similar sensual descriptions of the means employed by both Lady Wisdom and Tramp Folly toward completely antithetical ends—the one toward life, the other toward death.[35] Lady Wisdom appears as an alluring streetwalker in her own right, calling simple, sinful youth from the busiest city corners to follow her, love her, embrace her, and hold fast to her, and inviting them to her delectable table to share her freshly butchered meat and mixed wine.

Thus, the evangelistic (reaching out to sinners) and erotic (reaching out and "touching" sinners) overtones of the banquet scene in Luke 7 are not as foreign to Israel's sapiential symbolic universe as Simon might have thought. Nevertheless, problems persist from both Pharisaic and feminist perspectives. From the Pharisee's side, the fact remains that Jesus "carries on" with a woman who is not his wife in a house that is not his own in a place that is not his bedroom. The action occurs in Simon's home around Simon's private dinner table where the sinful woman has not been invited and where he may well have hoped to display the highest standards of temple piety. Whatever Simon may have enjoyed in his own bedchamber with his own wife (and there is no reason to think he was a prude), he cannot be happy that his table has taken on the appearance of a brothel, his dinner party spiced up with a jar of myrrh, and his pious plans tangled by a woman's unbound tresses (everyone knows that food and hair don't mix—isn't there some law about wearing hairnets?).

But Simon, poor fellow, is a hopeless literalist and not a very good feminist. What can you expect, then? He just does not appreciate the marvelous metaphor unfolding in his house of Woman Wisdom's wining, dining, and welcoming repentant sinners in warm embrace into the family of God. Admittedly, it takes a little effort to make the metaphor work. The woman in Simon's home does not fully fit the part of Lady Wisdom. She seeks, she embraces, she loves—but she does not speak a single word. In Proverbs, both Lady Wisdom and Tramp Folly carry out their vocations chiefly through enticing speech, soliciting the attention of prospective suitors through persuasive (seductive) rhetoric. In the Lukan story, however, the male Jesus plays this prophetic role, not the silent woman. Although not portrayed as the full incarnation of Divine Wisdom, as we see in Matthew and John, the Lukan Jesus does represent the principal heir and primary envoy of Lady Wisdom. His knowledge of Simon's unexpressed thoughts, his spinning of a clever parable, his welcome of a receptive sinner at the table, his pointed exposure of Simon's lack of love, and his authoritative pronouncement on the forgiveness of sins all vindicate his mission as Wisdom's supreme prophet.

As for the sinful woman, her acceptance and affirmation by Jesus signal her incorporation into the surrogate family of faith, the household of Divine Wisdom. She is thus a child of Mother Wisdom in her own right, but a clearly subordinate sister to Jesus whose feet she attends. Moreover, she is no prophet. After the birth narrative, Luke has scant interest in women prophets, as several recent studies have demonstrated.[36] Women may join the Jesus movement, but he prefers them to "choose the better part" of sitting silently and dutifully at his feet—which is exactly what the anointing woman does, as surely as Mary of Bethany (Luke 10:42). In the process, she becomes thoroughly objectified, a model to be viewed—"Do you *see* this woman?"—not a subject to be heard. While, as we have argued, she may be imagined as a genuinely positive model of love, faith, and action rather than a pitiful whore, a feminist critique still finds that Luke's portrayal of this figure remains problematic.

Co-text: What Kind of Passion Is This?

While the affectionate, anointing woman and receptive, reclining Jesus in Luke 7 can both be "vindicated" as "Wisdom's children" in (relative) conformity with traditional Jewish Wisdom texts like Proverbs, Song of Solomon, and Sirach, their respective roles in this erotic scene become more problematic with respect to a strand of Hellenistic-Jewish wisdom more closely intertwined with Greek moral philosophy. As a prime example, the reconfiguration of Maccabean martyr traditions in 4 Maccabees reflects a Stoic preoccupation with human emotions or "passions" (*pathē*) that appears to be egregiously undermined by the Lukan woman's gushy out-pouring of passion and, perhaps, by Jesus' complicity in this passionate ordeal as well.[37]

What particular sensations does 4 Maccabees aim to harness? The gamut of debilitating passions spring from two main sources: "The two most com-prehensive types of the emotions are *pleasure* and *pain*" (1:20). The "plea-sure" category—that seems most relevant to the Lukan anointing episode—subdivides into another pair of primary (primal) passions: "It is evident that reason rules over those emotions that hinder self-control, namely, *gluttony* and *lust*" (1:3). Gluttony and lust, gormandizing and wom-anizing, gastronomic (*gastrimargias*) and erotic excess, pose a formidable double threat to Wisdom's children, but one that can be successfully sur-mounted by reason and logic (*logismos*), manifested in self-discipline and self-control (*sōphrosynē* and *enkrateia*).[38] Just look at Joseph and Daniel: "the temperate (*sōphrōn*) Joseph," who, though "young and in his prime for inter-course, nullified the frenzy of the passions," particularly that of "sexual desire" for seductive women like "thy neighbor's—or thy boss's—wife" (2:1–6); and the courageous Daniel (and his three Hebrew cohorts) who stoutly refused to comply with the unreasonable (unlawful) dietary and devotional demands of a pagan ruler, even on pain of death.[39] Indeed, for both Joseph and Daniel and friends, mastering the urge of pleasure thrust them into battle with its partner in passion—pain—whether in the form of an Egyptian prison, a lion's den, or a fiery furnace. This savage emotion they also conquered, however, through virile valor (*andreia*), with not a little help, of course, from special heavenly agents. The martyrs (Eleazar and company) memorialized in 4 Maccabees were not so fortunate in the divine aid department (no lion-taming angel or flame-retarding fireman [or even "one like a fireman"] for them), but they more than made up for this deficiency with incredible displays of unflinching *andreia* in the face of brutal torture inflicted by the Seleucid tyrant, Antiochus IV.

If all of this pitched battle against passion seems to be a fundamentally male obsession, wrapped up with the very essence of masculinity, that's because it is.[40] Women were stereotypically regarded as inveterate emotional creatures by nature, ruled by their passions—often hysterically and irrationally—and void of sound reason. Such ancient perceptions of uncontrollable feminine feeling, extending to the realm of pleasure as well as pain, run counter to popular psychological thought since the Enlightenment, as Thomas Laqueur has observed with particular reference to women's (presumed) capacity for orgasm:

> The commonplace of much contemporary psychology—that men want sex while women want relationships—is the precise inversion of pre-Enlightenment notions that, extending back to antiquity, equated friendship with men and fleshliness with women. Women, whose desires knew no bounds in the old scheme of things, and whose reason offered so little resistance to passion, became in some [modern] accounts creatures whose whole reproductive life might be spent anesthetized to the pleasures of the flesh. When, in the late eighteenth century, it became a possibility that "the majority of women are not much troubled with sexual feelings," the presence or absence of orgasm became a biological signpost of sexual difference.[41]

But all was not utterly hopeless for the wanton "weaker sex" of antiquity. Certain rare and special women—like the mother of the seven Maccabean brother-martyrs—managed to rise above their passionate natures. But they did so entirely on men's terms, by becoming masculinized, like men, and thus denying their womanhood. Self-control and courage remained quintessentially male virtues, regardless of who practiced them. And so the remarkable Maccabean mother—who stoically witnessed the horrific execution of each of her seven sons, from eldest to youngest, without encouraging them to recant and spare their lives, and then threw herself into the fire as a brave act of self-martyrdom—was lauded in 4 Maccabees for *disregarding* her natural feelings and inclinations as a woman and displaying "*a man's courage* in the midst of her emotions." In fact, she herself is not the one praised as much as the masculine persona of "devout reason" that penetrates her heart or the "God-fearing Abraham" who set the standard for child-sac-rificing faith.[42]

> But devout reason, giving her heart *a man's courage in the very midst of her emotions*, strengthened her to *disregard*, for the time, her parental love. Although she witnessed the destruction of seven children and the ingenious and various rackings, this noble mother *disregarded all these because of faith in God*. For as in the council chamber of her own soul she saw mighty advocates—nature, family, parental love, and the rackings of her children—this mother held two ballots, one bearing death, and the other deliverance for her children. She did not approve the deliverance that would preserve the seven sons for a short time, but as the daughter of Abraham she remembered his fortitude. . . .
>
> If, then, a woman, advanced in years and mother of seven sons, endured seeing her children tortured to death, it must be admitted that devout reason is sovereign over the emotions. (15:23–28; 16:1)

In other words, if even a woman can be so controlled—made to appear so manly—then devout reason must really be something.

Specifically, this rational transformation (reason possession) of the Maccabean mother allowed her to stanch (disregard) the flood of emotions normally engulfing her "weaker sex" (15:5), such as her intense love for her offspring (a "deeper sympathy" than fathers feel by virtue of her intimate experiences of pregnancy and delivery, 15:4) and her concomitant anguish over her children's pain, readily issuing in a torrent of tears. "Though so many factors influenced the mother to suffer with them out of love for her children, in the case of none of them were the various tortures strong enough to pervert her reason" (16:11). Even when staring deep into the eyes of her beloved tormented sons, she shed nary a tear (16:16–20).

A colossal display of male control and courage, if there ever was one—but with a vital caveat: all of this dispassion was "for the time" (*proskairos*, 15:23)—temporary, aberrational, the exception that proves the rule, a des-perate measure locked into a desperate time. We mustn't make a habit of this; we mustn't expect more of our hysterical women than they can bear. And so, in an awkward and anticlimactic move, the author (or editor) of 4 Maccabees concludes his encomiastic narrative with the mother's flashback speech to her sons (before their vicious martyrdom), reminding them of her sexual history (just what every son is dying to know about his mother), beginning with her youthful chastity ("I was a pure virgin and did not go outside my father's house") and climaxing with her devotion to their father, her late husband, who faithfully instructed his sons to follow the path of courage and discipline blazed by Abraham, Joseph, Daniel, and other great heroes (no heroines) of the faith (18:6–19). In Dad's absence, Mom may have to make a few speeches and throw herself in the fire (without letting anyone "touch her body" [17:1], however—chaste to the bitter end), but this is scarcely the normal order of things. In fact its patent *ab*normality finally shames the despicable bully Antiochus the most: "If then a woman [of all things], advanced in years and mother of seven sons . . . has despised the fiercest tortures," (16:1–2), what kind of man must her torturer be? "O mother, soldier of God in the cause of religion, elder and woman! By steadfastness you have conquered even a tyrant, and in word and deed you have proved yourself more powerful than a man" (16:14). Shame, shame on him.[43]

Against this backdrop of a representative Hellenistic Jewish construction of gender and passion, the "loose" lady in Luke 7 fits conventional expectations of emotion-laden femininity—a slave to her passions. No tightly monitored, maternal, manly martyr here. Unlike the Maccabean hero(ine), the Lukan woman roams "outside her father's house" through the city and into another man's home who is clearly not her father or husband.[44] This story leaves open whether she has (or has ever had) a husband or children, but that would hardly be the reader's first guess. She seems unattached, except when she latches on to Jesus' body. And in this display, far from reining in her emotions, she oozes forth with lavish love expressed through unbridled tears, lips, and hair. Not a prostitute necessarily (see above), but certainly not a passionless, masculinized woman, either. The Lukan woman does match the Maccabean mother as an exemplar of *faith,* but she does so, significantly, *as* a woman. "And [Jesus] said to *the woman,* 'Your faith [exhibited in typical womanly ways] has saved you; go in peace" (Luke 7:50). No need for her to undergo an Abrahamic soul transplant; her female soul will do just fine.

How does Jesus fare in this story against the template of masculine self-mastery? On the one hand, he appears fully in control of his passions and the proceedings. He is the dominant speaker—indeed, the only public speaker in the scene[45]—calmly discerning and responding to Simon's internal critique with a clever parable and persuasive defense of the woman's behavior.[46] He proves to be the better man than Simon. And with respect to the woman, while Jesus justifies her emotional outburst, he does not match it. He passively receives her loving ministrations without requiting them. But there is another side to consider. Passive compliance, while in some sense passion-less, is not passion control—far from it in the masculine ideal. Joseph boldly resisted and pulled away from the lusty Mrs. Potiphar. Daniel and the Maccabeans refused to eat any of Nebuchadnezzar's or Antiochus's food. They just said "No"—that's what real men do. Jesus, however, while not initiating sexual contact or consummating the relationship, does not spurn the woman's erotic advances and actually affirms them; and while not breaking kosher laws (he's in a Pharisee's home, remember) or overeating, as far as we know, he is attending (yet another) banquet just after fending off charges of being "a glutton and a drunkard" (7:34). He's walking a bit of a moral tightrope here—not surrendering wholly to the twin pleasure traps of gluttony and lust, but not exactly tilting out on the mastery meter either, not the preeminent master of his own masculine domain that we might expect.[47]

What we need to test Jesus' and the woman's discipline rating more accurately is some real *pain,* that other major passion category alongside pleasure. The anointing woman has the pain of her "many sins," whatever those might be, pressing upon her, which she responds to with her flood of tears. Of course, weeping is an appropriate emotional product of grieving over sin, but it remains a sign of weakness—emotional weakness (sobbing) responding to moral weakness (sinning)—more typically associated with the "weaker sex." While a good move, repenting is not as good—not as noble or manly—as staunchly resolving not to sin in the first place. As for Jesus, he experiences no pain at all in the present scene, except perhaps (if we push it) the "mental anguish" of implied social criticism that, in any case, he handles quite easily. Overall, I imagine Jesus feels quite mellow after being doused with kisses and ointment.

The pain for Jesus, of course, comes later in what we commonly call his "passion," culminating in martyrdom on the cross. Now we're in manly Maccabean country. Jesus' *passions* are most thoroughly tested (and ironically limited) in his *passion,* that is, in Luke's passion narrative in the closing chapters of his gospel. But while Jesus' passion(s) come sharply into view in this material, the experiences of and with the anointing woman seem to be a distant memory. If we lament, with Schüssler Fiorenza, interpreters' historic neglect of another (the same?) anointing woman who does appear in Matthew's and Mark's passion accounts—with explicit dominical mandate to remember her forever (so much for what Jesus wants)—then we must weep and wail over her complete absence from Luke's passion story.[48] In fact, the anointing woman of Luke 7 exits as abruptly as she enters, to appear no more. "Do you see this woman?" Jesus asks. Yes, but you better look quick, because she will be never be seen again.

Or so it seems. But for those with eyes to see and with other senses (passions) turned on, this remarkable woman is not so quickly effaced. The flame of her passion is not altogether extinguished, nor the fragrance of her perfume deodorized. As Corley and Reid have both suggested, but not explored in any depth, flickers may be felt and whiffs sniffed of this woman's activity in Luke's passion narrative.[49] Specifically, her kissing and caressing, weeping and wetting, find evocative counterparts in the conduct of various characters—female and male, including Jesus—in Luke's final chapters. These are not perfect parallels, but rather suggestive, "loose" connections, appropriate perhaps to this (oft-perceived) "loose" woman whom interpreters find hard to "pin down." But possible links with Jesus' painful passion may help us to understand her better, to fill out her portrait, and to flesh out her passions in relation to other Lukan figures. Her match (or lack thereof) with Jesus, the primary Lukan hero, remains a paramount consideration. In order, however, to give this match maximum chance to work, we must overcome the dominant tendency in biblical study, both professional and popular, to drive a sharp wedge between Jesus' feelings of pleasure (if he had any) and pain (which he may have overcome but certainly experienced at the end of his life). In other words, we find it problematic to correlate Jesus' hedonic passions with his Stoic passion, or we thoroughly domesticate the former as tender *com*passion as we accentuate the fiery intensity and violent milieu of the latter. As Teresa Hornsby astutely avers:

> In biblical discourse there are extreme contradictions between the passion of Jesus' suffering and the passion of Jesus' pleasure. While non-violent, "gentle" passion is privileged in expressions of sexual relationships, it is ignored (or stigmatized) in biblical scholarship. A feminist biblical discourse could dissolve the barrier by, for example, listening to those who would consider that these two passions—one fierce, one tender—are equal.
>
> If the lavish adoration of the anointing woman is perceived as deviant, and it is, then this means that biblical scholarship has failed to recognize the potential of the Sacred in all excessive physicality. The interpreters of Christianity seem to be more comfortable explaining and propagating the violent passion of Jesus rather than acknowledging any other passion concerning Jesus' body.[50]

Perhaps we can push ourselves out of this narrow comfort zone a little by comparing and contrasting the physical and emotional reactions of the woman in Luke 7 with similar gestures in Luke's passion narrative.

KISSING AND CARESSING

While at first blush, the woman's intimate, tactile (*haptō*) maneuvers of kissing (*kataphileō*) and massaging (*ekmassō*) Jesus' feet appear to be totally unrelated and inappropriate to Jesus' painful passion, second glances reveal some suggestive links. A curious linguistic connection surfaces before the passion narrative per se in Jesus' final passion prediction: "[T]he Son of Man . . . will be handed over to the Gentiles; and he will be mocked and insulted and spat upon. After they have flogged (*mastigōsantes*) him, they will kill him, and on the third day he will rise again" (18:31–33). The verb *mastigoō* (flog), used only here in Luke's writings, is a cognate of *ekmassō* (wipe), used only in Luke 7 of the anointing woman's activity.[51] Apart from a formal etymological link, what semantic notions might associate these two terms? Both concern treatments of the body—in this case, Jesus' body—applied by others' hands and objects. The woman takes her locks in hand and buffs Jesus dry, while the Romans (will) grasp their lashes and beat Jesus bloody.[52] The former wiping removes sweat and grime from (*ek*) Jesus' feet, while the latter whipping draws sweat and blood from Jesus' back and chest. They thus depict diametrically opposing actions (the *ek* makes all the difference)—one a refreshing "toweling off," the other a debilitating "tearing up." And accordingly, the anointing woman represents the dramatic antitype of the Roman soldiers: her passionate, physical love for the holy prophet Jesus shames their torturous maltreatment of an innocent victim.

Coming to the passion narrative proper, covering the final days of Jesus' life, we encounter in the arrest scene more obvious "touching" moments reminiscent of the affectionate woman's story. Most notably, the arrest marks the only other occasion in Luke where someone kisses, or at least tries to kiss, Jesus. A kiss is just a kiss? Not when Judas and betrayal are in the air. Luke's story leaves tantalizingly open the motives of both Judas and Jesus as well as whether the kiss actually took place: "While he was still speaking, suddenly a crowd came, and the one called Judas, one of the twelve, was leading them. He approached Jesus to kiss him; but Jesus said to him, 'Judas, is it with a kiss that you are betraying the Son of Man?'" (23:47–48).Why does Judas make his move to kiss Jesus? Luke omits the feature found in Matthew and Mark that Judas employs the kiss as a means of identifying Jesus (unobtrusively) to the arrest party. Could this (attempted) kiss, then, be simply a customary form of greeting among Jesus and his disciples (akin to a handshake in modern American culture) or even a sign of last-minute confusion or regret on Judas's part (he can't help but be pulled to love the magnetic Jesus even as he plans to betray him)?[53] The wider Lukan context renders suspect such amiable possibilities. However common it became for the early Christians to "greet one another with a holy kiss,"[54] there is no profusion of kissing in Luke's gospel or sufficient evidence from external sources that kissing was the normal, everyday form of public salutation in ancient Mediterranean society.[55] In Luke, beyond Jesus' arrest, kissing only occurs in extraordinary, demonstrable love scenes between the anointing woman and Jesus and between the father and the prodigal son in Jesus' parable (7:38; 15:20).[56] Both accounts use the stronger term for kissing (*kataphileō*), denoting special warmth and pathos appropriate to the momentous reconciliation of sinners. Now Lord knows that Judas, whom Satan had recently entered (22:3), needs to be reconciled to Jesus, but it is very doubtful that this is on Judas's mind. He draws near not to shower Jesus' feet or neck with loving kisses but merely to give him a perfunctory peck on the cheek (the weaker, simpler verb *phileō*),[57] possibly out of habit or as a means of identification, but any rate, not out of any deep affection or remorse.

Jesus can hardly believe Judas's tactics: "Judas, *with a kiss* [*philēmati*, in the emphatic first position] you are betraying the Son of Man [You've got to be kidding]." As Raymond Brown observes, this is the only time in the gospel tradition that Jesus directly addresses Judas by name.[58] "Judas, I know you, I love you, I called you as one of the Twelve," Jesus seems to be saying. "We ate together, prayed together, worked together, and this is how you treat me?" While there may be traces of Jesus' unfailing compassion toward Judas in this personal exchange (as Brown suggests), consistent with the theme of forgiveness in Luke's passion narrative,[59] I think the more dominant tone is one of shock and disappointment. Such an ethos accounts best for the narrator's silence about the actual kiss, as if to erase it from memory, as if to say, "We're not going to perpetuate the travesty of this kiss, however slight and casual it might have been." Real kissing is reserved for real love, like that demonstrated by the anointing woman. No question there about whether it happened or why. It happened all right, again and again—"from the time I came in she has not stopped kissing my feet"—in stark counterpoint to Simon and Judas who "gave me no kiss" (7:45), or at least not one worth having. And it happened for the right reason: not to "kiss off," as Judas is wont to do with Jesus, or to "kiss up," like a sycophantic client to a potential patron, but rather to "kiss down," to borrow John Dominic Crossan's apt phrase, even as I reconfigure it in the woman's case.

Crossan evokes the world of imperial politics in ancient Rome where an inferior official might "kiss up" to a superior one who in turn might "kiss down" to the lesser to give the appearance of mutual friendship and promise of patronage.[60] Against that backdrop, Crossan contends the Gospels portray Judas "in the most shameful colors possible. For if, in that ancient Mediterranean world, to betray *after* a kiss was shameful, to betray *with* a kiss was infamous."[61] Or in my earlier language, to "kiss up" in order to "kiss off" is villainy in the extreme. But to "kiss down" as the woman does with respect to Jesus—in the spontaneous humility and penitence of a grateful child of God, not in the staged condescension and arrogance of a ruling patron—is the very model of loving discipleship.

Following the interrupted kissing of Jesus' cheek, the action quickly shifts to another physical action—the slicing of the slave's ear (this servant was part of the high priest's posse) by one of Jesus' followers. If the aborted kiss suggested even for a second the possibility of intimacy and friendship, the sword strike clearly signals the dominant sinister tone of the arrest scene. Violence trumps romance; pain conquers pleasure—except for Jesus' marvelous, tender response. All four gospels concur that Jesus promptly puts a stop to this butchery. This will not turn into a gang-style brawl; he will go quietly and calmly to his predestined martyrdom—a model of masculine dignity and self-possession throughout the ordeal. But only Luke supplies another touch, Jesus' more feminine, healing touch of the severed appendage (22:51). Danker surmises that Luke's use of a diminutive form (*ōtion*, "ear-let" or "ear lobe") "adds a note of pathos to the scene."[62] I'm not sure we can press that much emotional function into this form, but the scene has plenty of pathos regardless of how much ear flesh was lopped off. And it's the kind of pathos, the kind of touch (*haptō* again), evocative of the woman's earlier contact with Jesus. She doesn't heal him and he is certainly no enemy of hers, as the high priest's slave appears to be with respect to Jesus. But, nonetheless, her physical refreshment of Jesus through her tactile ministrations provides something of a pattern for Jesus' own restorative ministry. He who knew what it meant to be touched touches others—even his enemies (cf. 6:27–36)—with healing love. The link remains loose but sure—no other Lukan stories combine elements of kissing and touching.

Without the kissing element, one additional "touching" scene worth considering emerges at the end of Luke's narrative. Crucifixion has given way to resurrection, but without obliterating the effects of Jesus' suffering. His body, though transformed, still bears the marks of his humanity and passion—a vital point that Jesus wants his disciples to know, lest they mistake him for a dispassionate apparition beyond their realm of experience. And so he invites his company of followers—likely including women as well as men at this point[63]—to do exactly what the anointing woman had done on her own initiative, without Jesus' coaxing: "'Look at my hands and my feet; see that it is I myself. Touch me and see; for a ghost does not have flesh and bones as you see me have.' And when he said this, he showed them his hands and feet" (24:39–40). The verb for "touch" is not *haptō* this time, but *psēlaphaō*; however, its connotation of "handle" or "feel"—that is, prolonged, deliberative touching—fits the anointing-wiping-massaging activity of the woman in Luke 7 quite nicely, perhaps with less sexual-euphemistic overtone than *haptō*, but still capable of erotic nuance. As the woman had handled Jesus' soiled feet and thereby came to know him and his message of peace (7:50), so the risen Jesus finally summons his friends (could the woman be among them?) to handle his scarred feet[64] and thereby feel his "peace with them" (24:36).[65] And can it be mere coincidence that both events take place at dinner settings (7:36; 24:41–43)? Eating and touching, food consuming and man handling, in a sweet and sour mix of peace and passion, pleasure and pain, bind together the Lukan Jesus and his disciples with the anonymous anointing woman in the foreground of that relationship.

To recap, the woman who expresses deep loving emotion through demonstrable physical contact (kissing and wiping) represents an antitype of the villainous Judas (kissing) and the violent Romans (whipping) as well as something of a prototype for the benevolent Jesus (refreshing touch) and the bewildered disciples invited to probe Jesus' feet and hands. We turn now from the tactile manifestations of the woman's passion to the liquid elements—her outpouring of tears and ointment—and their possible seepage into Jesus' passion.

WEEPING AND WETTING

"As he came near and saw the city [of Jerusalem], he wept over it." This statement introduces a unique Lukan lament scene in which the crying Jesus cries out in anguish at the horrible fate awaiting Jerusalem "because you did not recognize the time of your visitation from God" (19:41–44). Here is the sole occasion in Luke's story where Jesus himself weeps, matching the anointing woman's emotional outburst (using the same verb, *klaiō*). But again the parallel is pliable: Jesus does not weep *for* himself—either for his past sins or for his imminent suffering—but rather for the ignorant Jerusalem that is about to inflict his suffering, reject its messianic king, and set itself up for unspeakable disaster. Stoutly disregarding his own pending demise, he weeps for the sin and suffering of Jerusalem in classic prophetic (especially Jeremiad) mode, the mode of a worthy "*man* of God."[66]

So Jesus' teary response can scarcely be judged as effeminate; yet in its overarching Lukan context, it retains some marked feminine affinities. From a wide narrative angle, the present lament scene slots between two other ominous reflections on Jerusalem's fate by Jesus. In the earlier passage (13:31–35), Jesus anticipates his rejection and death in Jerusalem with bitter yet tender regret that the city habitually spurns his protective, *maternal* care: "How often I have desired to gather your children together as a hen gathers her brood under her wings, but you were not willing!" (13:34). In the latter text (23:27–31), set right at the edge of The Skull where Jesus will die, he rechannels the weeping of the "daughters of Jerusalem" away from himself to the terrible destiny awaiting them and their children in this doomed city, thereby conjoining their present and future tears with his previous ones in 19:41–44. They must weep as he wept in solidarity with their excruciating grief over the tragic loss of their children.[67] A frustrated mother hen on the one side, and a devastated mother city on the other, frame Jesus' sobbing over Jerusalem with poignant and passionate feminine-maternal accents. And in the background of this picture we may detect outlines of the widow at Nain (7:12–13) along with Jairus and his wife (8:51–52), weeping for their dead children. Although not in this particular family portrait, still another woman provides a measure of inspiration for it.[68] Cast more as a child (of Wisdom) than as a mother, the anointing woman in Luke 7 nevertheless also knows well the overwhelming feeling of sorrow, fueled by intense love and spilling forth in a flood of tears.

The specific content of Jesus' lament in 19:42–44 and its immediate placement between two other emotionally charged scenes suggest further contacts with the episode in 7:36–50. The lament opens and closes with Jesus' consternation over Jerusalem's failure to grasp the opportunity for divine blessing.[69] It's a problem of knowing or recognizing (*ginōskō*) what should have been obvious: "If you, even you, had only recognized (*egnōs*) on this day the things that make for peace! (19:42). . . . because you did not recognize (*egnōs*) the time of your visitation from God" (19:44). By contrast, the prophet Jesus knows all too well what must now befall Jerusalem as a consequence of its ignorance. The city's chance for peace has passed; the crushing prospect of war looms on the horizon. Such language evokes ironic resonance with the anointing-woman scene. There, Simon the Pharisee dares to question Jesus' prophetic insight: "If this man were a prophet, he would have known (*eginōsken*) who and what kind of woman this is who is touching him" (7:39). Of course, Jesus knows perfectly well—better than Simon— the full dimensions of this woman's character. As well as being a sinner, she is a woman of deep faith and love who clearly recognizes "the time of God's visitation" to her in Jesus and thus may "go in peace" (7:50), unlike the ignorant and complacent leaders of Jerusalem.[70] She also models Jesus' response to such tragic, missed opportunity. Like her, he weeps (no gloating "I told you so").

Although (unlike her) he puts his grief into words, he offers no decorous, well-crafted eulogy. As Danker notes, "the very syntax of the Greek throbs with the agitation of his heart."[71] Its opening fragment, repeated emphasis on "you" (as if, "how could *you* do this!"), and "short, choppy sentences" convey a vivid sense of spontaneous, emotional orality.[72] Its "fractured syntax" betrays a broken heart.[73] Here we see and hear a truly passionate Jesus.

Such passion both coheres and clashes with surrounding incidents. The immediately preceding "triumphal" approach to Jerusalem (he doesn't actually enter yet) pulses with emotion, but it is not Jesus' and it is not sad. As Jesus rides on the colt in stately, royal fashion, "the whole multitude of the disciples" breaks out in jubilant chorus (19:37). Juxtaposed with this coronation procession, the ensuing lament scene appears to jolt the reader with a "fine dramatic contrast," as Fitzmyer observes.[74] But on closer inspection, the shift in tone may not be as dramatic as that, because in addition to depicting Jesus' regal dignity and the crowd's exultation, Luke appends the negative reaction of "some of the Pharisees in the crowd" and Jesus' sharp, prophetic retort (19:39–40). The Pharisees object to the people's public "emotional outburst"[75] over Jesus, consistent with Simon the Pharisee's implicit annoyance at the woman's passionate gushing over Jesus at a dinner party. And as Jesus verbally vindicated the woman's passion and put Simon in his place, so, as he nears Jerusalem, he affirms the crowd's display and rebuffs the Pharisee's anxiety: "I tell you, if these were silent, the stones would shout out" (19:40). Like his supporters, Jesus does not remain silent or sedate. He's already stirred up; his emotions are already churning. He's primed for weeping and lamenting as he contemplates stones that will thunder in anguish as they tumble down, not one left upon another (19:44), drowning out any joyous shouts they might produce for the moment.[76]

Following his tearful lament on the outskirts of the city, Jesus enters the temple in what again appears to mark a sudden shift in mood—from grief to anger, from sadness to madness, from weeping to whipping—as he commences to drive out the merchants from the temple precincts (19:45). Here we confront a manly Jesus, to be sure, but perhaps not one as self-controlled as he could be. While Luke does not over-dramatize Jesus' "temple tantrum" and quickly follows it with Jesus' sober prophetic utterance (19:46), the cluster of three scenes at the end of Luke 19 still retains traces of Jesus' emotional volatility—his surging passions within the passion—a swirling mix of love, sorrow, disappointment, and anger amid unmistakable displays of authority and dignity. Whether or not this passionate portrait feminizes Jesus in any way, it seems to me to strengthen rather than weaken his bond with the passionate woman of Luke 7.

Beyond this lament scene on the edge of Jerusalem, Jesus will shed no more tears, even as his own personal pain rapidly escalates and culminates in crucifixion. But other fluids will flow from his anguished body, and others will weep in response to his suffering. Further recalling the anointing woman's wetting and pouring, though handling no alabaster jar (*alabastron*) of ointment, Jesus does deal with an array of "cups" (*potērion*), both literal and metaphorical, containing various substances.[77]

The first of these cups—actually, a pair of them—appear at the Lord's Supper. Initially, Jesus offers a cup of wine to his apostles for them to share. He thus assumes the dual role of hospitable host and attending servant, with the accent on the servant model that he especially wants his followers to emulate ("divide it among yourselves. . . . I am among you as one who serves," 22:17, 27). But they are woefully slow to pick up on the point, concerned more about protecting their honorific status than on providing refreshing service (22:24–27). As such they align themselves with negligent Pharisaic hosts like Simon and other authority-conscious "benefactors," while, for his part, Jesus—"the one who serves"—associates himself more closely with the anointing woman who had previously served him.

After serving one cup of wine and a loaf of bread, the Lukan Jesus again takes "the cup"—this time, the "cup that is poured out" for his disciples as a token of his new blood-sealed covenant with them (22:20).[78] While it is possible that he decants more wine into one or more additional cups for the disciples to drink (again), the previous cup scene suggests a single, common vessel: just "a cup," with no accompanying jug or other containers mentioned (22:17)—hence, no "pouring" of the first cup. Unless we now assume in this second cup reference the awkward scenario that Jesus somehow "pours" wine from the one vessel down the disciples' throats, this new cup gesture more likely entails pouring out a measure of wine *on the ground* as a kind of sacrificial libation, reminiscent of various cultic rituals and portending his imminent self-offering of blood on the cross.[79] This selfless outpouring on others' behalf again links Jesus, at least loosely, with the woman who formerly doused his feet and the surrounding floor with her tears and ointment. He pours wine (*oinos*), not myrrh (*myron*), as a symbol, first and foremost, of bloody death, not of fragrant life. But the pouring out "for you" and the promise of drinking the fruit of the vine again when "the kingdom of God comes" intimates a vital nexus between life and death (22:18, 20). As Jesus was refreshed by the woman's lavish outpouring, so, in turn, he will renew his followers by his own passionate libation.

The next "cup" reference appears soon after the Lord's Supper incident as the setting shifts to the Mount of Olives. Here the vessel is symbolic, not tangible, but its clear association with Jesus' deadly destiny reinforces the bloody image of the wine cup and provides another occasion for monitoring Jesus' emotions in the face of pain. An obvious first impression—generated by Jesus' rather un-martyr-like and un-masculine request to be spared the cup—that he buckles under pressure and surrenders to debilitating passions is countered by several factors, pinpointed by Jerome Neyrey, concerning Luke's redaction of Mark.[80] For example, 1) Mark's attribution of distress, agitation, and anguish/grief (*perilypos*) of soul to Jesus (Mark 14:33–34) is transferred from Jesus to the somnolent disciples in Luke ("he found them sleeping because of grief [*lypēs*]," Luke 22:45; 2) while Mark has Jesus hurling himself on the ground (as if overwhelmed by the situation) in the presence of his three closest friends (Mark 14:35), Luke presents Jesus much more discreetly, "kneeling" to pray by himself, "about a stone's throw" from all the disciples (Luke 22:41);[81] 3) whereas in Mark, Jesus' prayer for relief stresses God's *ability* to alter the course of fate ("Abba, Father, for you all things are possible," Mark 14:36), in Luke the accent falls wholly on God's *sovereignty* ("Father, if you are willing . . . ," Luke 22:42); and 4) the unique (if authentic)[82] Lukan portrait of Jesus' *agōnia* manifested in prodigious sweat the size of "blood globules"[83] (sweating bullets, we might say) depicts not so much a craven anguish of soul as a courageous athletic struggle to conquer fear and foe, not unlike Eleazar and the other Maccabean martyrs: "Like a noble athlete the old man, while being beaten, was victorious over his torturers; in fact with his faced bathed in sweat, and gasping heavily for breath, he amazed even his torturers by his courageous spirit" (4 Macc 6:10–11). Thus it seems that, like Eleazar, the Lukan Jesus valiantly endures unjust punishment with his "own blood and noble sweat in sufferings even unto death" and thereby successfully "steers the ship of [rational] religion over the sea of the emotions" (4 Macc 7:1, 8).

Under this reading, Jesus' profuse outpouring of sweat represents a muscular and masculine emotional antithesis to the anointing woman's hysterical deluge of tears and frivolous decanting of perfume. Jesus battles Satan and the forces of evil;[84] she blubbers over her own sin and infatuation with Jesus. The two passions could hardly be more polarized.

But is this the only reading possible? Are there some connections, however loose, that might bring the two poles closer together? If we follow the standard compositional theory that Luke has altered Mark, then undoubtedly Luke has softened Mark's potentially negative presentation of a weak, distraught, uncontrolled Jesus. Or perhaps we should say that Luke *hardened* Mark's Jesus into a stronger, manlier figure. At any rate, Neyrey has made his redactional case. But I think he has overplayed the "absence of emotions" in

Luke's account. Hitting one's knees to pray may suggest less angst than falling on one's face, but kneeling need not signify total composure. The New Testament depicts various prayer postures (lying, kneeling, standing) with various emotional effects, depending on the situation. In Luke's parable of the Pharisee and the tax collector, for example, both parties *stand* alone to pray in the temple, but with opposite demeanors: one quite happy with himself; the other beside himself, beaten up with remorse, begging for mercy (18:9–14). In Luke's second volume, we discover various figures kneeling to pray, like Stephen (Acts 7:60) and Peter (9:40), whose supplications do reflect heroic courage and calm in the midst of death (Stephen's own and Tabitha's).[85] But there is also the moving farewell scene where Paul kneels to pray with the Ephesian elders amid a flood of emotions (including grieving) and passionate gestures (including weeping and kissing): "When he had finished speaking, he knelt down with them all and prayed. There was much weeping (*klauthmos*) among them all; they embraced Paul and kissed (*katephiloun*) him, grieving especially because of what he had said, that they would not see him again" (20:36–37). To be sure, the weeping, kissing, and grieving in this incident display the Ephesians' reactions to Paul (like the anointing woman's to Jesus), not those of Paul himself. But in the preceding speech that sets up the farewell, Paul conveys more than a little (com)passion of his own for the Ephesians, including a double reference to his "tearful" ministry among them (20:19, 31).

Thus, Jesus' kneeling at Olivet need not betray Stoic mastery of emotions, especially when conjoined with the agonizing and sweating that, again, need not *purely* signify heroic combat and conquest devoid of psychic anguish and anxiety. In Hellenistic Greek, *agōnia*—with or without *psychē*—may connote inner agony (soul distress) (2 Macc 3:14, 16; 15:19),[86] and there is no reason to deny that at least a touch of such distress attends Jesus' intense prayer struggle. In fact, the likelihood of emotional entanglement is heightened by Luke's modeling Jesus' passion after that of Isaiah's suffering servant, as Joel Green has demonstrated.[87] Leading into the Olivet episode, Jesus explicitly identifies his trials with those of the pathetic figure in Isa 53: "And he was counted among the lawless" (Luke 22:37; Isa 53:12). As even a cursory reading of this servant song discloses, its tenor is hopeful but not haughty, trusting but not triumphant. The focal figure is no mighty martyr but rather a humble human plagued (*anthrōpos en plēgē*) with suffering and "pain of soul" (*ponos tēs psychēs*) (Isa 53:3, 11). And so we must temper the superhero image of the Lukan Jesus with the servant portrait featuring outpoured sorrow and distress—not unlike that of the female servant who

ministered to him in Luke 7, except that Jesus suffers for others' transgres-
sions (*hamartias,* Isa 53:5), not his own.

Having considered scenes from Luke's passion narrative where Jesus
himself participates in some action of pouring and sweating, weeping and
wetting—reminiscent of the anointing woman's display toward him—we
turn finally to probe one poignant vignette where Jesus responds to
another's weeping, specifically to Peter's vexatious wailing in the wake of his
denying Jesus. Actually, Jesus' response to Peter triggers the weeping. After
"the cock crowed," marking the completion of Peter's three-fold denial predicted by Jesus, "the Lord turned (*strapheis*) and looked (*eneblepsen*) at
Peter" (22:60–61). Meeting Jesus' gaze tripped Peter's memory of the awful
forecast (which he had vigorously resisted), prompting him to "go out and
weep bitterly" (22:62). How does the "sinner"-apostle in the high priest's
courtyard compare here with the "sinner"-woman in Simon the Pharisee's
dining room?[88] Like her, Peter shows tearful remorse for his misconduct, but
unlike her, his shame drives him from Jesus' presence rather than to him. His
weeping is bitter; hers is better—better because it flows from a "greater love"
and stronger commitment to (faith in) Jesus. As with Peter, Jesus "turns"
(*strapheis*) to the woman and "looks"—or at least invites Simon to look ("Do
you see [*blepeis*] this woman?" 7:44); and soon thereafter she exits the house.
But unlike Peter, she goes "in peace" (7:50), not in pain.

All is not lost for Peter, however. A number of commentators stress that
Peter's weeping marks the beginning of his restoration, the first step in
answering Jesus' prayer that Peter's "faith may not fail" (22:32).[89] Thus Jesus'
"look" may be regarded as sympathetic as well as incriminating. If he had
had an opportunity to commend Peter's weeping, he would have, as surely as
he did the anointing woman's. But at this moment, Peter remains a work in
progress toward the goal of loving and faithful devotion that the woman has
already reached. Though unnamed, unvoiced, and unmentioned after Luke
7, a vestige of her remains as a model of true discipleship for Peter and the
apostles.

Conclusion

These and other tantalizing connections between the passionate woman in
Luke 7 and the passion(s) of Jesus himself on the one hand, and the experiences of Jesus' disciples on the other, are good and notable—but, perhaps,
not good enough. The links remain "loose," both in terms of substance and
distance. Jesus' acts of touching, weeping, perspiring, and pouring in the

Lukan passion narrative—all carried out with intense feeling (passion)—correlate with similar emotional displays by the anointing woman. No other character pair in Luke's gospel evinces such a close match of tactile and fluid gestures. But this is no perfect match, no partnership of equals. Jesus unequivocally remains the dominant, male authority, as is obvious in Luke 7, where the woman stays silent and stationed at Jesus' feet (like Mary of Bethany in 10:39–42). In the passion narrative, where the emotional focus shifts from pleasure to pain, Jesus' indomitable virility becomes less clear at times, as his deep love for his people (like a mother hen) and personal anguish of soul overwhelm him for a moment. As the Isaianic suffering servant, he does not wholly fit the bill of the heroic-Stoic Maccabean martyr, defiant and nonplussed in the face of unspeakable torment. But overall, the Lukan Jesus still dies with dignity and discipline—as the Lord's bold prophet (as well as servant), the model "man of God." He cries and sweats and pours out his anguish and affection—but not uncontrollably, unceasingly. Unlike the woman who "did not stop" flooding Jesus with her passion (7:45), Jesus stanches his passions at will in order to get on with God's business: "not my will but yours be done" (22:42).

As for the anointing woman's relationship to Jesus' disciples, her passionate kissing, crying, and caressing provide positive counter-patterns for the treacherous Judas (22:47–48), the cowardly Peter (22:62), and the fearful followers (24:36–39). She thus merits the badge of a loving and loyal "model disciple." But it's hard to see and remember the woman, much less the badge, by the end of Luke's narrative. To borrow Luke's language, a "great gulf" separates her story at the end of chap. 7 from the passion story in chaps. 22–24. By the time we wind through the long travel journey in Luke 9–19, the woman is easily forgotten. True, a group of anonymous women, whom, we belatedly learn, had "followed Jesus from Galilee" (23:49, 55–56) re-emerge at Jesus' cross and tomb. But these women are more of an afterthought than an integral part of the plot (oh, by the way—the women are still hanging around).[90] Should we infer the presence of the woman from Luke 7 in this bunch? Perhaps, although she receives no special mention (as do Mary Magdalene, Joanna, and Mary the mother of James [24:10]). But at least we have the *anointing* connection: the women "prepared spices and ointments" for Jesus' body (23:56). The woman's benevolent treatment of Jesus in Luke 7 is about to be reprised, it seems. The plan, however, hits a rather critical snag at the tomb: there is no body to anoint! The women's work is aborted. When Jesus' body does make a few special appearances—on the Emmaus road, in a Jerusalem room, there is still no anointing. This myrrh remains unpoured and the women's mission unfulfilled. Accordingly, the women are shuffled to the background in favor of Cleopas, Simon, and the eleven apostles—men all, although not very perceptive or brave men at this stage—who, we assume (and Acts confirms) will bear the main responsibility of carrying on Jesus' mission. "Do you see this woman" at the end of Luke's gospel? Only if we use a wide-angle lens, and then only allusively, tangentially, loosely. Deviant labels stick like crazy glue: sadly, once a "loose" woman, always a "loose" woman.

Notes

1. See Barbara E. Reid, *Choosing the Better Part?: Women in the Gospel of Luke* (Collegeville, MN: Liturgical Press, 1996), 115; "'Do You See This Woman?': Luke 7:36–50 as a Paradigm for Feminist Hermeneutics," *Biblical Research* 40 (1995): 42–43.

2. See the summary of traditional criticism on this passage in Joseph A. Fitzmyer, *The Gospel According to Luke I–IX* (Anchor Bible 28; New York: Doubleday, 1981), 684–88; see also Robert Holst, "The One Anointing of Jesus: Another Application of the Form-Critical Method," *Journal of Biblical Literature* 95 (1976): 435–46.

3. A narrative-critical approach meticulously modeled in Robert C. Tannehill, *The Gospel According to Luke* (vol. 1 of *The Narrative Unity of Luke-Acts: A Literary Interpretation*; Foundations and Facets; Philadelphia: Fortress, 1986), 116–19, 177–78; and Joel B. Green, *The Gospel of Luke* (New International Commentary on the New Testament; Grand Rapids: Eerdmans, 1997), 305–15.

4. Fitzmyer, *Gospel of Luke I–IX*, 684.

5. E.g., see Craig A. Evans and James A. Sanders, *Luke and Scripture: The Function of Sacred Tradition in Luke-Acts* (Minneapolis: Fortress, 1993); John A. Darr, *On Character Building: The Reader and the Rhetoric of Characterization in Luke-Acts* (Literary Currents in Biblical Interpretation; Louisville, KY: Westminster/John Knox, 1992), 28–29, 156–58; David P. Moessner, ed., *Jesus and the Heritage of Israel: Luke's Narrative Claim upon Israel's Legacy* (Harrisburg, PA: Trinity Press International, 1999); Moessner, *Lord of the Banquet: The Literary and Theological Significance of the Lukan Travel Narrative* (Harrisburg, PA: Trinity Press International, 1989).

6. Dorothy A. Lee, "Women as 'Sinners': Three Narratives of Salvation in Luke and John," *Australian Biblical Review* 44 (1996): 1–15.

7. Thomas L. Brodie, "Luke 7,36–50 as an Internalization of 2 Kings 4,1–37: A Study in Luke's Use of Rhetorical Imitation," *Biblica* 64 (1983): 57–85.

8. D. A. S. Ravens, "The Setting of Luke's Account of the Anointing: Luke 7.2–8.3," *New Testament Studies* 34 (1988): 286.

9. I borrow and adapt the analytical categories of "inner-text," "inter-text," and "co-text" employed variously by Joel B. Green, "Discourse Analysis and New Testament Interpretation," in *Hearing the New Testament: Strategies for Interpretation* (ed. Joel B. Green; Grand Rapids: Eerdmans, 1995), 183–96; *Gospel of Luke*, 11–20; and Vernon K. Robbins, *The Tapestry of Early Christian Discourse: Rhetoric, Society, and Ideology* (London: Routledge, 1996), 27–33.

10. "Sinner" is thus both a moral and social designation: morally, it identifies someone who consistently falls short of God's holy will (sinner as wicked); socially, it marks someone who violates community norms (sinner as outsider). See the discussion in James D. G. Dunn, *Jesus, Paul, and the Law: Studies in Mark and Galatians* (Louisville, KY: Westminster/John Knox, 1990), 71–79; M. J. Wilkins, "Sinner," in *Dictionary of Jesus and the Gospels* (ed. Joel B.

Green, Scot McKnight, and I. Howard Marshall; Downers Grove, IL: InterVarsity, 1992), 757–60; David A. Neale, *None But the Sinners: Religious Categories in the Gospel of Luke* (Journal for the Study of the New Testament: Supplement Series 58; Sheffield, UK: Sheffield Academic Press, 1991), 135–47, 191–94.

11. Edwin M. Schur, *Labeling Women Deviant: Gender, Stigma, and Social Control* (New York: McGraw-Hill, 1984), 51–132; see the convenient summary in Table 2, p. 53.

12. Male slaves also tended to the refreshment of guests' feet and other amenities in Greco-Roman antiquity, but such service was quite typical for female slaves as well. See Richard I. Pervo, "Wisdom and Power: Petronius' *Satyricon* and the Social World of Early Christianity," *Anglican Theological Review* 67 (1985): 313–15.

13. Schur, *Labeling Women Deviant,* 53–59.

14. The image of the "hysterical woman" was a common ancient stereotype reflected elsewhere in Luke's writings (e.g., Luke 24:10–11; Acts 12:14–15). See Margaret Y. MacDonald, *Early Christian Women and Pagan Opinion: The Power of the Hysterical Woman* (Cambridge, UK: Cambridge University Press, 1996), discussed briefly in n. 18 in the next chapter.

15. On the Pharisees' concern for ritual purity in common table-fellowship, see Jacob Neusner, *Judaism in the Beginning of Christianity* (Philadelphia: Fortress, 1984), 56–58; Neusner, *From Testament to Torah: An Introduction to Judaism in Its Formative Age* (Englewood Cliffs, NJ: Prentice-Hall, 1988), 33–35; Dunn, *Jesus, Paul and the Law,* 62–71.

16. The syntax places some emphasis on the invitation: the term for "asked" (*ērōta*) is the very first Greek word in the sentence and, indeed, in the entire story.

17. Teresa J. Hornsby exposes a tendentious pattern of scholarly analysis of Luke 7:36–50: "Although Luke's text leaves gaps and hence offers readers a variety of ways to interpret the anointing woman's presence and performance at Simon's house, scholars choose predominantly to depict her as an intrusive prostitute who acts inappropriately and excessively. It is scholars, not Luke, who make of this figure a 'public woman.'" While I agree that there is little textual basis for the "prostitute" label (see more below), I think Luke's depiction does suggest the woman is "intrusive" from Simon's vantage point; at any rate, one term does not automatically imply the other (prostitutes might be welcome in certain settings, and guests can be unwelcome for a host of reasons other than their sexual orientations). "The Women Is a Sinner/The Sinner Is a Woman," in *A Feminist Companion to Luke* (ed. Amy-Jill Levine; Feminist Companion to the New Testament and Early Christian Writings 3; London: Sheffield Academic Press, 2002), 128.

18. See the analysis of the social scenarios governing Luke 14:15–24 in Richard L. Rohrbaugh, "The Pre-Industrial City in Luke-Acts: Urban Social Relations," in *The Social World of Luke-Acts: Models for Interpretation* (ed. Jerome H. Neyrey; Peabody, MA: Hendrickson, 1991), 125–49; and Stuart L. Love, "Women and Men at Hellenistic Symposia Meals in Luke," in *Modelling Early Christianity: Social-Scientific Studies of the New Testament and Its Context* (ed. Philip F. Esler; London: Routledge, 1995), 198–204.

19. See Kenneth E. Bailey, "Through Peasant Eyes," in *Poet & Peasant* and *Through Peasant Eyes: A Literary-Cultural Approach to the Parables in Luke* (comb. ed.; Grand Rapids: Eerdmans, 1980), 3–6; and Charles H. Talbert, *Reading Luke: A Literary and Theological Commentary on the Third Gospel* (New York: Crossroad, 1986), 86.

20. Kathleen Corley marshals considerable evidence for the common presence of prostitutes and other assorted female escorts at Hellenistic banquets but does not, in my judgment (see more below), make her case that the particular "sinner"-woman in Luke 7 fits this profile. *Private Women, Public Meals: Social Conflict in the Synoptic Tradition* (Peabody, MA: Hendrickson, 1993), 24–79, 121–26; and "Prostitute," in Green, McKnight, and Marshall, eds., *Dictionary of Jesus and the Gospels,* 643.

21. See Jerome H. Neyrey, "Ceremonies in Luke-Acts: The Case of Meals and Table Fellowship," in Neyrey, ed., *The Social World of Luke-Acts,* 361–87.

22. Cf. Gen 20:6; Prov 6:29 (LXX).

23. Turid Karlsen Seim, *The Double Message: Patterns of Gender in Luke and Acts* (Nashville, TN: Abingdon; Edinburgh, UK: T and T Clark, 1994), 93–94. For a similar discussion of the erotic features of this story, see my *What Did Jesus Do?*, 107–10.

24. See Ruth 3:4, 7–10; Amy-Jill Levine, "Ruth," *Women's Bible Commentary* (ed. Carol A. Newsom and Sharon H. Ringe; 2nd ed.; Louisville, KY: Westminster/John Knox, 1998), 88–89. 1 Cor 12:21–23 appears to correlate the feet and genitals as "members of the body that seem to be weaker" or "less honorable" (in need of covering) but in fact "are indispensable" to the body's well-being.

25. See Bailey, "Through Peasant Eyes," 6–10.

26. According to Num 5:11–32, a wife suspected of being unfaithful to her husband is to be brought to trial before the Lord's priest, who will "dishevel her hair" and compel her to drink "the water of bitterness that brings the curse." If the water treatment (torture?) has no effect, she is deemed innocent. Because of the sexual focus of this ordeal, Alice Bach suggests that the hair-messing gesture functions less as a sign of mourning than as a public reenactment of the woman's alleged immorality: "The half-disrobed woman with disheveled hair, appearing as though she had been caught in an intimate act. . . ." "Introduction to a Case History: Numbers 5:11–31," in *Women in the Hebrew Bible: A Reader* (ed. Alice Bach; New York: Routledge, 1999), 461.

27. Green, *Gospel of Luke*, 310.

28. The verb *ekmassō* (to wipe/massage away/from), appears in the imperfect form in Luke 7:38, indicating a continuous and repetitive "massaging" of Jesus' feet. For these suggestive linguistic points, see Judith K. Applegate, "'And She Wet His Feet with Her Tears': A Feminist Interpretation of Luke 7.36–50," in *Escaping Eden: New Feminist Perspectives on the Bible* (ed. Harold C. Washington, Susan Lochrie Graham, and Pamela Thimmes; New York: New York University Press, 1999), 80.

29. For a helpful summary of sociological studies of "deviance as social product" and the relevance of such studies to New Testament scholarship, see John M. G. Barclay, "Deviance and Apostasy: Some Applications of Deviance Theory to First-Century Judaism and Christianity," in Esler, ed., *Modelling Early Christianity*, 114–27; and Malina and Neyrey, "Conflict in Luke-Acts: Labelling and Deviance Theory," in Neyrey, ed., *Social World of Luke-Acts*, 97–122.

30. On the pattern of "interrupting the labelling process" through "neutralization," see Malina and Neyrey, "Conflict in Luke-Acts," 108, 117–18; and Evelyn R. Thibeaux, "'Known to Be a Sinner': The Narrative Rhetoric of Luke 7:36–50," *Biblical Theology Bulletin* 23 (1993): 153.

31. On the social tendency to tag outsiders with a single deviant "master status," overriding all other positive and negative qualities, see Howard S. Becker, *Outsiders: Studies in the Sociology of Deviance* (New York: Free Press, 1963), 32–34; Edwin M. Schur, *Interpreting Deviance: A Sociological Introduction* (New York: Harper & Row, 1979), 231–40; Malina and Neyrey, "Conflict in Luke-Acts," 101; F. Scott Spencer, "The Ethiopian Eunuch and His Bible: A Social-Science Analysis," *Biblical Theology Bulletin* 22 (1992): 155–56.

32. Amy-Jill Levine astutely observes that this vindication of Mother Wisdom by her child Jesus reverses the customary focus in Hellenistic Judaism on Woman Wisdom's function as the prime vindicator of her offspring, the "defending mother" (Sir 4:11) and "powerful patroness/advocate of the unjustly accused" (Wis 10:14). In Luke 7:35, "the roles of dominant and victimized are therefore inverted; Wisdom becomes the mother who must be justified by her children." Levine, "Second Temple Judaism, Jesus, and Women: Yeast of Eden," *Biblical Interpretation* 2 (1994): 31–32.

33. See Elizabeth A. Johnson, *Friends of God and Prophets: A Feminist Theological Reading of the Communion of Saints* (New York: Continuum, 1998), 41–45.

34. J. Duncan M. Derrett observes the numerous connections between the anointing woman in Luke 7 and the female lover in the Song of Songs, but pushes the parallel in an unnecessarily allegorical direction: "The woman . . . who is ready to worship his [Jesus'] body, is certainly the Beloved of the Song of Songs, in other words the ideal Jerusalem, the ideal Israel, the

questing soul. . . . Our woman worships Jesus as the Bridegroom, at last ready (in the eye of *faith*) for the Beloved." *New Resolutions of Old Conundrums: A Fresh Insight into Luke's Gospel* (Shipston-on-Stour, UK: Peter Drinkwater, 1986), 131–32.

35. Gale A. Yee, "'I Have Perfumed My Bed with Myrrh': The Foreign Woman (*'iššâ, zārâ,*) in Proverbs 1–9," *Journal for the Study of the Old Testament* 43 (1989): 53–68; *Poor Banished Children of Eve: Woman as Evil in the Hebrew Bible* (Minneapolis: Fortress, 2003), 149–53.

36. See, e.g., Reid, *Choosing the Better Part?*; and chap. 6, "Out of Mind, Out of Voice," in this volume.

37. On the portrayal of masculine and feminine ideals in 4 Maccabees, see especially Moore and Anderson, "Taking It Like a Man," 249–73; Mary Rose D'Angelo, "*Eusebeia*: Roman Imperial Family Values and the Sexual Politics of 4 Maccabees and the Pastorals," *Biblical Interpretation* 11 (2003): 147–57; and Robin Darling Young, "The 'Woman with the Soul of Abraham': Traditions about the Mother of the Maccabean Martyrs," in *"Women Like This": New Perspectives on Jewish Women in the Greco-Roman World* (ed. Amy-Jill Levine; SBL Early Judaism and Its Literature 1; Atlanta, GA: Scholars Press, 1991), 67–81.

38. See 4 Macc 1:30–31—"Observe now, first of all, that rational judgment is sovereign over the emotions [*pathōn*] by virtue of the restraining power of self-control [*sōphrosynēs*]. Self-control [*sōphrosynē*], then is dominance [*epikrateia*] over the desires [*epithymiōn*]." Diana M. Swancutt observes that in Greek (especially Stoic) and Roman moral philosophy, "the regulation of desire" or passion was a major "ideological matrix" controlling the understanding of proper gender relations: "The winning strategy in this battle with passion was an ethic of self-management called self-mastery (*enkrateia*), and the goal was *sōphrosynē*, 'moderation' or 'self-restraint' in the use of sex." Swancutt, "'The Disease of Effemination': The Charge of Effeminacy and the Verdict of God" [Romans 1:18–2:16], in *New Testament Masculinities* (ed. Stephen D. Moore and Janice Capel Anderson; Semeia Studies; Atlanta: SBL, 2003), 202–3. Abraham Smith notes that these two terms "most often associated with self-mastery" in Greco-Roman antiquity are both applied to Paul in the book of Acts: "*enkrateia*, or self-control [Acts 24:25], and *sōphrosynē*, or restraint [Acts 26:25]." Smith, "Full of Spirit and Wisdom': Luke's Portrait of Stephen (Acts 6:1–8:1a) as a Man of Self-Mastery," in Asceticism and the New Testament (ed. Leif E. Vaage and Vincent L. Wimbush; New York: Routledge, 1999), 98. See also Moore and Anderson, "Taking It Like a Man," 252–65.

39. David is also extolled for his extraordinary dietary restraint, refusing—though he was "extremely thirsty"—to indulge his "irrational desire for the water in the enemy's [Philistines'] territory" (4 Macc 3:6–18; cf. 2 Sam 23:13–17; 1 Chron 11:15–19).

40. See especially Moore and Anderson, "Taking It Like a Man."

41. Thomas Laqueur, *Making Sex: Body and Gender from the Greeks to Freud* (Cambridge, MA: Harvard University Press, 1990), 3–4.

42. On the Abraham connection see also 4 Macc 14:20 ("But sympathy for her children did not sway the mother of the young men; she was of the same mind as Abraham") and Young, "The 'Woman with the Soul of Abraham,'" 73–81.

43. Cf. Moore and Anderson, "Taking It Like a Man," 273: "4 Maccabees does modify the elite, hegemonic concept of masculinity by elevating self-mastery over mastery of social inferiors. Yet the martyrs master Antiochus in effect, so that mastery of others is still central and still celebrated. The irony of 4 Maccabees is that a feeble, flabby old man, a gaggle of boys, and an elderly widow—all persons who should rate low on the hierarchical continuum of (masterful) masculinity and (mastered) femininity—triumph over someone who should be at the privileged end of the continuum."

44. Contra Hornsby, I argued above that the Lukan story does intimate the intrusive or invasive nature of the anointing woman's presence in Simon's house. While the precise relationship between Simon and this woman is left vague (how did he know who she was?), Hornsby's musing ("The Woman Is a Sinner," 127) that the woman "could be a part of Simon's household, she could even be Simon's girlfriend for all we know" seems far-fetched in the context of Luke's

narrative. The Pharisees in Luke may be proud, greedy, and hypocritical in a variety of ways, but womanizing and consorting with "sinners" of any stripe are not among their reported tendencies; indeed, their aversion to table-fellowship with "sinners" consistently sets them apart from Jesus (see 5:30; 7:29–30; 15:1–2).

45. See Mary Rose D'Angelo, "'Knowing How to Preside over His Own Household': Imperial Masculinity and Christian Asceticism in the Pastorals, *Hermas*, and Luke-Acts," in Moore and Anderson, eds., *New Testament Masculinities*, 294: "In this work [Luke-Acts], the primary marker of masculinity is fitness to speak in public and for the community."

46. The only other speaking that occurs in this episode (apart from Simon's talking "to himself," 7:39) is in response to Jesus' teaching: Simon answers Jesus' question in 7:43, and the guests talk "among themselves" in 7:43 about Jesus' extraordinary claim to forgive sins. In any event, Jesus takes rhetorical charge of the proceedings.

47. Sitcom junkies might recognize in "mastering one's domain" an allusion to a classic *Seinfeld* episode dealing with sexuality.

48. Elisabeth Schüssler Fiorenza, *In Memory of Her: A Feminist Theological Reconstruction of Christian Origins* (10th Anniversary Edition; New York: Crossroad, 1994), xliii–xliv. Mary Rose D'Angelo posits two reasons for Luke's suppression and/or rearrangement of Mark's story of the anointing woman: "First, apologetic concerns probably led the author to avoid the implication that Jesus accepted messianic anointing, thus eliminating any grounds for the political charge that Jesus claimed to be the messianic king (Luke 23:1–2). Second, the Gospel's prophetic Christology is likely to have inspired the author to cast Jesus, rather than the woman, as a prophet." D'Angelo, "Luke 7:36–50—Woman Who Anoints Jesus," in *Women in Scripture: A Dictionary of Named and Unnamed Women in the Hebrew Bible, the Apocryphal/Deuterocanonical Books, and the New Testament* (ed. Carol Meyers, Toni Craven, and Ross S. Kraemer; Grand Rapids: Eerdmans, 2001), 441.

49. Corley, *Private Women*, 128–30; Reid, *Choosing the Better Part?*, 122; "Do You See This Woman?" 48–49.

50. Teresa J. Hornsby, "Why Is She Crying?: A Feminist Interpretation of Luke 7.36–50," in Washington, Graham, and Thimmes, eds., *Escaping Eden*, 100.

51. See Warren C. Trenchard, *Complete Vocabulary Guide to the Greek New Testament* (rev. ed.; Grand Rapids: Zondervan, 1998), 68, for a list of cognate forms of *mastigoō*, including *mastizō* (strike with a whip, scourge) and *mastix* (whip, lash, suffering), both used in Luke's second volume with respect to Paul: "The tribune directed that he [Paul] was to be brought into the barracks, and ordered him to be examined by flogging (*mastixin*). . . . But when they tied him up with thongs, Paul said to the centurion, who was standing by, 'Is it legal for you to flog (*mastizein*) a Roman citizen who is uncondemned?'" (Acts 22:24, 25).

52. Actually, the flogging of Jesus is threatened by Pilate in Luke 23:16, 22, but never explicitly carried out in the narrative; rather the scourging quickly gives way to the even more brutal assault of crucifixion demanded by the crowd (see 23:13–25). Both Jesus and his followers in Acts receive various physical beatings from the authorities, both Jewish and Roman.

53. See a full discussion of the interpretive options in Raymond E. Brown, *The Death of the Messiah: From Gethsemane to the Grave* (Anchor Bible Reference Library; New York: Doubleday, 1994), 252–55.

54. Rom 16:16; 1 Cor 16:20; 2 Cor 13:12; 1 Thess 5:26; 1 Pet 5:14.

55. Brown, *Death of the Messiah*, 255, speaks of "a reticence about public kisses in Greco-Roman society; mostly they are described in scenes of reconciliation or of relatives meeting after a separation."

56. See also the emotional reconciliation scenes, involving both kissing and weeping, between brothers Jacob and Esau in Gen 33:4 and father Jacob and son Joseph in 50:1.

57. "Note that Luke uses *philein* for 'kiss' and thus avoids the added warmth of Mark's *kataphilein*." Brown, *Death of the Messiah*, 258–59.

58. Ibid., 259.

59. See Luke 22:31–32, 51; 23:34, 40–43; 24:47; Brown, *Death of the Messiah*, 259.

60. John Dominic Crossan, *Who Killed Jesus?: Exposing the Roots of Anti-Semitism in the Gospel Story of the Death of Jesus* (New York: HarperCollins, 1995), 70–73. He cites (from Josephus) the example of Herod the Great's "kissing up" to Emperor Augustus's chief military deputy, Marcus Vipsanius Agrippa: "Herod went up to him [Agrippa] and embraced him in grateful acknowledgement of his friendly attitude towards himself. To this too Agrippa responded in friendly fashion and behaved like an equal, putting his arms around Herod and embracing him in turn" (Josephus, *Jewish Antiquities* 16.61). As Crossan stresses, Agrippa is indeed only acting "*like* an equal"; as the emperor's right-hand man, "he could probably make or break Herod at will" (p. 72).

61. Crossan, *Who Killed Jesus?*, 72.

62. Frederick W. Danker, *Jesus and the New Age: A Commentary on St. Luke's Gospel* (rev. ed.; Philadelphia: Fortress, 1988), 357.

63. References in Luke's resurrection stories to "the eleven and to all the rest" (Luke 24:9) and "the eleven and their companions gathered together" (24:33) assume a wider community of Jesus' followers assembled with the apostles, probably including women as well as men. See Robert J. Karris, "Women and Discipleship in Luke," *Catholic Biblical Quarterly* 56 (1994), 13–19.

64. There is no explicit emphasis in Luke 24:39–40 on touching the *nail prints* in Jesus' hands and feet, as we find in the Thomas story in John 20:25–27 (actually, it's hands and side in the Fourth Gospel—no feet), but the immediate backdrop of Jesus' crucifixion in Luke 23 implies that Jesus presents his *scarred* extremities as proof of his identity.

65. Some early manuscripts omit the "peace be with you" (*eirēnē hymin*) reference in Luke 24:36, but on the whole, external attestation is strong, and the frequent overlaps between the Lukan and Johannine passion and resurrection narratives (see "peace" greeting in John 20:19, 21) favor retaining the "peace" reference in Luke. See Bruce M. Metzger, *A Textual Commentary on the Greek New Testament* (2nd ed.; Stuttgart: Deutsche Bibelgesellschaft, 1994), 160.

66. See the description of Elisha—"Then the man of God wept" (2 Kgs 8:11). On the prophet Jeremiah weeping over the fate of Jerusalem, see, e.g., Jer 9:1; 14:17. On the connection between the weeping Lukan Jesus and suffering Old Testament prophets, see Robert C. Tannehill, *Luke* (Abingdon New Testament Commentaries; Nashville, TN: Abingdon, 1996), 286; and David L. Tiede, *Prophecy and History in Luke-Acts* (Philadelphia: Fortress, 1980), 78–86.

67. Tannehill, *Luke*, 286, also adds Luke 21:20–24 to the cluster of texts signifying Jerusalem's tragic destiny.

68. Unlike his response to the anointing woman, Jesus tells both the widow at Nain and the parents of the dead daughter in Capernaum "not to weep" (7:12; 8:52). However, such a reaction is not a criticism of their bereavement, but rather an anticipation of his imminent resuscitation of their deceased children (7:13 and 8:52).

69. On the *inclusio* or framing pattern in this lament related to Jerusalem's "not knowing," see Tannehill, *Luke*, 284–85; R. Alan Culpepper, "The Gospel of Luke," in *The New Interpreter's Bible* (vol. 9; Nashville, TN: Abingdon, 1994–98), 372.

70. While the people of Jerusalem at large come within the orbit of Jesus' concern, a special emphasis falls on the obstinacy of "the chief priests, the scribes, and the leaders of the people" (Luke 19:47; 20:1–2).

71. Danker, *Jesus and the New Age*, 314.

72. Tannehill, *Luke*, 285.

73. Tiede, *Prophecy and History in Luke-Acts*, 79, 86.

74. Joseph A. Fitzmyer, *The Gospel According to Luke X–XXIV* (Anchor Bible 28A; New York: Doubleday, 1985), 1253; see also Tannehill, *Luke*, 284: "At this point [19:41–44] there is a sharp shift in mood from rejoicing to lament."

75. See Danker's lively assessment of the Pharisees' reaction to Jesus (*Jesus and the New Age*, 313): "They [the Pharisees] are typical of leaders who are allergic to demonstrations or what

they term 'emotional outbursts'; they much prefer 'orderly' discussion, preferably under the adjudication of carefully selected committees, which practically guarantee hardening of institutional arteries and obsolescence of the gospel."

76. On the connection between the stones in 19:40 and 19:44, see Danker, *Jesus and the New Age*, 314: "The reference to stones crying out is filled with pathos, anticipating as it does the terrible doom predicted in v. 44."

77. I surveyed the various "cup" references in the gospels' passion narratives in *What Did Jesus Do?*, 115–19.

78. Because of the unusual cup-bread-cup sequence, there is varying manuscript evidence surrounding the proper reading of Luke 22:17–20. For a summary of the evidence and support of the authenticity of the longer text with the double-cup arrangement, see Metzger, *Textual Commentary*, 148–50.

79. See Tannehill, *Luke*, 315–16, citing Lev 4:18, 25, 30, 34; Num 28:7–9, 14, 24; and Sir 50:15 as possible parallels.

80. Jerome H. Neyrey, "The Absence of Jesus' Emotions—the Lucan Redaction of Lk 22,39–46," *Biblica* 61 (1980): 153–71; *The Passion According to Luke: A Redaction Study of Luke's Soteriology* (New York: Paulist Press, 1985), 49–65.

81. See also Luke Timothy Johnson, *The Gospel of Luke* (Sacra Pagina 3; Collegeville, MN: Liturgical Press, 1991), 351: "The description [in Luke 22:41] emphasizes Jesus' control and lack of emotional turmoil. . . . rather than 'fall on the ground' (Mark 14:35) or 'fall on his face' (Matt 26:39), he [Luke] has Jesus simply sink to his knees."

82. Again there is a textual question about the originality of the sweating scene (22:43–44) to Luke's account. The United Bible Societies translation committee retained the text in qualifying brackets (functioning like an asterisk) in the fourth revised edition, reflecting their respect for the passage's "evident antiquity and its importance in the textual tradition," but also its absence from several key ancient manuscripts (see Metzger, *Textual Commentary*, 151). In *Death of the Messiah*, 181–82, Brown opines that "on purely textual grounds . . . the weight of the evidence moderately favors omission," but on stylistic grounds, "clearly the passage is more easily explained stylistically if Luke wrote it" (see full discussion, pp. 180–86). In any case, the passage has obvious relevance for the present study, focusing on Jesus' emotions.

83. The apt phrase derives from Johnson, *Gospel of Luke*, 352. The language does not suggest a literal oozing of blood but rather a simile accentuating the "huge drops" *like* (*hōsei*) "blood globules" (*thromboi haimatos*) flowing from Jesus' body.

84. Luke 22:3 clearly identifies Judas as a pawn of Satan. The presence of the strengthening angel in 22:43 adds to the cosmic dimension of Jesus' struggle.

85. On Stephen as an exemplary "man of self-mastery," see Abraham Smith, "Full of Spirit and Wisdom."

86. 2 Macc 3:16: "To see the appearance of the high priest was to be wounded at heart, for his face and the change of his color disclosed the *anguish of his soul* (*kata psychēn agōnian*)."

87. Green, "Jesus on the Mount of Olives (Luke 22.39–46): Tradition and Theology," *Journal for the Study of the New Testament* 26 (1986): 29–48; *Gospel of Luke*, 777–78.

88. Recall Peter's introduction in Luke as a "sinner" (5:8); here he continues to live up to that reputation; see Fitzmyer, *Gospel According to Luke X–XXIV*, 1460–61.

89. Tannehill, *Luke*, 328; Johnson, *Gospel of Luke*, 362; Richard S. Ascough, "Rejection and Repentance: Peter and the People in Luke's Passion Narrative," *Biblica* 74 (1993): 358–59.

90. Richard Bauckham, *Gospel Women: Studies of the Named Women in the Gospels* (Grand Rapids: Eerdmans, 2002), 199, views the evidence much more positively than I do: "Luke does not introduce the women at 8:2–3 so that readers may forget them again until 23:50, but so that readers may journey with them in Jesus' company all the way to the cross." Ignoring the women for sixteen chapters seems to me like a weak narrative technique for keeping them in the readers' minds. Perhaps as long as they remain still and quiet, the women can tag along with Jesus and the male disciples throughout the journey.

CHAPTER 6

Out of Mind, Out of Voice:
Slave-Girls and Prophetic Daughters
in Luke-Acts

The days when one could glibly speak of "Luke"[1] as women's best New Testament friend are decidedly past, especially when due weight is given to the book of Acts as a sequel to the Lukan gospel. Two scholars from the University of Oslo—one older (emeritus) and male, the other younger and female—illustrate the shift toward a more critical view of women's roles in Luke-Acts. In 1983 (English translation, 1984), Jacob Jervell argued that Luke is not interested in women as women, but merely as faithful "daughters of Abraham" or "Jewesses" representative of the revitalized people of Israel gathered by Jesus.[2] Thus what matters for Luke is women's ethnic and religious identity, not their gender. Within the structure of the new community, conventional gender roles remain fixed. Women constitute the "passive," "hearing" sector of the community, thoroughly subordinate to male authority and discourse. The book of Acts particularly enforces this arrangement, as men dominate all of the speeches and assume all of the key leadership positions in the early church. In short, in Jervell's estimation, "there is neither the entitlement of women to equal rights nor any emancipation of women" in Luke's narratives.[3]

A decade later, Turid Karlsen Seim offered a more extensive and nuanced, though still critical, assessment of gender relations in Luke-Acts. Generally, she concludes that "it is a preposterous simplification to ask whether Luke's writings are friendly or hostile to women . . . [they] cannot be reduced either to a feminist treasure chamber or to a chamber of horrors for women's theology."[4] On the one hand, Seim disagrees with Jervell's notion that women function simply as a cipher for "Jewish disciples"; as she sees it, patterns of pairing women and men within Christian communities suggest that women possess some kind of positive, independent status as women in Luke's work. On the other hand, Seim detects a strong element of male priority in the areas of proclamation and leadership, laced with considerable irony. Women have the right and ability to speak and rule within the believing community, but by and large men will not hear or follow them—a fact of social life that Luke may lament on some level but is not eager to change. And so we are left to sort out Luke's "double message" (Seim's title) regarding women's roles in early Christianity.[5]

I hope to decode further this complex message by focusing on one important aspect of women's ministry examined by both Jervell and Seim and by many others—the right to *speak* or *prophesy*—as practiced by one group of lower-class females who have received little attention—slave-girls or maidservants.[6]

Impetus for this investigation comes from Peter's citation of Joel's programmatic prophecy on the day of Pentecost: "I will pour out my Spirit upon all flesh, and your sons and your daughters shall prophesy, and your young men shall see visions, and your old men shall dream dreams. Even upon my slaves, both men (*doulous*) and women (*doulas*), in those days I will pour out my Spirit; and they shall prophesy" (Acts 2:17–18). Through double emphasis[7] this passage establishes prophetic utterance by all people, including women and men—both daughters and sons, female slaves and male slaves—as a major sign of the Spirit's outpouring in the last days. Strategically situated in the middle of the two-volume Lukan narrative, the Joel citation provides both a *review* of past events and a *preview* of coming attractions.[8] The review takes us back to the beginning of the third gospel in which three women, designated as either "daughter/descendant" (*thygatēr*) or "slave/servant" (*doulē*), function as inspired prophets heralding the new era of salvation dawning with the birth of Jesus: Elizabeth, "one of the daughters of Aaron" (1:5); Mary, the humble "slave" of the Lord (1:48); and Anna, "the daughter of Phanuel" (2:36). Both Elizabeth and Mary deliver prophetic speeches (1:41–45) under the explicit impulse of the Holy Spirit (1:35, 41); in Anna's case, however, although she is the only one of these women to be specifically labeled "a prophet," we hear only a brief, third-person summary of her proclamation (2:38) and no reference to her imbuement with the Spirit. In these respects she is dramatically overshadowed by Simeon, thrice anointed with the Spirit (2:25, 26, 27), whose mouth pours forth "amazing" words of praise and prophecy to the young Jesus and his parents in the preceding scene (2:28–35).

From this point forward in Luke's gospel, women's prophetic vocation further wanes. Jesus emerges as the supreme prophet of God whom women heed and serve with their hands and purses, but not with their voices (e.g., 4:38–39; 7:11–16; 8:2–3; 10:38–42; 21:1–4). When a vocal woman like Martha dares to speak out in Jesus' presence, she is rebuked for not following the "better" silent option of attentive sister Mary (10:38–42). When Mary Magdalene and other women seem to reclaim their voice at the end of the story as the first witnesses to the empty tomb, the male apostles dismiss their report as an "idle tale" (24:11).[9] In short, as Barbara Reid concludes, after setting the prophetic stage for the infant Messiah, "the women who speak in the rest of the gospel are reprimanded by Jesus or are disbelieved."[10]

While women's prophecy appears to diminish over the course of Luke's gospel, the announced fulfillment of Joel's promise at the outset of Acts leads us to anticipate a fresh revival of such activity. Mary the mother of Jesus suddenly comes back on the scene as part of the early praying community in Jerusalem (1:14). We perk up our ears for another prophetic song (like the Magnificat in Luke 1:46–55); but as it happens, we hear not a single additional note from her or about her as Acts unfolds. Moreover, there is a conspicuous dearth of other active women prophets in Acts. The expectations raised by the Joel citation are frustrated; the previewed inclusive scenario is never fully realized.

In Peter's next Jerusalem speech after Pentecost, he addresses "males" (*andres*)/"brothers" (*adelphoi*) only and refers to them as "*sons* (*huioi*) of the prophets" of Israel (3:12, 17, 25). The daughters have dropped out of the picture.[11] In Acts 5 we eventually hear a woman's voice—Sapphira's—but what she says is a *lie* and what results from her fraudulent utterance is her immediate *death*. The famous, or rather infamous, first words from a woman in Acts are her last! This is scarcely an encouraging sign to women speakers. In Acts 21 we finally encounter the prophetic daughters we have been looking for—Philip the evangelist's "four unmarried daughters who had the gift of prophecy" (21:9). Unfortunately, however, when Paul comes to their Caesarean home, he receives guidance concerning his ensuing visit to Jerusalem from an itinerant *male* prophet (Agabus) from Judea (21:10–11), while Philip's resident prophetic daughters remain mute in the background.

If daughters do not fare particularly well as prophets in Acts, what about "my female slaves" (*tas doulas mou*) also destined to receive the Spirit of prophecy according to Joel's agenda? If we limit our search strictly to the word *doulē*, then we find no examples of female slaves/servants in Luke or Acts, speaking or otherwise, outside of Mary in the birth narrative. But if we expand our linguistic scope slightly to include the close synonym, *paidiskē*, denoting "slave-girl,"[12] and also extend the socio-religious boundary beyond metaphorical handmaids of the Lord ("my [= God's] slaves")[13] to include any literal, working slave-girls, whatever their ties to the believing community, then we discover some interesting cases.

On three occasions—one in the Lukan passion narrative (22:56), the other two in the middle chapters of Acts (12:13–15; 16–18)—a *paidiskē* makes an announcement: *her voice is heard.* And what each slave-girl says is absolutely reliable: *she speaks the truth.* But, like the women witnesses to the empty tomb, each vocal slave-girl encounters resistance to her message: *her word is squelched or challenged in some way.* Shadows of doubt are even cast on the character and competence of each slave-girl as a witness: *she is stigmatized in some fashion as a suspicious, if not dangerous, deviant.*

Literary and Social Frameworks

Investigating more particular literary and social dimensions of these intriguing cases will allow us to build a more comprehensive portrait of vocal maidservants in Luke-Acts. On the literary side, we must be alert to the following issues:

NARRATION

Is the speech of the slave-girls emphasized in the narrative through direct citation or veiled through indirect report? Is their testimony isolated or embedded in dialogue?[14] Are the slave-girls given any opportunity to argue their case, defend their word, as Peter and the apostles, Stephen, and Paul do at some length in Acts?

LOCATION

Where do the slave-girl scenes occur in the developing structure of the narrative (plot)? How do they fit with surrounding material (context)? Within the respective scenes, where do the slave-girls deliver their messages (settings)? For example, do they speak up within closed (inside) or open (outside) spaces, and how do such areas typically function in the narrative? Is "inside" a protected haven and "outside" a hazardous zone for women's speech? Or, vice versa, is "inside" a restricted cell and "outside" a liberating environment, a breath of fresh air?[15]

CHARACTERIZATION

What does the narrative disclose, through either direct or indirect description, about these vocal slave-girls beyond the *paidiskē* label? Are they brought to the fore and identified by proper name or left in the background as anonymous figures? How do their reported actions correlate with their speech? How do they stack up, either by comparison or contrast, with other characters in the story?[16]

MOTIVATION

In analyzing the Lot narrative in Gen 19, David Gunn has effectively focused on the element of "desire" or motivation as a key to exploring the nexus between plot and character: "Who desires what and when? In what ways are the desires that drive the story fulfilled?" Such an approach, Gunn avers, has the advantage of taking seriously the perspectives and influences of multiple characters within the story, not just those of the supposed protagonist.[17] Applied to our investigation of prophetic slave-girls in Luke-Acts, we ask: What do they hope to achieve by their announcements? Why and to what extent are their aims more frustrated than fulfilled?

Our profile of three *paidiskai* in the Lukan narratives may be further sharpened by probing various social questions.

STATUS AND OCCUPATION

What kind of masters do these young women serve, and what is the precise nature of their work? Within the prevailing patriarchal-hierarchical structure of first-century Mediterranean households, servant-girls would clearly rank at the bottom of the ladder, subordinated by their gender and age[18] as well as by their slave class. In such a position, they were especially vulnerable to exploitation and abuse by their employers (cf. Luke 12:45).[19] As for their duties, Deborah Sawyer has observed that maidservants in the Greco-Roman world performed a variety of household tasks, including not only standard menial chores of cooking, cleaning, and sewing, but also various functions surrounding the care and training of their masters' children. Moreover, some female slaves operated outside the domestic sphere, serving their owners' business interests in the public marketplace.[20] Kathleen Corley has further called attention to the preponderance of slave-women among prostitutes in brothels and entertainers at banquets.[21]

RACE AND RELIGION

Are the vocal slave-girls and their masters in the Lukan narratives Jewish or Gentile, and how do they relate to various religious groups?[22] Are they included among the followers of Jesus in Luke or the emerging Christian congregations in Acts? Are they part of "God-fearing" households (worshiping the God of Israel), either Jewish or Gentile, accepting or rejecting Jesus Messiah? Or are they associated with some "pagan" Greco-Roman network, completely outside the sphere of Judaism? Most importantly, do these ethnic-religious distinctions make any difference in the reception of the slave-girls' messages?

GENDER AND LOCATION

Cultural analyses of "public" and "private" space in the ancient Mediterranean world focus not only on physical settings (indoor/outdoor), but also on social boundaries related to gender roles, kinship ties, and honor-shame codes.[23] Philo of Alexandria sketches a common division in elite, Eastern (Greek) Mediterranean societies[24] between male-dominated "public" areas—where men (household heads) jockey for honor and standing in the civic arena (*polis*); and female-restricted "private" (or domestic) spheres—where women preserve their proper sense of shame and modesty within the family unit (*oikos*).

> Market-places and council-halls and law-courts and gatherings and meetings where a large number of people are assembled, and open-air life with full scope for discussion and action—all these are suitable to men both in war and peace. The women are best suited to the indoor life which never strays from the house, within which the middle door is taken by the maidens as their boundary, and the outer door by those who have reached full womanhood. (*Special Laws* 3.169)[25]

Within this scenario, "public" speaking (open-air life with full scope for discussion) was largely a male prerogative, indeed, the principal means of acquiring and defending masculine honor. Women could express their opinions within the household, but outside this realm, vocal women ran the risk of being tagged as shameless tattlers, busybodies, and threats to the social order (cf. 1 Tim 5:13–14).

However, while Philo endorses the primary seclusion and domestication of elite women, he also, as Shelly Matthews discerns, "allows for some destabilization of the public/private binary"—especially in the realm of religious observance:

> A woman, then, should not be a busybody, meddling with matters outside her household concerns, but should seek a life of seclusion. She should not show herself off like a vagrant in the streets before the eyes of other men, *except when she has to go to the temple,* and even then she should take pains to go, not when the market is full, but when most people have gone home, and so like a free-born-lady worthy of the name, with everything quiet around her, make her oblations, and offer her prayers to avert the evil and gain the good. (*Special Laws* 3.171)[26]

Still, Philo permits women's public display of religion only for "free-born ladies" under the strictest circumstances of limited crowds and "everything quiet around her." Vocal slave-girls are doubly cropped from this picture.

Understanding the people of God as an inclusive, "fictive" kinship group based in believers' homes (Luke 8:19–21; 11:27–28; Acts 2:42–47; 5:42; 12:12–17; 16:14–15, 30–34, 40; 20:20), the Lukan Jesus and his early followers appear to blur prevailing gender-oriented, public-domestic dichotomies. Jerome Neyrey may overstate the case that "there was *no* 'public' Christian world for males or females. They met in 'private' space and adopted the customs appropriate for households and kinship groups."[27] But the evidence for a strong "house-church" focus is clear in Luke-Acts, potentially offering more room for women, both slave and free, to speak and be heard. In light of cultural stereotypes, we must determine whether the vocal maidservants in Luke-Acts speak out decorously in "private" kinship circles, where they might expect a tolerant if not sympathetic hearing, or more brazenly in agonistic "public" forums of male discourse, where their opinion would more likely be dismissed and derided.

DEVIANCE AND DENUNCIATION

How exactly is the witness of the respective slave-girls repudiated? Is it simply ignored or more directly attacked? A common strategy for invalidating testimony involves impugning the character of the speaker through name-calling (labeling) and other insinuations of social deviance. To what extent are the slave-girls in Luke-Acts judged to be "out of bounds" of "normal" society and thus effectively rendered "out of voice"? Who are the particular "agents of censure," and what interests of theirs seem to be threatened by the maidservants' testimony?[28]

The High Priest's Servant-Girl (Luke 22:54–62)

The initial *paidiskē*, an anonymous slave in the Jewish high priest's household, emerges as the first of three speakers who identify Peter as an associate of the arrested Jesus, prompting Peter's notorious denials. The setting for this scene is the high priest's *aulē* in Jerusalem (22:55), denoting either the courtyard or a corridor within his official residence or perhaps the entire palace.[29] The audience around the servant girl and Peter includes Jesus, the arrest party—previously identified as "the chief priests, the officers of the temple police, and the elders" (22:52)—and presumably other household servants.[30] Thus, while in one sense the slave-girl speaks in the appropriate domain of a private home where she and other female servants work, in another sense she raises her voice presumptuously in an official, public venue—the palace or court of the high priest (*archiereus*)—before a group of male religious authorities.

The public nature of the scene is reinforced by the slave-girl's third-person accusation—"*This man* (*houtos*) also was with him" (22:56)—clearly announced to the assembly, contrasted with the limited second-person address to Peter in the other gospels—"*You* (*su*) also were with Jesus."[31] What does she hope to gain by such an announcement? While no specific motives are exposed in the immediate context, certain inferences may be made in connection with a sinister, diabolical plot disclosed in preceding narratives. At the beginning of the chapter, the narrator reveals that the "chief priests and officers of the temple police" had cut a deal with Satan-inspired Judas Iscariot to destroy Jesus (22:1–6). Again, just before his arrest, the Lukan Jesus predicts that Satan will severely test the loyalty of the disciples and that Peter in particular will fail the test by thrice dissociating himself from Jesus (22:31–34). Against this backdrop, the slave-girl emerges as the *agent of Satan* intent on undermining Peter's faith and discipleship. Moreover, by virtue of her household tie with the malevolent high priest and her explicit association of Peter with Jesus ("This man [Peter] was also with him [Jesus]"), she also appears to endorse Satan's violent aims against the Jesus movement, hoping to implicate Peter along with Jesus as rebels worthy of death.[32]

Loretta Dornisch resists such a deviant, demonic portrait of the vocal maidservant, separating her out from the other nefarious characters in the trial scene.

Once again, the young woman who is learning is the one who has the keenness of recognition. In contrast, those who should recognize and acknowledge him [Jesus]—Peter, the leader of the disciples; those who are in charge of Jesus' body; the body of elders of the people, both chief priests and scribes; deny him, mock him, beat him, curse him, blaspheme him, betray him, trap him, and witness against him. The young maidservant recognizes him. She tries to enable Peter to recognize him, but Peter replies, "I know him not." The contrast seems clear both in the tradition and in the teachings being handed on to new generations of Christians.[33]

While the high priest's slave-girl does not threaten Jesus as directly or as destructively as her master does (together with other Jewish officials, Judas, and Peter), she in no way stands apart from the proceedings as a favorable witness to Jesus. Her "recognition" cannot be equated with faith or "acknowledgement," such as we find, for example, in the dramatic "recognition" (finally!) of the risen Jesus by the Emmaus travelers (24:28–32). However, Dornisch's point that the maidservant in some sense creates an opportunity for *Peter* to experience renewed recognition of Jesus is more on target. Even if she functions as Satan's tool in testing Peter, as suggested above, she does not force Peter to succumb to cowardice. Testing sets the stage for growth as well as failure, depending on the response of the one being tested. The slave-girl's announcement concerning Peter's alliance with Jesus is absolutely true (no false witness here). She forces Peter to face the truth and act upon it.

Unfortunately, in answering the slave-girl's challenge, Peter flatly disavows any knowledge of Jesus, a tactic designed to protect his honor and preserve his life by distancing himself from a deviant criminal. Ironically, while the high priest's maidservant speaks the truth, Jesus' chief apostle utters a barefaced lie. The unique form of Peter's denial in Luke is noteworthy for our interests in that he personally counters his challenger in gender-specific terms: "*Woman (gynai)*, I do not know him" (22:57). The next two accusations, which essentially echo the first, come from individual *male attendants,* unlike in the other gospels, which either stick with the original woman (Mark 14:69) or introduce another female servant (Matt 26:71) or a band of servants and guards (John 18:25) in round two, and put forward a group of bystanders as the accusers (Matt 26:73/Mark 14:70) in round three. (Only John 18:25 parallels Luke 22:59–60 in presenting the final questioner as one of the high priest's male servants.) Peter's second and third retorts in Luke closely match his first, using a vocative form appropriate to his challengers' gender: "*Man (anthrōpe)*, I am not!" (22:58); "*Man (anthrōpe)*, I do not know what you are talking about!" (22:60). As Joseph Fitzmyer observes, this transparent pattern of two male witnesses counterbalancing one female witness makes the Lukan version of Peter's trial "even more official than the Marcan," that is, more in line with conventional rules of evidence in Jewish courts, which valued the corroborative testimony of two or three men over the dubious word of women, certainly that of a lone servant-girl.[34]

Mary's Maidservant, Rhoda (Acts 12:12–17)

The next scene to be considered features a slave-girl named Rhoda who announces (indirectly) Peter's surprising appearance at the gate of her mistress's residence following his miraculous release from prison and imminent execution at the hands of King Herod (cf. Acts 12:1–11). Unlike the previous slave-girl, who acted as a pawn in Satan's scheme to ensnare and destroy Peter, the current maidservant functions as a witness to Peter's rescue from bondage and death effected by "the angel of the Lord" (12:1–7), motivated simply by her exuberance over the good news she has to proclaim. She is in fact so "overjoyed" that she rushes to tell the assembly of Peter's presence before letting him inside the gate! (12:14).[35] Moreover, unlike the previous household tie with the high priest and other temple officials inimical to Jesus, Rhoda serves a leading Jewish-Christian woman—Mary the mother of John Mark—who hosts a large gathering of praying believers in her Jerusalem home (12:12).[36] It is before this prayer group, presumably interceding on Peter's behalf, that Rhoda makes her startling but truthful announcement of Peter's arrival.

Once again, the proclamation scene appears to be set on the threshold of domestic and public space. It begins not with Rhoda's speaking, but with her *hearing* Peter's knock and then "[his] voice" coming from the street *outside* the "outer gate." Leaving Peter standing outside, Rhoda then "ran in" (probably through the courtyard) to make her announcement to the assembly (12:13–14). She serves, then, as a bridge between the public, hostile regime of King Herod (outside)[37] and the private, supportive fellowship of the Christian community (inside). However, even this latter, household realm, where Rhoda delivers her message, is not unambiguously "private." For the setting is not simply Mary's household, but a house *church* gathered in Mary's home, a congregation of "many" praying disciples from various households, including men as well as women.[38] Although ideally these believers are knit together in one home-based "fictive" family (cf. 2:42–47; 4:32–34),[39] it is difficult not to imagine that the conglomeration of multiple "real" families under one roof would still create something of a "public" scenario in which rules of social exchange might be more restrictive than in individual house-holds. We may recall, for example, the famous Corinthian case where Paul (or his editor/interpolator) prohibited women from speaking "in church" (meeting presumably in a large residence), advising them instead to discuss spiritual matters with their husbands "at home" (their own private abodes) (1 Cor 14:34–36). In any case, Rhoda's testimony comes under the collective scrutiny not only of Mary and her immediate relatives, but of the entire prayer group assembled in Mary's house.

Despite her accurate report stemming from sincere motives and deliv-ered to a sympathetic audience whom we expect to be thrilled over news of Peter's safety (the answer to their prayers!),[40] Rhoda fares no better as a wit-ness in Mary's home than the slave-girl in the high priest's courtyard. Twice she confronts blatant denials of her testimony, first in the form of personal ridicule—"You are out of your mind"—and then, when she sticks to her story, in the form of metaphysical reproof—"It is his angel" (his guardian angel presumably, who somehow resembles Peter's form but, from the per-spective of the skeptical assembly, is not doing a very good job of protecting his charge, since they assume Peter's body remains in jail awaiting execution; or maybe they think the guardian angel is lost and needs directions to Herod's prison!).[41] The poor girl is either too hysterical[42] or too naïve to trust her judgment; being "out of mind" renders her "out of voice." No mat-ter that Peter himself (not his angel or apparition) has been banging on the gate the whole time ("Peter continued knocking," 12:16), rapping out a con-firming signal of Rhoda's message. Only when the group belatedly opens the gate and sees Peter for themselves do they believe her report.[43]

Moreover, it is *Peter's voice* that ultimately persuades. He not only appears alive before the confused assembly but motions for them "with his hand [the same hand whose knuckles are rubbed raw from knocking?] *to be silent*" and "describe[s]" for them the details of his deliverance (12:17). In the process, Peter silences Rhoda as well and effectively usurps her role as witness. Recall-ing, too, that from the start Rhoda's testimony was based on "recognizing *Peter's voice*" (12:14), we find her word being wholly bracketed (stifled) by Peter's in the story.

The assembly's dubious reaction to Rhoda's "mad" report is closely par-allel to the apostles' dismissal of the women's witness to Jesus' empty tomb in Luke 24 as an "idle tale." Only when Peter went to the tomb and saw the vacant burial clothes did he consider that the women might have a point (24:11–12). Now, in an intriguing switch of roles in Acts 12, Peter plays Jesus' part: he is the one miraculously released from the jaws of death preparing to reveal himself to distraught supporters who think he is gone. And again, the female testimony to his "resurrection" is scorned until confirmed by a larger company of eyewitnesses that includes males.

The typological link between Jesus and Peter continues with the acts of commissioning and departing. After his death and resurrection, Jesus commissioned the eleven apostles to be his authoritative witnesses just before going away (*poreuomai*) into heaven (Acts 1:8–11). Peter then promptly moved to replace the deceased apostle Judas with another *man* (*anēr*) who had followed Jesus since the days of John (1:21–22), thus restoring the Twelve as the leading body of messianic witnesses. Now in Acts 12, the loss of James, another member of the Twelve, to Herod's sword creates another vacancy in the apostolic circle (12:2). Once more Peter steps forward to address the leadership crisis, this time following his own impending death and "resurrection." Will he look to the influential householder Mary or even to the slave-girl Rhoda, who has proven herself a faithful, enthusiastic witness? As it happens, Peter treats Mary and her house church as little more than a messenger service and halfway house. Just before "he departs and goes (*poreuomai*) to another place," he orders the community in Mary's home to report his recent experience to "*James* [another James] *and the brothers* (*adelphois*)" (12:17). As Robert Wall has argued, this sudden introduction of James by name only assumes readers' knowledge of his leading position in the Jerusalem church and hints at a larger role to come in the story of Acts. Rather than restoring the Twelve after losing one of its members, Peter now seems to be *transferring* the authority and responsibility of the Twelve to another cohort of male ministers in Jerusalem under the headship of James.[44] In any case, Mary and Rhoda are never heard from again in Acts, while James later emerges as a major voice in two key Jerusalem councils (15:13–21; 21:17–26).

The Merchants' Fortune-Telling Slave-Girl (Acts 16:16–18)

The third and final slave-girl to be examined publicizes the mission of Paul and associates in the city of Philippi. Unlike the two previous *paidiskai* employed in the household of a Jewish master or mistress in Jerusalem, this slave-girl works for a group of Roman "owners" (*kyrioi*) in the Philippian marketplace. She generates considerable profits for these masters on the public streets—a kind of prostitution[45]—by her special ability to unveil divine secrets (16:16). Such mantic prowess stems from the "Pythian spirit" that possesses her, a spirit linked with the serpent-slaying Apollo, thought to inspire the famous oracles at Delphi uttered by female prophets.[46] The girl is thus doubly bound by socioeconomic and psycho-spiritual forces.

While a public, commercial setting provides the main locus of the Philippian slave-girl's activity, we also discover that she meets the Pauline missionary party as they are heading "to the place of prayer (*proseuchē*)" and tags along with them for several days (16:16, 18). This raises questions concerning her association with Lydia and other God-fearing women whom Paul sought out at "a place of prayer (*proseuchē*) in the previous scene (16:13). Strikingly, what emerges is a clear contrast between Lydia and this slave-girl in terms of social status and religious function.[47] Unlike the exploited Pythian slave, Lydia is a merchant of some independent means, dealing in expensive purple cloth and managing her own household (16:14–15).[48] Despite her higher social location,[49] however, as well as her provision of hospitality (an important form of service in Luke-Acts, exemplified by Jesus and Paul, along with various women),[50] when it comes to the vital ministry of proclaiming the word, Lydia functions solely as a *passive hearer and helper* of Paul. The story stresses her aural response to Paul's message through a double reference, the second of which intensifies her passivity by crediting "the Lord" as the one who "open[s] her heart to listen eagerly to what was said by Paul" (16:14). Lydia also has a brief speaking part, but the words she utters are suppliant rather than prophetic, thoroughly subject to Paul's authority ("If you have judged me to be faithful to the Lord, come and stay at my home," 16:15).[51]

In contrast to Lydia's affirmed role as passive hearer and helper, the prophetic slave-girl appears as an *active announcer and annoyer* of Paul, whose persistent proclamation prompts Paul to silence her by exorcising the Pythian spirit (16:18). What is it exactly that the slave-girl says, and why does she say it? Her oracle seems to be perfectly orthodox by Lukan standards: "These men are slaves of the Most High God (*tou theou tou hypsistou*), who proclaim to you a way of salvation (*hodon sōtērias*)" (16:17). This announcement closely recalls the prophetic vocation of John the Baptist, sketched by Zechariah under the inspiration of the Holy Spirit (cf. Luke 1:67): "And you, child, will be called the prophet of the Most High (*hypsistou*); for you will go before the Lord to prepare his ways (*hodous*), to give knowledge of salvation (*sōtērias*) to his people . . . " (Luke 1:76–77). Indeed, much as John paved the path of Jesus' saving mission around the Jordan ("Prepare the way [*hodon*] of the Lord . . . all flesh shall see the salvation of God [*to sōtērian tou theou*]," Luke 3:3–6), the slave-girl heralds the coming of Paul in Philippi.[52] What does she hope to accomplish by this publicity? Two possible, opposite options present themselves: either she sincerely wants to honor Paul and companions as authentic messengers of the God of Israel, whom she now confesses publicly as the "Most High God," supreme over Apollo and other

Greco-Roman deities;[53] or she maliciously sets out to expose Paul's monotheistic (Yahwistic) mission in hopes of stirring up anti-Judaic hostility and driving Paul out of the city. The sparse narrative leaves the matter tantalizingly open. Reimer's conclusion that the slave-girl's "following" Paul indicates her discipleship is plausible, but not certain.[54] Simon Magus, after all, "stayed constantly with Philip" the evangelist before being unmasked as a greedy charlatan by Peter and John (8:12–24). It is not always easy to distinguish between true and false disciples (cf. 20:29–30).[55]

Paul's petulant expulsion of the Pythian spirit obviously demonstrates that *he* has a problem with this prophetic slave-girl, but it is not altogether clear why he has a problem (shouldn't he appreciate the "free advertising"?)[56] or what that problem might be. Is he "very much annoyed" (16:18) simply with her persistent nagging chatter (shut up, already!), like the proverbial "continual dripping of rain,"[57] or does he object to something more substantial? In the only other New Testament occurrence of *diaponeomai* in Acts 4:2, the chief priests and Sadducees become "much annoyed" over the heretical teaching of the apostles concerning Jesus' resurrection. In Paul's case, however, as we have seen, there seems to be no major theological point to dispute in the slave-girl's testimony.[58] Alternatively, Paul may well be bothered not so much by the content of the slave-girl's message as by the source: her prophecy springs from an alien spirit of divination, not from the Holy Spirit of God. We know of cases from Luke's gospel where Jesus delivered victims from harmful, unclean spirits who patently spoke the truth about him (Luke 4:31–37; 8:26–39).[59] However, the scenario in Acts 16 diverges from these incidents at key points: the spirit possessing the slave-girl is never labeled "unclean";[60] it does not remonstrate with Paul, as the spirits did with Jesus: "Let us alone! What have you to do with us!" (indeed, recall that the Pythian spirit wants to stay close to Paul[61]); and we do not know precisely how the spirit is damaging the slave-girl other than supplying a prophetic gift that enables her owners—the real oppressors—to exploit her.[62]

Another critical question arises as to whether Paul does the slave-girl any real favor by casting out the Pythian spirit. He shuts her up, puts her out of work, and then the story drops her completely, as Gail O'Day, Clarice Martin, and Kathy Chambers (Williams) have observed.[63] She may be freed from her oppressive employers, but does she find a home—a supportive, fictive family—in the liberating community of God's people? Does she enter into the "way of salvation" that she herself proclaimed? We do not know: the narrative leaves us, the readers, to worry about the girl's fate.

Williams goes so far as to suggest that, following the comedic trope of the "humorous rape," Paul the exorcist may be viewed as "violating" the slave-girl and "stripping" her of her livelihood; but then, instead of fulfilling the concomitant convention of marrying the shamed girl and making an honest woman out of her, Paul abandons the de-possessed (de-flowered) slave-girl.[64] While affirming the critical point about Paul's shameful lack of attending further to this girl whose life he has just turned "upside down" (cf. Acts 17:6), I am more skeptical about interpreting his exorcism as an unwarranted violation. The slave-girl had already been penetrated by the Pythian spirit and pimped by her Philippian owners before encountering Paul. Thus, in Lukan terms at least, she needs precisely the kind of liberation from these oppressive forces that Paul provides. But she also needs (again, in Lukan terms) a nurturing community of fellowship and sustenance in which to grow and thrive—and this Paul appears to fail at miserably.

Obviously, many issues remain unsettled in this strange story. But in any case, we are left with one disturbing fact: for whatever reason, a prophetic slave-girl proclaiming the good news of God's salvation—as envisioned in the Joel citation at Pentecost—is ultimately silenced and forgotten.

Conclusion

The three proclaiming slave-girls in Luke-Acts come from various worlds—Jewish, Jewish-Christian, and Greco-Roman—both hostile and friendly to the "way" of Jesus; they speak in various settings—palace (*aulē*), house (*oikia*), and marketplace (*agora*)—for various possible reasons—to condemn and destroy, to encourage and excite, to herald or expose; and they are driven by various impulses—satanic malice, joyous emotion, and a Pythian spirit. Amid this diversity, however, these slave-girls remain bound together as a trio of vocal women who speak the truth but have their word spurned by Peter or Paul—the leading spokesmen in the church—or by a local Christian community. All three *paidiskai* convey their message through direct or indirect speech, but after their report is challenged in some way, they have no further opportunity for rebuttal or clarification. In fact, they are never heard from again.

As for the form of the resistance to the slave-girls' reports, once again variety reigns: their testimonies are alternately denied, mocked, corrected, substantiated (by male witnesses), or throttled. But in any event, maidservants' voices are consistently more suppressed than celebrated in Luke-Acts. Thus, while the infancy narrative in Luke 1–2 and especially the Joel citation in Acts 2 provide idealistic support for prophetic women in general and servant women in particular, their vision is ultimately overwhelmed by pragmatic considerations. Women may have the right and gift to speak, but few audiences—even in the church—are willing to hear them.

Rhoda's case is most telling in this regard. She stands out from the other two slave-girls in both characterization and context: she is the only one dignified by a personal name, and she makes her announcement in the most private, the most pervasively Christian, and thus the most ostensibly supportive of the three settings. If the Joel-Pentecost script is to be played out anywhere, it would seem to be here—in Mary's *oikia* of prayer, rather than in the high priest's *aulē* or the Philippian *agora*. But, remarkably, however optimal the conditions for a favorable hearing, Rhoda's witness is stifled and stigmatized as surely as that of the other slave-girls. Demonized as being "out of her mind" differs in form but not in substance from sinister associations with satanic schemes and Pythian prophecies.

Of course, the implied Lukan author does not agree that Rhoda is deranged. Her witness to Peter's presence, as surely as Mary Magdalene's witness to the risen Jesus, is perfectly reliable. But by giving Rhoda no direct lines in Acts 12[65] (the other two *paidiskai* at least speak a few words) and no appearances (much less speech) anywhere else in the narrative, Luke seems to capitulate to prevailing social and cultural practices rather than rise above them. The Joel banner of liberation for female slaves still hangs in a prominent spot in Acts 2 as a wistful hope of how things might (should) be in the future, but for all practical purposes in the present life of the Lukan community, it functions as little more than window-dressing.

In his examination of *The Origins of Christian Morality* in the first two centuries of the common era, Wayne Meeks charts the prevailing trend in early Christianity to reflect rather than resist traditional social structures, focusing on three separate groups—lower-class prophets, women, and slaves—which we have combined into one group of prophetic slave-girls.

> True, a *prophet* of the lowest social class might receive in a trance a "revelation of the Lord" and with it the right to speak and give direction to the household assembly—but everyone still knew to whom the house belonged.
>
> True, *women* sometimes took on exceptional roles of leadership in the new movement—but there were soon strong reactions against that.
>
> True, in an exceptional case the apostle could write to a householder that he should welcome back his delinquent *slave* "no longer as a slave, but more than a slave, a beloved brother" (Philem. 16), but elsewhere he treats slavery as a matter of indifference: "You were a slave when called? Never mind" (1 Cor. 7:21). Soon Paul's disciples and other leaders as well would be repeating the old rules of Greek household management,

"Slaves, be submissive . . . to your masters; likewise, wives, be submissive to your own husbands . . ." and so on (1 Pet. 2:8–3:7).[66]

Although differing in style and tone from the blunt exhortations in the Petrine and Pauline letters, the suggestive Petrine and Pauline narratives in Luke-Acts that resist slave-girls ultimately reinforce the same hierarchical norms.

Notes

1. I utilize the conventional tag of "Luke" to designate the common author of Luke and Acts without assuming his/her identity as Luke the physician or any other particular historical figure.

2. Jacob Jervell, "The Daughters of Abraham: Women in Acts," in *The Unknown Paul: Essays on Luke-Acts and Early Christian History* (Minneapolis: Fortress, 1984), 146–57. In the same year (1983), Elisabeth Schüssler Fiorenza published her landmark volume, *In Memory of Her: A Feminist Theological Reconstruction of Christian Origins* (10th Anniversary Edition; New York: Crossroad, 1994), which also exposed the Lukan redactional tendency to delimit women's contributions to the development of early Christianity (pp. 49, 160–62).

3. Jervell, "Daughters of Abraham," 154.

4. Turid Karlsen Seim, *The Double Message: Patterns of Gender in Luke and Acts* (Nashville, TN: Abingdon; Edinburgh, UK: T and T Clark, 1994), 249. Jane Schaberg represents the "chamber of horrors" approach in her assessment that the Lukan gospel, because it *appears* to be so interested in women characters yet consistently confines them to subservient roles, "is an extremely dangerous text, perhaps the most dangerous in the Bible." Schaberg, "Luke," in *Women's Bible Commentary* (ed. Carol A. Newsom and Sharon H. Ringe; 2nd ed.; Louisville, KY: Westminster/John Knox, 1998), 363.

5. See also Turid Karlsen Seim, "The Gospel of Luke," in *A Feminist Companion* (vol. 2 of *Searching the Scriptures;* ed. Elisabeth Schüssler Fiorenza; New York: Crossroad, 1994), 728–62; Barbara E. Reid, *Choosing the Better Part?: Women in the Gospel of Luke* (Collegeville, MN: Liturgical Press, 1996); and Mary Rose D'Angelo, "Women in Luke-Acts: A Reductional View," *Journal of Biblical Literature* 109 (1990): 441–61.

6. The first wave of feminist studies of Luke-Acts focused primarily on named, high-ranking women characters possessing a measure of wealth and independence (e.g., Mary Magdalene, Mary and Martha of Bethany, Joanna, Tabitha, and Lydia). Lower-class figures, such as anonymous widows and slave-girls, tended to be overlooked. See my "Neglected Widows in Acts 6:1–7," *Catholic Biblical Quarterly* 56 (1994): 715–33. More recently, James M. Arlandson, in *Women, Class, and Society in Early Christianity: Models from Luke-Acts* (Peabody, MA: Hendrickson, 1997), has stressed the need for biblical scholars to appreciate the variegated class positions across the spectrum of society held by women in early Christianity generally and within Luke-Acts in particular. In examining underclass women in Luke's writings, Arlandson concentrates on prostitutes, widows, the sick and demon-possessed, and those marginalized by ethnic status and persecution (pp. 151–93). He acknowledges the significance of female slaves in Luke-Acts, but treats them more lightly, mostly in a brief appendix, pp. 195–99; cf. 123–26, 151.

7. The second "and they shall prophesy," at the end of the citation, has been added to the LXX source.

8. On this preview/review technique, see Robert C. Tannehill, "Israel in Luke-Acts: A Tragic Story," *JBL* 104 (1985): 69–85; Robert C. Tannehill, *The Narrative Unity of Luke-Acts: A Literary Interpretation* (vol. 1 of *The Gospel According to Luke;* Foundations and Facets; Philadelphia: Fortress, 1986), 21–23.

9. Seim, *Double Message,* 150–63, observes that, in addition to having their testimony rejected by male apostles, the women in Luke are never explicitly commissioned as witnesses to the resurrection, as we find in Mark 16:7.

10. Reid, *Choosing the Better Part?,* 52.

11. Jervell, "Daughters of Abraham," 154.

12. See Walter Bauer, William F. Arndt, F. Wilbur Gingrich, and Frederick W. Danker, *A Greek-English Lexicon of the New Testament and Other Early Christian Literature* (2nd ed.; Chicago: University of Chicago Press, 1979), 604.

13. Cf. Seim, *Double Message,* 170.

14. See Robert Alter, *The Art of Biblical Narrative* (New York: Basic Books, 1981), 63–87.

15. See Mieke Bal, *Introduction to the Theory of Narrative* (Toronto: University of Toronto Press, 1985), 44–45; Mark Allan Powell, *What Is Narrative Criticism?* (Minneapolis: Fortress, 1990), 70–71; and compare the sociocultural boundaries of "public" and "private" territory sketched below.

16. See Adele Berlin, *Poetics and Interpretation of Biblical Narrative* (Winona Lake, IN: Eisenbrauns, 1994), 3–42, 59–61.

17. David M. Gunn, "Narrative Criticism," in *To Each Its Own Meaning: An Introduction to Biblical Criticisms and Their Application* (ed. Steven L. McKenzie and Stephen R. Haynes; Louisville, KY: Westminster/John Knox, 1993), 180.

18. The youth of the *paidiskē* is implied in its form as a diminutive of *pais* (child/servant; see Bauer, Arndt, Gingrich, and Danker, *Greek-English Lexicon,* 604).

19. Tal Ilan, *Jewish Women in Greco-Roman Palestine* (Peabody, MA: Hendrickson, 1995), 205–11, particularly notes the subjection of female slaves to sexual abuse, assumed (and challenged) in Jewish sources from the Greco-Roman period (e.g., "Be not ashamed . . . of meddling with his [another man's] servant-girl—and do not approach her bed" [Sir 41:17, 22]; "The more maidservants, the more lewdness" [*Mishnah Avot* 2:7]). One segment of Job's extended protest of innocence illustrates both the typical vulnerability of female slaves in the ancient world and the commitment of Israel's God of mercy and justice to defend their cause alongside that of destitute widows and orphans: "If I have rejected the cause of my male or female slaves, when they brought a complaint against me; what then shall I do when God rises up?" (Job 31:13–14; cf. vv. 16–23; and Arlandson, *Women, Class, and Society,* 99–102). Carolyn Osiek and David Balch call attention to the planned breeding of slave-women to produce additional slaves (children), which an owner might retain, trade, or sell, like any other commodity. Osiek and Balch, *Families in the New Testament World: Households and House Churches* (The Family, Religion, and Culture; Louisville, KY: Westminster/John Knox, 1997), 78–79.

20. Deborah F. Sawyer, *Women and Religion in the First Christian Centuries* (London: Routledge, 1996), 27–31.

21. Kathleen Corley, *Private Women, Public Meals: Social Conflict in the Synoptic Tradition* (Peabody, MA: Hendrickson, 1993), 15, 48–52.

22. Ilan, *Jewish Women,* 207–8, persuasively challenges the common opinion that Palestinian Jews in the Second Temple era would only employ non-Jewish servants (so-called "Canaanite slaves"). The situation was more fluid: both Jews and Gentiles could own either Jewish or non-Jewish maidservants.

23. See Karen Jo Torjesen, *When Women Were Priests: Women's Leadership in the Early Church and the Scandal of Their Subordination in the Rise of Christianity* (San Francisco, CA: HarperSanFrancisco, 1993), 5–7, 38–43, 59–65, 111–76; Jerome H. Neyrey, "What's Wrong with this Picture?: John 4, Cultural Stereotypes of Women, and Public and Private Space," *Biblical Theology Bulletin* 24 (1994): 77–91; Corley, *Private Women,* 24–79; Bruce Malina and Jerome H.

Neyrey, "Honor and Shame in Luke-Acts: Pivotal Values of the Mediterranean World," in *The Social World of Luke-Acts: Models for Interpretation* (ed. Jerome H. Neyrey; Peabody, MA: Hendrickson, 1991), 41–44; Margaret Y. MacDonald, *Early Christian Women and Pagan Opinion: The Power of the Hysterical Woman* (Cambridge, UK: Cambridge University Press, 1996), 13–47.

24. Osiek and Balch, *Families in the New Testament World*, 36–47, observe that women in ancient Western Roman society potentially had more freedom of movement than those in the Eastern Greek world, as did peasant women cross-culturally and -geographically by virtue of the fact that their smaller (often single-room) dwellings afforded little space for segregation. However, this study focuses on slave-girls working in elite, Eastern Jewish and Greek environments, where notions of gender-divided space more usually applied.

25. Cited in Osiek and Balch, *Families in the New Testament World*, 44.

26. See the citation and discussion of this passage from Philo in Shelly Matthews, *First Converts: Rich Pagan Women and the Rhetoric of Mission in Early Judaism and Christianity* (Stanford, CA: Stanford University Press, 2001), 84–85.

27. Neyrey, "What's Wrong with This Picture?," 78 (emphasis added).

28. See Malina and Neyrey, "Conflict in Luke-Acts."

29. See Luke Timothy Johnson, *The Gospel of Luke* (Sacra Pagina 3; Collegeville, MN: Liturgical Press, 1991), 357; Raymond E. Brown, *The Death of the Messiah: From Gethsemane to the Grave* (Anchor Bible Reference Library; New York: Doubleday, 1994), 593.

30. The priestly arrest party identified in Luke 22:52 represents the closest antecedent for the ambiguous "they" in 22:54, 55. Among the Synoptics, only Luke places Jesus in the *aulē* of the high priest as an immediate witness to Peter's interrogation and denials. Cf. 22:61; Brown, *Death of the Messiah*, 589–95.

31. This contrastive pattern extends to all three accusations. Whereas the forms of address in Matthew and Mark follow the sequence "you"/"this man"/"you," in Luke they run "this man"/"you"/"this man."

32. See Joseph A. Fitzmyer, *The Gospel According to Luke X–XXIV* (Anchor Bible 28A; New York: Doubleday, 1985), 1460: "The servant girl . . . ha[s] played the role of Satan in Peter's *peirasmos*—associating Peter with the 'guilty' Jesus, soon to be accused."

33. Loretta Dornisch, *A Woman Reads the Gospel of Luke* (Collegeville, MN: Liturgical Press, 1996), 215, cf. pp. 212–15.

34. Fitzmyer, *Gospel According to Luke X–XXIV*, 1460. Cf. Deut 19:15; Josephus, *Jewish Antiquities* 4.129; *Mishnah Rosh HasShanah* 1.8.

35. On this and other humorous, slap-stick elements in the Rhoda tale associated with the *servus currens* (running slave) stock character within ancient Greco-Roman situation comedies, see Kathy Chambers, "'Knock, Knock—Who's There?': Acts 12:6–17 as a Comedy of Errors," in *A Feminist Companion to Acts* (ed. Amy-Jill Levine; Feminist Companion to the New Testament and Early Christian Writings 6; London: Sheffield Academic Press, 2004); and J. Albert Harrill, "The Dramatic Function of the Running Slave Rhoda (Acts 12.15–16)," *New Testament Studies* 46 (2000): 150–57. However, while agreeing on the wider comedic milieu informing Rhoda's story, Chambers and Harrill sharply diverge over the particular function of Rhoda's portrayal in its Lukan context: Chambers maintains that the Rhoda episode at least partially subverts the stereotypical lampooning of bungling running servants, whereas Harrill thinks "Luke has created a highly conventionalized sequence of action elaborated not to uplift slaves (or women) but to entertain with humour that dishonours them"(p. 151). My reading is closer to Chambers's more positive reading of Rhoda's conduct, while still acknowledging (as Chambers also does) a counter-tension in Luke's ideology supporting the status quo ("Luke is no social revolutionary"; see more below).

36. Although, as Ivoni Richter Reimer observes, the text does not explicitly identify Rhoda as Mary's slave, the reference to Mary's "house" just before Rhoda's introduction strongly implies this relationship (12:12–13). Reimer, *Women in the Acts of the Apostles: A Feminist Liberation Perspective* (Minneapolis: Fortress, 1995), 241–42. On Mary's apparent wealth and prominence,

suggested by her ownership of at least one domestic servant and a sizeable residence adjoined by a courtyard opening to the street through an "outer gate" (*pylōn*, 12:13), see Schüssler Fiorenza, *In Memory of Her*, 166–67; Arlandson, *Women, Class, and Society*, 138–40; and Gail R. O'Day, "Acts," in Newsom and Ringe, ed., *Women's Bible Commentary*, 399.

37. In the larger narrative of Acts 12:1–19, the public city-domain where Herod violently asserts his power is bounded by two gates: 1) the "iron gate" (*pylē*) to the prison through which Herod intended to "bring out" Peter for execution (12:4, 10); and 2) the "outer gate" (*pylōn*) to Mary's home through which Peter gains ultimate refuge from Herod's plot. On the sequence of inside-outside moves in this story, see F. Scott Spencer, *Acts* (Readings: A New Biblical Commentary; Sheffield, UK: Sheffield Academic Press, 1997), 125–26.

38. The term for "many" (*hikanoi*) in 12:12 is masculine, encompassing both male and female congregants. Note also the masculine plural pronoun for "them" (*autois*) in 12:17.

39. See Neyrey, "What's Wrong with this Picture?," 78 (cited above).

40. Of course, just because the congregation prayed for the imperiled Peter (12:5, 12) does not mean they necessarily expected that he would be released, still less that he was now standing outside the very house where they were gathered. In any case, a measure of surprise over Rhoda's wondrous report is understandable; more troubling is the sharpness and stubbornness of the assembly's reaction, discussed below.

41. As Christopher R. Matthews explains, "a person's guardian angel was thought to resemble the person protected" (cf. Matt 18:10). Matthews, "The Acts of the Apostles," in *The New Oxford Annotated Bible: New Revised Standard Version with the Apocrypha* (ed. Michael D. Coogan; 3rd ed.; New York: Oxford University Press, 2001), 207. Further irony surrounding the assembly's mistaking of Peter for an angel emerges from the fact that it was none other than an "angel of the Lord" who orchestrated Peter's release from prison (Acts 12:7–11).

42. The image of the "hysterical woman"—easily duped and given to excess in matters of religious experience—was a common stereotype in ancient Greco-Roman society. Margaret MacDonald (*Early Christian Women*, 1–8, 104–9) has investigated the influence of such a stereotype on pagan judgments of early Christian origins, such as Celsus's critique that Christianity began with the "fantastic tale" of resurrection promulgated by "a hysterical (*paroistros*) female" (Mary Magdalene) and others "deluded by the same sorcery" (Origen, *Contra Celsum* 2:55). However, the basic charge of "mania" or "madness" as a means of discrediting a witness could be applied to men as well as women. In the New Testament, for example, the verb used to denote the assembly's labeling of Rhoda as insane (*mainomai*) also appears in the Johannine Jews' denunciation of Jesus ("He has a demon and is out of his mind [*mainetai*]," John 10:20), Festus's dismissal of Paul (Acts 26:24), and outsiders' mockery of excessive glossalalists (1 Cor 14:23).

43 . As Chambers makes clear in "Knock, Knock—Who's There?," it is the free congregants in Mary's home, not Rhoda, who are the ultimate butts of the joke for failing to believe the absolutely reliable report of the slave-girl regarding Peter's whereabouts. When the assembly ("they," not Rhoda) "opened the gate and saw him [Peter], *they* were amazed" (12:17)—in others words, *they* were the ones truly "out of their minds" (*exestēsan*), while Rhoda was thoroughly vindicated; contra Harrill in "Dramatic Function," who mismatches Rhoda with comedic "running slaves" who typically blather on and on about some fictional event in hopes of wheedling some reward out of their masters; on the contrary, Rhoda succinctly speaks the truth (she's actually given no lines of direct speech) with no assumed ulterior motives other than informing the group of Peter's presence at the gate.

44. Robert W. Wall, "Successors to 'the Twelve' According to Acts 12:1–17," *Catholic Biblical Quarterly* 53 (1991): 628–43.

45. Cf. Matthews, *First Converts: Rich Pagan Women*, 89: "The report that she earns money for her masters by her performance on the city streets also indicates that her work is not clearly differentiated from prostitution."

46. See Howard Clark Kee, *To Every Nation Under Heaven: The Acts of the Apostles* (New Testament in Context; Harrisburg, PA: Trinity Press International, 1997), 195–97; F. F. Bruce,

The Book of Acts (New International Commentary on the New Testament; rev. ed.; Grand Rapids: Eerdmans, 1988), 312; Johnson, *Gospel of Luke*, 293–94.

47. I do not push this contrast between Lydia and the slave-girl beyond the categories of social status and religious function to include a moral disjunction between a "good girl" (Lydia) and a "bad girl" (pythoness), as do Jeffrey L. Staley, "Changing Woman: Postcolonial Reflections on Acts 16.6–40, *Journal for the Study of the New Testament* 73 (1999): 126–28; and Robert M. Price, *The Widow Traditions in Luke-Acts: A Feminist-Critical Scrutiny* (Society of Biblical Literature Dissertation Series 155; Atlanta, GA: Scholars Press, 1997), 225–34. Price even goes so far (too far, in my judgment) to suggest that Luke has divided one historical woman named Lydia into two—the good hostess and her "evil twin" (p. 229). The fact that the slave-girl, for all her "annoyance" of Paul, still speaks the truth—in Lukan terms! (see more below)—complicates a wholly negative assessment of her character. She appears as an unfortunate (exploited) and irritating (to Paul) figure, to be sure, but not as a necessarily "bad" and "evil" villainess.

48. Kathy Chambers Williams, "At the Expense of Women: Humor [?] in Acts 16.14–40," in *Are We Amused? Humour about Women in the Biblical World* (ed. Athalya Brenner; New York: T & T Clark, 2003), 88, juxtaposes Lydia as one who "draws in revenue" from her occupation and the slave-girl who operates as a "source of revenue" for her owners.

49. Studies by Luise Schottroff, "Lydia: A New Quality of Power," in *Let the Oppressed Go Free: Feminist Perspectives on the New Testament* (Gender and the Biblical Tradition; Louisville, KY: Westminster/John Knox, 1993), 131–37; and Ivoni Richter Reimer, *Women in the Acts of the Apostles*, 98–113, have nuanced our understanding of Lydia's social status. Despite her apparent wealth and independence, Lydia may have otherwise occupied a rather lowly, marginal place in the wider community by virtue of her association with the despised, "dirty work" of cloth dyeing conducted outside the city limits. Still, as a homeowner and businesswoman, she certainly ranked higher than household servants she might have employed or the Pythian slave-girl controlled by businessmen within the city. In *First Converts: Rich Pagan Women*, 88, Shelly Matthews positions Lydia within a middling "'quasi-elite' class" comprised of "persons of low status" who had "achieved a measure of respectability" through a profitable trade. For additional discussion of Lydia's social location, see the next chapter in this book.

50. Lydia's hospitality is evident at the end of the Philippian narrative (16:40) as well as at the beginning (16:15). On others' hospitality in Luke and Acts, see especially Luke 9:10–17; 15:1–2; 22:27 (Jesus); 10:38–42 (Martha and Mary); Acts 10:22–48 (Cornelius); 16:27–34 (Philippian jailer); 17:5–9 (Jason); 18:2–3 (Priscilla and Aquila); 18:7 (Titius Justus); 21:8–14 (Philip); 21:16 (Mnason); 28:7–10 (Publius); 28:30–31 (Paul). For fuller discussion, see Spencer, *The Portrait of Philip in Acts: A Study of Roles and Relations* (Journal for the Study of the New Testament: Supplement Series 67; Sheffield, UK: Sheffield Academic Press, 1992), 250–62.

51. Williams, "At the Expense of Women," 88, correctly observes that Lydia's offer of hospitality in 16:15 is a vigorous one, presented by the narrator as something she "urged" (*parekalesen*) or "prevailed" (*parebiasato*) upon the Pauline party to do. Williams further avers that the second verb (*parabiazomai*) intimates the use of "intense pressure" on Lydia's part, almost as if she "forced" Paul to stay with her, in marked contrast to Paul's "forcing" the slave-girl to be quiet in the ensuing scene. I'm not certain we can "force" that much meaning into *parabiazomai* here, and in any case, I lay heavier accent in the text on the content of direct speech accorded to Lydia, reflecting her primary sense of submission to Paul's authority and judgment about whether she is a worthy host.

52. Although different verbs are used, the slave-girl's "cry[ing] out" (*krazō*) her oracle (Acts 16:17) echoes "the voice of one crying out (*boōntos*) in the wilderness" forecast by Isaiah and fulfilled by John the Baptist (Luke 3:4).

53. *Hypsistos* (Most High) was a common title for the supreme deity in the ancient world in both Jewish and pagan contexts. The LXX amply attests its application to YHWH, the one true God of Israel (notably in Psalms and Sirach); Greco-Roman sources reveal the usage of *Hypsistos* with reference to Zeus and various other gods while also acknowledging the Jews'

appropriation of the term for their deity. See the analyses of the relevant literary and inscriptional data in Paul R. Trebilco, "Paul and Silas: 'Servants of the Most High God' (Acts 16.16–18)," *Journal for the Study of the New Testament* 36 (1989): 51–58; Trebilco, *Jewish Communities in Asia Minor* (*Society for New Testament Studies Monograph Series* 69; Cambridge, UK: Cambridge University Press, 1991), 127–44; and Reimer, *Women in the Acts of the Apostles,* 161–65.

In the New Testament, most of the evidence clusters in the Lukan writings (Luke 1:32, 35, 76; 6:35; 8:28; Acts 7:48; 16:17). Reimer contends that all of these texts refer to the Most High God of Israel, in line with LXX usage; thus, in the case of Acts 16:17, "we may suppose that the slave girl refers to this Jewish God and no other" (p. 165). Trebilco is more cautious, however, contending that in a *Gentile* setting, the slave-girl's proclamation of "the Most High God"—in the construction *ho theos ho hypsistos*—would have been "misleading" and "vague," representing "a far less specific and meaningful title than it was for the Jews" ("Paul and Silas," 58–65). While Trebilco has demonstrated on a historical level the potential ambiguity of the *Hypsistos* reference in first-century Philippi, on the level of the Lukan narrative he has overplayed the significance of the linguistic distinction between *ho theos ho hypsistos* and simply *ho hypsistos* (the latter clearly identifying the Jewish God in Luke 1:32, 35, 76; 6:35; Acts 7:48) and underplayed the parallels between the slave-girl's message and 1) John the Baptist's vocation (discussed above; cf. Luke 1:76–77; 3:3–6); and 2) the truthful recognition by the Gerasene demoniac (a Gentile) of Jesus' filial tie to "the Most High God" (*ho theos ho hypsistos*) in Luke 8:28 (see further below).

54. Reimer, *Women in the Acts of the Apostles,* 156–68.

55. See Spencer, *Portrait of Philip,* 122–26.

56. The happy "free advertising" reference derives from Richard I. Pervo, *Profit with Delight: The Literary Genre of the Acts of the Apostles* (Philadelphia: Fortress, 1987), 63.

57. Cf. Prov 19:13; 27:15 (applied to the contentious wife). In the flow of the Acts narrative, Paul's annoyance is related most directly to the slave-girl's repetitive announcements "for many days" (18:18a).

58. While affirming that the slave-girl speaks the truth about the missionaries' vocation as servants of God and instruments of salvation, Kee, *To Every Nation,* 197, suggests that she does not declare the whole truth. Specifically, she does not mention the "crucial factor" in mediating divine salvation—"the name of Jesus"—through which Paul proceeds to expel the prophetic spirit (16:18).

59. In the first case, the possessed man accurately confesses to Jesus: "I know who you are, the Holy One of God" (Luke 4:34); in the second, the demoniac correctly identifies Jesus as "Son of the Most High God" (8:28).

60. Reimer, *Women in the Acts of the Apostles,* 156–60, 167, 170.

61. Interestingly, while the Gerasene demoniac wants to follow Jesus only *after* he is delivered (Luke 8:38), the Pythian slave-girl already follows Paul *before* he expels the spirit from her (Acts 16:17).

62. Cf. Reimer, *Women in the Acts of the Apostles,* 173: "We should further observe that it is not the 'Pythian' spirit who enslaves the woman. It is her owners who enslave her and who profit financially from her ability to prophesy. Nevertheless, the spirit that is expelled from her has kept the slave girl in her state of slavery" (cf. 165–67).

63. O'Day, "Acts," 310–11; Clarice J. Martin, "The Acts of the Apostles," in Schüssler Fiorenza, ed., *Searching the Scriptures,* 2:784–85.

64. Williams, "At the Expense of the Woman," 83–87.

65. Cf. Chambers, "Knock, Knock—Who's There?": "She [Rhoda] does not 'lecture' her social betters; to the contrary, they silence her. Indeed, the narrative never presents Rhoda's voice in direct discourse."

66. Wayne A. Meeks, *The Origins of Christian Morality: The First Two Centuries* (New Haven, CN: Yale University Press, 1993), 49–50 (emphasis mine).

CHAPTER 7

Women of "the Cloth" in Acts: Sewing the Word

How to Curse a Treacherous Villain: Witness David's fivefold declamation of the house of Joab after the latter's vengeful murder of the diplomatic Abner:

> *May the house of Joab never be*
> *without one who has a discharge,*
> *or who is leprous,*
> *or who holds a spindle,*
> *or who falls by the sword,*
> *or who lacks food! (2 Sam 3:29)*

At the heart of this ominous list of disasters, flanked by paired imprecations of dreaded disease (discharge/leprosy) and death (war/famine), is the surprising threat of spinsterhood. Is "holding a spindle" really a fate equal to, if not worse than, death?[1] It was, apparently, in the macho, militaristic culture of ancient Israel's Davidic kingdom. Spinning, weaving, knitting, and other forms of textile labor were quintessentially women's work—domestic drudgeries that no self-respecting commander like Joab would be caught dead doing. To consign his male descendants to such effeminate employment would effectively emasculate Joab's legacy; it would be difficult to imagine any more shameful fate in that society.[2]

This scenario reflects a pervasive stereotype, confirmed in both literary and material remains, concerning the production of clothing in the ancient Mediterranean world: such arduous labor was performed principally by women in the private confines of the patriarchal household. In short, women were responsible for clothing their families in conjunction with other standard domestic chores such as cooking, cleaning, and childcare.[3]

166

While women's historic preoccupation with spinning and sewing can scarcely be denied, questions may be raised regarding the relationship of such labor to other spheres of activity beyond the domestic environment. In her analysis of women's roles within early Christianity, Luise Schottroff invites us to explore a "triple track" of possible channels for women's work: 1) "providing for others," 2) "earning an income," and/or 3) "building up the congregation."[4] Alternatively, we may relate Schottroff's first category to domestic/menial duty in the home; the second to public/commercial work in the marketplace; and the third to religious/communal service in the church. This heuristic framework leads us to wonder whether women's textile labor in biblical antiquity ever extended beyond the domestic realm into the wider commercial and religious sectors and, if so, how did such pursuits undergird and/or undermine women's traditional roles within the family and in male-dominated society at large.

Interestingly, within the androcentric world of the New Testament book of Acts, we discover three prominent Jewish-Christian women of "the cloth"—Tabitha, Lydia, and Priscilla—who utilize their textile skills—sewing tunics, dyeing fabrics, and stitching tents—in various business ventures within the Roman marketplace and in ministerial efforts within the Christian community. The domestic status, both marital and maternal, of these women is uncertain, except for Priscilla's identity as Aquila's wife; but clearly, though working with cloth in their homes, they are not monochrome, housebound "spinsters." This study aims to provide a multilevel profile of these women of "the cloth" in Acts in terms of Schottroff's triad of domestic, commercial, and religious spheres of occupation.

The pun on "the cloth"—while anachronistic to Acts—particularly focuses our attention on the interplay between women's domestic and religious identities and between "material" and "spiritual" forms of service. While Acts can scarcely be read as endorsing full-dress "ordained" ministry for women or anyone else beyond the Twelve (cf. 1:15–26), cloth-dealing women like Tabitha, Lydia, and Priscilla, who also actively participate in synagogue and church, provide excellent cases for reflecting on the nexus between matter and spirit, hand and heart, labor and ministry. Such reflection on the ideological implications of "women's traditional textile work" coordinates with what Elaine Hedges has shown to be "a widespread and peculiarly interesting development in contemporary feminist thinking." Writing in 1991, she observed:

In the past two decades visual artists and art historians, social historians, folklorists, poets and novelists, and most recently literary critics and theorists have discovered in the processes and products of the spindle, shuttle, and needle a major source for understanding women of the past, and as well, a source of subject matter and of images and metaphors for new creative work.[5]

As for religious scholars, Hedges cites the pioneering efforts of Mary Daly to redefine women's spiritual experience in terms of a radical appropriation of "spinning" as a root metaphor for the "creative enterprise of mind and imagination" and "connectedness within the cosmos."[6] More recently, Elizabeth A. Johnson has tapped into a similar metaphorical heritage in designing her own "feminist-theological" vision, no less creative than Daly's but much more interwoven with classical Christian tradition:

> Feminist artisans and poets have been designing evocative metaphors for the creative work women do. Spinning, weaving, and quilting, all taken from women's domestic chores, provide an evocative description of scholarship as it seeks to articulate new patterns from bits of contemporary experiences and ancient sources. In the spirit of these metaphors, this exploration attempts to braid a footbridge between the ledges of classical and feminist Christian wisdom.[7]

Feminist interpreters of the New Testament and Christian origins have also turned for fresh inspiration and guidance to women's work of weaving, spinning, and quilting, discovering that more than etymology links the production of textiles and texts. Building on the insights of poet Adrienne Rich[8] and literary critic Nancy Miller,[9] Elisabeth Schüssler Fiorenza has employed a "hermeneutics of remembrance" that "resemble[s] the activity of a quiltmaker who stitches all surviving historical patches together into a new overall design."[10] Balancing this creative and connective dimension of feminist biblical-historical research is a counteractive and deconstructive component that "seeks to move against the grain" (or "read against the weave," in Miller's terms) "of the androcentric text to the life and struggles of women in the early churches."[11] Applied to the study of Luke-Acts, Schüssler Fiorenza detects that the ostensible pattern of women's equality and even leadership in the early church—suggested, for example, by Jesus' acceptance of wealthy women patrons (Luke 8:1–3) and by his special affirmation of Mary's discipleship (10:38–42)—is effectively "undercut" or unraveled by the overall dominance in Acts of male preachers of the word and male officers of the church.[12]

In a similar fashion, appreciating the close analogy between "putting together a text" and "the weaving of a textile," Brigitte Kahl offers a "materialist-feminist" reading of Luke both in light of intertextual threads with the Old Testament and against the weave of Luke's own narrative fabric.[13] The birth stories in Luke 1, for example, betray a "close interwovenness" with well-known biblical narratives from Genesis and Samuel. At the same time, Luke creates a new "feminist-egalitarian" pattern out of these materials:

> The age-old rivalry between one woman and another woman, between firstborn and younger son, which is inherent in the rules of patriarchy, finally turns into sisterhood and brotherhood: Hagar and Sarah, Leah and Rachel, Hannah and Penninah as well as Cain and Abel, Ishmael and Isaac, Esau and Jacob finally become reconciled in Elizabeth and Mary, John and Jesus.[14]

Unfortunately, this magnificent, inclusive web is severely stretched and strained in the balance of Luke's work. Clear marks of "repatriarchalization" predominate from Luke 2 to the end of Acts. What began in the Magnificat as a female prophet's (Mary) revolutionary announcement of liberation for the poor and oppressed in occupied Palestine is "fully replaced by a socially neutral 'gospel for the Gentiles'" proclaimed by the male missionary (Paul) in the heart of imperial Rome (Acts 28:28–31). Still, as Kahl argues, the radical vision of Luke 1 remains "as something like a 'feminist code' woven into the texture of the biblical 'textile,'" functioning as a persistent, obstinate "challenge to reinterpret and reanimate the Pauline gospel for the Gentiles by the 'original' spirit of an inclusive and ecumenical justice and liberation for poor men and women."[15]

These feminist-critical appropriations of textile work rooted in historical analysis and postmodern literary theory guard against the trap of romanticizing the ancient tradition of women's weaving as some sort of pristine model of modern women's liberation. Focusing on the American scene, Hedges has demonstrated that women's celebration of textile labor as a stimulus to independent creative and scholarly endeavors is largely a recent phenomenon, emerging in the last half of the twentieth century. Before that, aspiring female artists and intellectuals encountered the stereotype of the stay-at-home seamstress as a marked "deterrent to ambition and achievement." When daring to branch out in new directions, with a pen, say, rather than a needle, thoughtful women had to assure the male hierarchy that nothing was really changing, that their new ventures were just "an innocuous extension of domesticity."[16] Hence we find adroit nineteenth-century writers like Harriet Beecher Stowe deprecating their compositions as an "ill-arranged patchwork" of characters and even concealing their "scribblings" in a sewing basket, the perduring symbol of "proper" ladies' labor.[17]

If this "adversarial relationship"[18] between women's textile and textual work, between their domestic, commercial, and religious "weavings," characterized nineteenth-century American society, how much more, we might imagine, would such conditions have typified the first-century Eastern Mediterranean world. In any event, in assessing the various roles of women of "the cloth" in Acts, it is incumbent that we firmly anchor such investigation in the ancient historical and literary contexts under-girding this material.

Weaving the Contexts

In narrowing ideological proximity to the portraits of Jewish-Christian women of "the cloth" in Acts, three broad "intertexts" merit examination: 1) pagan Greek and Roman classics;[19] 2) Jewish scriptures in Greek (LXX);[20] and 3) the Christian Gospel of Luke, the "first" volume in the Luke-Acts set (cf. Acts 1:1; Luke 1:3).[21]

Two poetic renditions of Greek mythology are particularly relevant to tracking the thread between women's domestic, religious, and other creative outlets of textile work. The first encounter between a man and woman in Homer's *Odyssey* features a conflict between Telemachus and Penelope, the son and wife of the long absent hero, Odysseus. In this scene, the "wary and reserved" Penelope emerges from her upstairs chamber deeply offended by the musical entertainment being offered to her son and suitors in her own home. She demands that the bard "break off this song" about returning warriors, since it only served to deepen her grief over Odysseus's loss. In response, Telemachus, shamed by Penelope's intrusion, puts his mother back in her place in no uncertain terms:

> *So, mother*
> *go back to your quarters. Tend to your own tasks,*
> *the distaff and the loom, and keep the women*
> *working hard as well. As for giving orders,*
> *men will see to that, but I most of all:*
> I *hold the reins of power in this house.*
> *(1.409–414)*[22]

Clearly, Telemachus believes that women should diligently and silently carry out their weaving duties in the home, isolated from and subordinate to male rulers. And Penelope agrees!: "she withdrew to her own room . . . and took to heart the clear good sense in what her son had said" (1.415–416). Later, however, she uses her weaving skills not only to confirm her domestic identity but also to connive against her suitors and control her own destiny. She announces that she cannot remarry in good conscience until she has completed weaving a burial shroud for her departed husband's father, Laertes. The project winds up extending over three years, because each night Penelope secretly unravels her web, then starts anew the next morning. When Penelope is finally exposed, one of her deceived suitors, Antinous, cannot help but admire this "matchless queen of cunning" who has so frustrated his plans: "she persists in tormenting us, quick to exploit the gifts Athena gave her—a skilled hand for elegant work, a fine mind and subtle wiles too— we've never heard the like" (2.127–130). Here is the tension: on the one hand, Penelope's weaving "wiles' reinforce her exclusive, chaste devotion to her lord and husband Odysseus, even in his assumed death; on the other hand, they also demonstrate her considerable god-given intellectual and political talents, which exceed her expected manual-domestic skills.[23]

Athena's patronage of women's textile labor is also the subject—and problem—of the tale of Arachne spun by the first-century Roman poet, Ovid (43 BCE–17 CE). In Book VI of *The Metamorphoses,* Arachne is introduced as a young woman of lowly birth, the daughter of a common Lydian artisan who made his living as a purple-dyer. Arachne herself becomes known throughout Lydia for her consummate skills at all levels of cloth production—carding, spinning, weaving, embroidering. Whether she used these talents to enhance her father's business or to supplement the family's income is never mentioned. In any event, she captures the attention of admiring nymphs as well as mortals and is assumed to be great Athena's prize pupil. Arachne, however, spurns such tutelage, and defiantly challenges Athena to a weaving duel. So each contestant—girl and goddess—fashions her finest tapestry out of gold and purple threads. Athena's displays a central battle scene between herself and Neptune, establishing her superior claim to the city of Athens, surrounded in each corner by vivid depictions of divine retribution against human, especially female, pride. Arachne's work intricately details a series of gross violations of mortal women by rapacious gods. The two tapestries thus inscribe the basic power struggle within conventional divine/human and masculine/feminine hierarchies.[24]

At the end of the day, Arachne both wins and loses. Shockingly, she wins the battle in Ovid's account (a notable reversal from earlier versions) by

virtue of her "flawless" creation, conceded by Athena and "even Envy person-
ified"; ultimately, however, she loses the war, as an irate Athena bashes
Arachne four times on the forehead and transforms her into a spider. That
will teach uppity young women who dare to step outside their proper
domestic sphere of modest, mortal, menial weaving. But that may not be the
whole story. The fact that Arachne's work outstrips Athena's in the latter's
"masculine, military mode" and that even as a spider she continues to spin
her web (to "exercise her old-time weaver-art") may suggest Ovid's admira-
tion for Arachne's subversive activity, perhaps as a model for his own "verbal
tapestries" and "skillful ecphrases of textile skill," as Ann Rosalind Jones surmises.[25]

In considering the Old Testament context, we have already noted the traditional image of spinning as domestic women's work lying behind David's
curse of Joab's lineage (2 Sam 3:29). A wider survey of biblical literature both
sharpens and complicates this basic portrait. The first attempt at sewing
comes very early in the Bible with the famous fig-leaf project, carried out by
the man and woman *together* (Gen 3:7) just before God stipulates a gender-
divided system of labor (3:16–19). In this new order, however, nothing is said
about who should be responsible for clothing duties. As it happens, *God
himself* takes on the role of tailor, outfitting the first couple in leather coats to
replace their pathetic leaf coverings (3:21).[26]

Perhaps this sets the stage for certain links between worship and weaving
that emerge in the construction of various curtains, screens, coverings, hang-
ings, and vestments for use in Israel's tabernacle in the wilderness, following
a detailed pattern that "the Lord commanded Moses" in Exod 35–40. Initially, colored yarns, fine linen, and goats' hair were provided by "all the skillful women [who] spun with their hands" (35:25).[27] Thus we find biblical
precedent for weaving both as women's work and as a channel for women's
worship of YHWH, as was also true in the service of Asherah (2 Kgs 23:7),
Artemis, and other ancient female deities.[28] In building YHWH's tabernacle,
however, while women supplied the raw materials, the task of producing and
finishing the grand project fell primarily to two divinely inspired crafts*men*,
Bezalel and Oholiab (Exod 35:35–40). To what extent they were aided by
other weavers, male or female, is not certain.[29] Perhaps women labored
strictly in a cottage industry, working out of their homes to provide fabrics
for professional male artisans. In any case, if women did participate in making priestly vestments, they certainly did not wear them.

Not surprisingly, the ideal wife in Prov 31 diligently works in the home
to manufacture clothing for her family. Indeed, the poem presents spinning
wool and flax as the woman's first specific duty (31:13) and thereafter adds

three supplemental references to textile labor (31:19, 21–22, 24) interlaced with other standard household responsibilities for providing food, tending children, and honoring her husband. Beyond this domestic realm, however, the female paragon also "engages in public economic enterprise"[30] and in certain expressions of religious service. On the commercial front, "she makes linen garments and sells them; she supplies the merchant with sashes" (31:24); in terms of ministry, the same hands that hold the distaff/spindle reach out to clothe the poor/needy (31:19–20), and as a mortal model of Woman Wisdom, the "capable wife . . . opens her mouth with wisdom" to "teach" the simple to "fear the Lord" (31:10, 26, 31).[31] Still, we must be careful not to make too much of this woman's independence: her business efforts, while "profitable" (31:18), seem limited to a cottage avocation (supplying cloth goods to merchants); and her conveyance of wisdom, while praiseworthy, seems directed chiefly to children within her household (31:27). Throughout the ode, the woman's remarkable achievements in textile and other types of employment redound to the pleasure and glory of her husband, who sits among the ruling elders "in the city gates" (31:23; cf. vv. 11–12, 28).[32]

From this idyllic portrait of a happy, honored husband supported by his wise, weaving wife, we turn to a messier snapshot of marital conflict surrounding women's textile work in the book of Tobit (2:11–14). The once prominent Assyrian exile, Tobit, now stripped of all his property and stricken blind for his tenacious devotion to Jewish law, bemoans the added disgrace of having to depend on his wife's (Anna) income from selling material she had woven.[33] The struggle comes to a head one day when Anna receives not only the usual wages from her employers, but also "a young goat for a meal." Tobit angrily accuses his wife of stealing the animal and demands she return it at once. Insisting that the goat was a charitable "gift," Anna lashes back at her husband: "Where are your acts of charity? Where are your righteous deeds? These things are known about you!" (2:14). Formerly proud of his many good deeds—including feeding the hungry and clothing the naked (1:16)—Tobit cannot even manage to feed and clothe himself now. What does he have to show for all his piety?[34]—a wife forced to peddle homespun goods that he also thinks (wrongly) is a thief! There is little left for Tobit now except to pray for death (3:1–6).

Once again, certain tensions emerge. The male ideal of a submissive, weaving, stay-at-home wife is challenged by the reality, borne of necessity, of women's earning wages from textile labor, wages paid by businessmen other than their husbands.[35] Still, Anna is scarcely an example of a successful career woman. She works at a subsistence level and stays firmly rooted in the home ("she cut off a piece she had woven and *sent it to the owners,*" 2:14). Overall, she appears to be no happier about her situation than Tobit.

Moving to the Gospel of Luke, the final and most immediate literary context for interpreting Acts, we come up empty in searching for comparative cases of women engaged in cloth work. We encounter women in many other traditional domestic occupations—cooking, catering, cleaning, childbearing—but no spinning, weaving, or the like. On closer examination, however, some important relevant material emerges. While women are not specifically cast as seamstresses in Luke, Jesus twice employs sewing metaphors to depict the kingdom of God. First, to illustrate the fundamental breach between an eroding social, political, and religious establishment—coming apart at the seams—and the restorative eschatological kingdom of God, Jesus cites a general maxim of sewing practice: "No one [*oudeis,* a generic masculine plural pronoun] tears a piece from a new garment and sews it on an old garment" (Luke 5:36; cf. 5:27–39). Second, Jesus more specifically describes the activity of God the Father as a tailor (reminiscent of Gen 3) clothing the destitute in his inclusive royal household:

> Consider the lilies, how they grow: they neither toil nor spin; yet I tell you even Solomon in all his glory was not clothed like one of these. But if God so clothes the grass of the field, which is alive today and tomorrow is thrown into the oven, how much more will he clothe you—you of little faith! . . . Do not be afraid, little flock, for it is your Father's good pleasure to give you the kingdom. (Luke 12:27–28, 32)

These images of sewing and spinning from the lips of the male Jesus pertaining to the kingdom of God the Father scarcely eradicate the pattern of weaving as typical women's work. Luke does not liberate women from domestic duty, but he does significantly ennoble household service (*diakonia*) as a paradigm of honorable divine and human activity, both male and female, governing even the ministry of Jesus himself: "I am among you as one who serves (*diakonōn*)" (22:27).[36] Alongside feeding and table-waiting, clothing the poor—including sharing one's own clothes as well as making new garments—constitutes a major expression of true religious piety in Luke (cf. 3:11; 6:29–30).[37]

Having explored the broad tapestry of women's textile work from Greco-Roman, Jewish, and Lukan sources, we are now prepared to examine the particular texture of stories of cloth-handling women in Acts along domestic, commercial, and religious lines. While seeking to coordinate this material with relevant contexts and intertexts, we must remain open to the possibility that depictions of women of "the cloth" in Acts might also run "against the weave"—as Schüssler Fiorenza and Kahl have put it—of previous literary patterns.

Tabitha: The Charitable Seamstress

The Tabitha story, set in the Christian community at Joppa, features the resuscitation from death of a beloved female disciple (*mathētria*)[38] known chiefly for her abundant "good deeds and the alms which she made (*epoiei*)"[39]—especially garments that "she made" (*epoiei*) for needy widows (Acts 9:36, 39). While it is commonly assumed that such philanthropy intimates Tabitha's status as an independent, wealthy patroness,[40] the fact that she actually *makes* the clothing, as Reimer observes, rather than gives from her own surplus, may suggest a more lowly social location.[41] In truth, we know little about Tabitha's identity beyond the fact that she is a Jewess with an Aramaic name meaning "gazelle" ("Dorcas" in Greek, 9:36), which, contrary to early interpreters, probably has nothing to do with her being light on her feet.[42]

As for Tabitha's domestic status, her appearance as a single, autonomous woman, without male supporters, has prompted some readers to classify her as a widow. But the term for "widow," *chēra*, commonly used in Luke and Acts, is never applied to her; she helps poor *chērai*, but not necessarily as one of them.[43] If not a *chēra*, which Luke reserves for particularly destitute widows,[44] we can perhaps surmise that Tabitha is financially better off than the widows she assists; but again, that does not automatically make her an opulent aristocrat.

We also do not know where Tabitha resided before her death. Since her corpse is prepared and laid in "a room upstairs," it is often thought that she had owned this two-story dwelling. But neither of the two references to the upper room (*hyperōon*, 9:37, 39) specifically labels it as *her* quarters. Moreover, upper rooms are common gathering places for early Christian communities or "house churches" in Acts (1:13; 20:7–12; cf. Luke 22:12). As such, the upper room may also represent a suitable site for mourning and memorializing respected members of the community—like Tabitha—who had died.[45] It is still possible, of course, that Tabitha hosted the Joppan congregation in her own home (as we will see later with Lydia and Priscilla), but that scenario is never made explicit in the text.

Wherever she lived, we can safely presume that Tabitha produced her hand-sewn tunics and cloaks[46] out of her domicile. How many garments she made and how organized or how extensive her outreach to widows might have been, we do not know. Arlandson's suppositions that she had "a small team helping her" manufacture "a sizeable surplus of goods" and that "she also sold part of the surplus to those capable of buying it, thereby making a profit" constitute pure speculation.[47] We have no accounting of the number of widows Tabitha was supplying or even whether she was their sole provider, and commercial interests—which Luke often discusses elsewhere—play no role in the present narrative.

The primary significance of Tabitha's work in Acts 9 lies in its *religious* dimension. The performance of "good works and acts of charity" such as clothing the naked reflects standard Jewish piety demanded of God-fearing persons, both male and female (cf. Tob 1:17; 4:16; Matt 25:36–46; Acts 10:1–2). Domestic manufacturing of garments to help the poor especially recalls the model of the ideal woman in Prov 31 sketched above (31:19). In Luke's gospel, John the Baptist's first requirement of penance for would-be converts was that "whoever has two coats (*chitōnas*) must share with anyone who has none" (3:11). Tabitha goes one better by not merely lending an extra coat but by actually making multiple new coats for needy widows (*chitōnas*, Acts 9:39).[48] Active caretaking of vulnerable widows represents another hallmark of Jewish piety, exemplified by YHWH himself (Exod 22:22–23; Ps 68:5; Prov 15:25) and his prophets, Elijah (1 Kgs 17:8–24), Elisha (2 Kgs 4:1–37), and Jesus (Luke 7:11–17; 18:1–8; 20:45–21:6).[49] Although, admittedly, the male apostle Peter gets star billing in Acts 9 for assisting the widows at Joppa by restoring their deceased benefactress—mirroring the resuscitation miracles of Elijah, Elisha, and Jesus—Tabitha obviously plays a vital supporting role. Widows owed their clothing most directly to *Tabitha's* diligent labor, both before and (presumably) after her death (Peter immediately leaves and turns to other business, 9:43–10:23).

Apart from their concern over Tabitha's subordination to Peter in Luke's story, certain feminist critics have also been suspicious of Luke's apparent hesitance to characterize Tabitha's work as *diakonia* or "ministry"—a "good work" (*ergon agathon*), to be sure, but not bona fide "ministry." The problem is further complicated by Luke's willingness to describe the care of hungry widows by a seven-*man* committee as *diakonia* (Acts 6:1–7).[50] Why not use the same term for Tabitha's service? While Luke often employs some form of *diakonia/diakoneō* to identify authentic ministry, he is not limited to it. For example, in a key text summarizing Jesus' entire ministry, Luke announces through Peter—"he [Jesus] went about doing good (*euergetōn*)" (Acts 10:38)—using a verb form (*euergeteō*) closely related to Tabitha's "good works" (*erga agatha*); and Tabitha's "almsdeeds" (*elēmosynai*) are matched by the God-fearing Cornelius in the next story (10:2, 4) and by the missionary

Paul later in Acts (24:17). Furthermore, a salient feature of *diakonia* in Luke's writings stresses a "holistic" rather than dichotomized view of religious "ministry" or "service." As we have seen, the Lukan Jesus who proclaims the gospel does so as "one who serves [at table]" (*ho diakonōn*, Luke 22:27); and "serving tables" (*diakonein trapezais*) and "serving the word" (*diakonia tou logou*) comprise complementary forms of true ministry (Acts 6:2, 4).[51] Such a perspective fits well with the focus on the home/household (*oikos*) as the primary locus of Christian fellowship, worship, and care, thus breaking down, to some extent, traditional domestic and cultic boundaries.[52] Therefore, while on one level, Tabitha's benevolent clothing of widows appears to be merely an "innocuous extension of domesticity,"[53] on another level, fully appreciating Luke's pastoral emphasis on caring materially for every member of God's household, such work may not be so innocuous or quotidian after all.

Is this to say that Luke takes us to the brink of women's ordination, that had there been the tradition of ministers donning "the cloth" at that time, Tabitha could have worn it as easily as Peter? Not exactly. As we have already suggested, Luke's ideals of equal ministerial opportunity for men and women often run "against the weave" of the actual stories he spins, particularly when it comes to who really has *a say* in church affairs.[54] Likewise, the ideal that acts of charity speak as loudly as actual words of proclamation becomes frayed in light of Acts' mounting preference for the latter form of ministry. It is difficult to ignore that a lot of speechmaking goes on in Acts and that it all comes from male voices. Reimer's opinion that labeling Tabitha a "disciple" implies her role as a missionary-proclaimer of the gospel stretches the meaning of the term beyond what it can bear.[55] Peter stands out as the sole spokes*man* in this story and, indeed, throughout much of the first half of Acts. The old Puritan commentator, Matthew Henry, got it right when he asserted, "Tabitha was a great doer, [but] no great talker"—right, that is, on the final level of Luke's narrative, but not necessarily from the view of history behind the story and certainly not from that of modern feminist critics.[56]

Lydia: The Hospitable Purple-Dealer

The Lydia story presents a God-fearing "dealer in purple cloth" (*porphyropōlis*), transplanted from Thyatira to Philippi, who welcomes the message proclaimed by Paul, receives baptism along with her household, and hosts the visiting missionaries and new community of believers in her home (Acts 16:13–15, 40). Again we encounter a single woman of "the cloth," with no mention of male kin. Whether Lydia was widowed, divorced, or married to a forgettable husband is anyone's guess.[57] In any event, in contrast to Tabitha's ambiguous domestic status, Lydia clearly functions as the head of "her household" (*oikos autēs*) and owner of "my home" (*oikos mou*) (16:15).

Other dimensions of Lydia's identity remain a matter of debate,[58] including the significance of her name. It is commonly noted that she bears a regional rather than an individual appellation—"a certain Lydian woman"—befitting someone of "servile origin."[59] The area of Lydia in western Asia Minor in fact encompassed the city of Thyatira, where the character Lydia formerly resided. We may also recall another famous cloth-working girl from Lydia and daughter of a humble purple-dyer, who, however, is also remembered by her given name (Arachne). Some inscriptional evidence also attests to "Lydia" as a personal as well as a place name, supporting Ben Witherington's contention that Luke intentionally highlights Lydia in Acts 16 as a wealthy, independent, *named woman,* prominent in her own right.[60]

However we evaluate her name, the key factor in determining Lydia's social location concerns her occupation. Here we move beyond Tabitha's homespun sphere of charitable garment making to truly commercial production and distribution of material goods, specifically, purple-tinted fabrics. Of course, we might still picture Lydia's running her business out of a home office and workshop where she employed members of her household.[61] But more seems to be involved than a simple cottage operation like that carried out by Tobit's wife, Anna, and the woman of Prov 31. For one thing, Lydia does not have to reckon with a husband (like Tobit) hassling her about her work or being preoccupied with his own public honor. And whereas the dutiful wife of Proverbs outfits her family in elegant crimson and purple fashions to support her husband's high position *within the city gates* (an ancient "dress for success" strategy; Prov 31:21–23), the purple-peddling Lydia may well live and work where she worships—in a marginal spot *outside the city gates* (Acts 16:13). Also, whereas the women in Proverbs and Tobit supply local merchants with cloth goods, Lydia functions more like a merchant herself, having transferred her business from Thyatira—a well-known center for dyed textiles[62]—to the booming Roman colony of Philippi.

Most commentators, like Witherington, assume that Lydia's employment in the purple trade brought her considerable wealth and prestige, making her one of the "high-standing" women Luke likes to feature (Acts 13:50; 17:4, 12), even though he does not explicitly label Lydia as such. The logic runs that, since purple garments were expensive items fit for kings and other elites, purple merchants must also have been rather well to do, perhaps even part of Caesar's civil service.[63] In short, a luxury product makes a lucrative profit. A somewhat quirky variation on this theme arises in Lillian Portefaix's suggestion that Lydia's profession, while lucrative, was still "entirely connected to the feminine sphere," since purple dye was purchased chiefly by wealthy women for party dresses, cheek rouge, and lipstick. Accordingly, "a woman dealer in purple needed to be well dressed herself in order to advertise her goods as her appearance would place her high in the estimation of other women."[64] Such a profile makes Lydia out to be something of a first-century Avon lady or Mary Kay representative (with the exception, presumably, that she ran around in a purple chariot instead of a pink one).

An entirely different strand of recent feminist-historical analysis challenges not only Lydia's supposed engagement in male-dominated commercial affairs, but also her high social standing. Both Schottroff and Reimer make a fundamental class distinction between purple-wearers and purple-workers.[65] The exploitation and marginalization of textile laborers is a sad but staple element of social life up to the modern day. In the ancient world, Plutarch clearly stated the common opinion: "Often we take pleasure in a thing, but we despise the one who made it. Thus we value aromatic salves and purple clothing, but the dyers and salve-makers remain for us common and low craftspersons."[66] In the case of purple-dyeing, the stigma was compounded by the filthy, "sordid," smelly process of extracting dye from plants or mollusks and treating materials with animal urine. It was a business typically zoned outside city limits, geographically matching the marginal social location of its practitioners. Purple-dyers might well have been wealthier than other artisans, but money was not the only or even supreme status marker in the ancient world.[67]

The case for Lydia's lower social status can be made, of course, only if we assume that her purple business included processing the dye and producing the colored fabrics as well as selling them.[68] We cannot be certain, but placing Lydia "outside the gate by the river" (16:13)—where smells would not offend those with noses in the air and plenty of water would be available for treating garments—supports the identity of a peripheral artisan. If it be objected that Luke would never portray his missionary heroes lodging with such folk, we need only recall Peter's sojourn in the house of Simon the tanner (9:39; 10:6, 32), another profession of questionable odor.[69]

Whatever the demands of Lydia's occupation, they do not distract her from an active religious life. As Tabitha was introduced as a "disciple," Lydia first appears as a "worshiper of God" (*sebomenē ton theon*), probably denoting here a pious Gentile sympathizer with the Jewish faith,[70] perhaps even a proselyte (cf. 13:43; 17:4, 17; 18:7). Appropriately, Paul first encounters Lydia along with other worshiping women "on the sabbath day" at a riverside "place of prayer" (*proseuchē*) or synagogue. As Bernadette Brooten has established, women's participation, even leadership, in synagogue services is amply attested in Luke's text and environment (cf. Luke 13:10–17; Acts 17:4, 10–12; 18:26).[71] While we do not know Lydia's precise role in the Jewish assembly, we do learn of her significant contribution to the new community of believers in Paul's gospel. She stands out as the first Christian convert on Macedonian soil and chief patron of the visiting missionaries and the emerging Philippian church congregating in her house. Along with being head of her economic household, Lydia apparently holds a similar place of authority in the fictive family of faith that she hosts, comprised of both male and female members ("brothers," *adelphoi,* 16:40).[72] Far from being a perfunctory service, hospitality constitutes an honorable, indispensable form of ministry in Luke and Acts, which leading figures like Jesus and Paul not only benefit from, but also practice.[73] In Lydia's case, her hospitality certainly goes beyond mere maid service to represent a courageous act of support in a politically charged situation. As Schottroff puts it:

> Each detail of the story speaks of Lydia's power. . . . She "compelled" Paul and other men to be her guests. She took initiative to such an extent that even our source—Acts—briefly cites her speech. . . . She insisted on having a house church in her home, knowing well that she thereby became conspicuous in the city and could possibly be persecuted for it. . . . The power growing in this community was not the kind that makes others small but a power that is shared and wants to make others great when they are small and in misery. Lydia's "compelling" was an expression of a power not directed toward rule but toward justice.[74]

While personally applauding this assessment of Lydia's "power" and wishing that it were so, I fear that it glosses over less liberating aspects of Luke's story. Lydia's "speech," as Schottroff calls it, simply recounts Lydia's offer of hospitality, and (as noted in the previous chapter) it remains subservient to Paul's will and authority ("if you have judged me to be faithful to the Lord," 16:15). Even if her persistent "urging/persuading" reflects a degree of boldness, Lydia's reported discourse hardly measures up to the standards of Peter or Paul's sermons in Acts. And her wider involvement with the dynamic proclamation of God's word is much more passive than active. A double emphasis falls on her "listening" to Paul's message, and even here she does not receive full credit: "*the Lord* opened her heart to listen" (16:14).[75] As elsewhere in Luke and Acts, despite the ideal of women prophets (Luke

1:26–56; Acts 2:17–18), the "better part" assigned to women is usually that of silent listening rather than of eloquent proclaiming.[76]

While Lydia's clothing business does not hinder her religious pursuits, is there any sense in which it might actually enhance her ministry? Unlike Tabitha, for whom making clothing for the poor *was* her ministry, Lydia does not, as far as we know, donate any of her purple goods to charity; indeed, supplying the rich with fancy garments might even be viewed as legitimating an oppressive hierarchy ("There was a rich man who was dressed in purple . . . ," Luke 16:19–31). At the risk of over-interpreting the Lydia account, I suggest a possible metaphorical link between her purple work and her church work, inspired by the tradition (sketched above) of women's textile labor as a model of women's wider creative endeavors. As Lydia employed her household in transforming ordinary materials into regal purple fabrics through a washing-dyeing process, so she leads her household—and others who gather in her house—to spiritual renewal through Christian faith and baptism. Paul himself might well have regarded Lydia's home as an inclusive center for "Jew and Greek, slave and free, male and female"—for all who "were baptized into Christ" and "clothed with Christ" (Gal 3:27–28).[77]

Priscilla: The Teaching Tentmaker

The story of Priscilla features a woman employed alongside her husband Aquila as a tentmaker, who hosts the itinerant missionary Paul in her home in Corinth, journeys with Aquila and Paul to Ephesus, and participates in catechizing another traveling teacher, an erudite Alexandrian named Apollos (Acts 18:1–4, 18–28). Unlike the two preceding women of "the cloth," Priscilla's marital status is clear and consistent. She is the wife of Aquila, a Jew from Pontus, and never appears apart from him (18:2, 18, 26). Interestingly, however, in two of the three named references in Acts, Priscilla is cited first (18:18, 26), matching the exact pattern of Paul's letters.[78] This inversion of the typical "Mr. and Mrs." order may point to Priscilla's dominance in the relationship, in terms of either social status,[79] ministerial function, or both. In any case, she is no subordinate cipher in the most reliable text (the revised Western version is another story).[80] Like the other Christian couple featured in Acts, the ill-fated Ananias and Sapphira, Aquila and Priscilla appear as collaborative associates in business and ministry.[81] Priscilla does not, however, simply follow her husband's lead as Sapphira did (all the way to her grave).

According to the most natural reading of the text, the partnership between Priscilla and Aquila extended to their craft of tent making: "he [Paul] stayed with *them* [*autois,* Aquila and Priscilla], and he was working [with them], for by trade *they were tentmakers (ēsan skēnopoioi)*" (18:3). There is no good grammatical reason to exclude Priscilla from the "they/ them" team. On socio-historical grounds, however, Ronald Hock has argued that "tent making" in this context referred primarily to the stout, manual— that is, manly—labor of leatherworking, as opposed to the more delicate occupation of weaving linen performed chiefly by women.[82] While Hock provides some valuable insights into the manufacture of leather goods in the ancient world, he goes too far in constructing unnecessarily sharp labor and gender dichotomies.[83] The great leather-linen debate, for example, is largely moot, as Jerome Murphy-O'Connor has shown. Why not both means of making tents and related goods? In addition to the evidence that Hock marshals for leatherworking, Murphy-O'Connor details the demand for colored, woven linen ship sails—like Cleopatra's royal purple sail in her voyages with Mark Antony—and decorative linen awnings draped around forums and theaters as sunscreens—such as the "star-spangled, sky blue" curtains around Nero's amphitheater in Rome.[84] We may recall similar tapestries of dyed linen and goats' hair (along with tanned hides and fine leather), fashioned by skilled women and men, adorning the wilderness tabernacle (Exod 35:23–26). Also, actual tents used for market booths and temporary lodging— at the popular Isthmian Games near Corinth, for example—could be made of durable canvas as well as of leather. In sum, tentmakers like Paul, Aquila, and Priscilla were probably "equally at home in sewing together strips of leather or different weights of canvas," using various awls, knives, needles, and waxed threads in the process.[85] Such work was unquestionably strenuous, time-consuming, even slavish, as Paul himself attests (1 Cor 4:10–12; 9:6, 19; 2 Cor 4:5; 6:5, 10; 11:27; 1 Thess 2:9), but there is no reason to think that Priscilla and other women were not up to the task (cf. Rom 16:3–4). There is also no reason to assume that Priscilla, Aquila, and other tentmakers were especially well-off economically or socially. Like other members of the humble, toiling artisan class, they may have struggled to make ends meet and been snubbed by ruling elites and leisured aristocrats.[86]

The religious service of Priscilla and Aquila may be tracked in three stages of increasing authority. First, they provide material support in the form of lodging and employment for the itinerant missionary Paul, who proclaims his message in the local Corinthian synagogue and in the nearby home of the God-fearing Titius Justus (Acts 18:1–8). At this stage, Priscilla and Aquila's ministry in Corinth seems more limited than Lydia's in Philippi: the married couple make no converts, from their household or otherwise, and their residence does not appear to be the headquarters of a "house church."[87] In the second stage, however, their involvement intensifies as they accompany Paul to Ephesus and are left in charge of the developing mission there when Paul moves on to other areas (18:18–23). At this point, Priscilla and Aquila function much like Barnabas, Timothy, Silas, and other Pauline missionary partners. Finally, their leadership becomes most evident in a climactic encounter with another visiting teacher, the "eloquent" and "enthusiastic" Apollos of Alexandria. While teaching "accurately concerning the things of Jesus" in the Ephesian synagogue, Apollos needed more advanced, sophisticated instruction. Enter the master teachers, Priscilla and Aquila (note the order), who "took him aside and explained the way of God to him *more accurately*" (18:24–26). This is as close as we get in Acts to a woman proclaiming the word to a man. To be sure, the scene is normalized somewhat by the presence of her husband; but, nonetheless, Priscilla takes the lead and more than holds her own in debating and correcting the learned Alexandrian scholar. Whether she (and Aquila) "take him aside" in a corner of the synagogue[88] or in their home[89] is uncertain; in any case, Priscilla takes the initiative and assumes the role of an authoritative teacher—although not before a public audience (she functions more as a private tutor).[90]

How might her teaching and tent making correlate? Here we may rely more on logical inference than metaphorical imagination. Recent appraisals of tent making in the Pauline world have accented its particular compatibility with missionary vocations and various intellectual pursuits.[91] The portability of requisite tools of the trade and high demand for its products in bustling urban centers made tent making an apt profession for itinerant evangelists. Priscilla and Aquila would thus be able to transfer their business and ministry from Rome to Corinth to Ephesus with relative ease. The tent-making workshop itself, perhaps located at the front or first floor of a residence, would afford a reasonably quiet and relaxed atmosphere for concurrent work and conversation with customers and other visitors, not only about the job at hand but also about the issues of the day. The shop of Simon the shoemaker became a famous venue for philosophical discussion in Athens, including such notables as Socrates and Pericles. Other Cynic philosophers also combined artisanship and scholarship, stitching and teaching, establishing the craft shop "as a conventional social setting for intellectual discourse."[92] Paul's reminder to the Thessalonians that "we worked night and day . . . *while* we proclaimed to you the gospel of God" (1 Thess 2:9) may also intimate a more direct link between manual labor and evangelical witness than is often assumed.[93] Sewing cloth or leather to make tents may go hand in hand with sowing the word or gospel to make disciples.

Stitching the Pieces Together

In our sampling of weaving stories from Greco-Roman, Jewish, and Lukan sources, we uncovered certain tensions between women's textile work as isolated domestic labor in support of the patriarchal family, on the one hand, and as a wider creative outlet for both economic profit and religious service, on the other. The three working women of "the cloth" in Acts negotiate these tensions in both similar and distinctive ways.

On the *domestic* front, all three women seem to ply their craft, at least partly, in a residential setting. That is, they use their homes as a base of operation, a workshop of sorts. Beyond this common foundation, however, different household structures emerge: Tabitha appears to work alone as a single woman; Lydia seems to be equally independent of paterfamilial rule at the same time she manages a working household of her own; and Priscilla labors alongside—but not subordinate to—her husband and at least one other male employee and household guest (Paul).

The *commercial* extension of domestic cloth production also varies: whereas Tabitha simply gives away her garments to needy widows, both Lydia and Priscilla market their goods for profit. While these two women's textile businesses may have brought them a measure of financial security, as hard-working artisans engaged in menial labor they probably did not enjoy high status among society's true, leisured nobility. Luke is happy to identify upper-crust women within early Christianity when he can; the fact that he does not so label Tabitha, Lydia, and Priscilla likely means that they did not fully fit the bill.

All three women of "the cloth" stand out as models of *religious* devotion, but each illustrates her own unique interface between textile work and Christian ministry. Tabitha's case offers the most direct and material connection: clothing widows *was* her ministry, the prime evidence of her "good deeds" and discipleship. Lydia's purple business, by contrast, while not incompatible with ministry, seems related to it only in an indirect and metaphorical fashion: handling dyed garments may be compared symbolically to hosting baptized converts. Finally, inference and circumstantial evidence suggest a plausible tie between Priscilla's tent making and her missionizing and teaching: her manual occupation provided an optimal setting for her ministerial vocation.

However we parse the precise relationship between women's cloth work and religious service in Acts, a clear case is made for "braiding a footbridge," to reprise Elizabeth Johnson's happy image, rather than driving a wedge between so-called "menial" and "spiritual" pursuits. I might wish that Luke had woven tighter specific links between women's practical service and *prophetic* opportunities, between sewing cloth and sowing the word. Priscilla's portrayal as a teaching tentmaker points in the right direction; unfortunately, it stands too alone in Acts and too much in the shadow of Paul's dominant witness. If Christian women are ever to fit "the cloth" of ordained ministry as easily as men, they must be given a great deal more authoritative voice than Luke allows. Still, it is good for all in the church, both men and women—especially for those within heavily word-centered traditions—to be reminded that acts of service can themselves speak volumes. As the earthly Jesus announced to his disciples in the upper room—"I am among you as one who serves"—so the risen Jesus embodied in Tabitha might well have proclaimed in another upper room—"I am among you as one who *sews*."

Notes

1. Some ambiguity surrounds the meaning of the Hebrew text. P. Kyle McCarter Jr., in *II Samuel* (Anchor Bible 9; Garden City, NY: Doubleday, 1984), 118, suggests that one who "clings to a crutch" makes better sense in the present context, presumably because it depicts another physical impairment to military service. Bruce C. Birch, however, notes that one who "holds a spindle" (NRSV) aptly fits the situation by "imply[ing] men who are not fit for battle and must do women's work." "The First and Second Books of Samuel," *New Interpreter's Bible* (vol. 2; Nashville, TN: Abingdon, 1998], 1225.

2. See David D. Gilmore, "Introduction: The Shame of Dishonor," in *Honor and Shame and the Unity of the Mediterranean* (ed. David D. Gilmore; Washington, DC: American Anthropological Association, 1987), 2–21; F. Scott Spencer, "The Ethiopian Eunuch and His Bible: A Social-Science Analysis," *Biblical Theology Bulletin* 22 (1992): 156–58. On the perpetuation of this stigma into the Roman period, note the assessment of Judith P. Hallett, "Women's Lives in the Ancient Mediterranean," in *Women and Christian Origins* (ed. Ross Shepard Kraemer and Mary Rose D'Angelo; New York: Oxford University Press, 1999), 33–34: "Roman authors such as Cicero and Ovid emphasize that the representation of wool-working as a quintessentially female pursuit served as a form of distinguishing proper female from proper male behavior: each author characterizes men as effeminate and homosexually passive merely by attributing them with working in wool."

3. Hallett, "Women's Lives," 33, stresses that this stereotype of women-as-weavers cut across class boundaries in the ancient world: "Employing symbolic designations for women as a group, most notably by associating all women with wool-working, was perhaps the most visible way of erasing class distinctions and of positing a domestically defined gender unity among all females." See further Elizabeth W. Barber, *Women's Work: The First 20,000 Years: Women, Cloth, and Society in Early Times* (New York: Norton, 1994); Carol Meyers, *Discovering Eve: Ancient Israelite Women in Context* (New York: Oxford University Press, 1988), 142–49; Cf. Phyllis A. Bird, *Missing Persons and Mistaken Identities: Women and Gender in Ancient Israel* (Overtures to Biblical Theology; Minneapolis: Fortress, 1997), 59.

4. Luise Schottroff, Silvia Shroer, and Marie-Theres Wacker, *Feminist Interpretation: The Bible in Women's Perspective* (Minneapolis: Fortress, 1998), 199.

5. Elaine Hedges, "The Needle or the Pen: The Literary Rediscovery of Women's Textile Work," in *Tradition and the Talents of Women* (ed. Florence Howe; Urbana: University of Illinois Press, 1991), 338.

6. Mary Daly, *Gyn/Ecology: The Metaethics of Radical Feminism* (Boston: Beacon, 1978), 389–90; cf. entire concluding chapter, "Spinning: Cosmic Tapestries," pp. 385–424; Hedges, "Needle," 339.

7. Elizabeth A. Johnson, *She Who Is: The Mystery of God in Feminist Theological Discourse* (New York: Crossroad, 1992), 10; cf. Shannon Shrein, *Quilting and Braiding: The Feminist Christologies of Sallie McFague and Elizabeth A. Johnson in Conversation* (Collegeville, MN: Liturgical Press, 1998).

8. Rich's poetry, replete with vivid textile imagery, has been appropriated by a number of modern feminist thinkers, religious and otherwise. For a useful synopsis of her work, see Hedges, "Needle," 348–54.

9. Nancy K. Miller, "Arachnologies: The Woman, The Text, and the Critic," in *The Poetics of Gender* (ed. Nancy K. Miller; New York: Columbia University Press, 1986), 270–95.

10. Elizabeth Schüssler Fiorenza, *But She Said: Feminist Practices of Biblical Interpretation* (Boston: Beacon, 1992), 52–54; cf. her "The 'Quilting' of Women's History: Phoebe of Cenchreae," in *Embodied Love: Sensuality and Relationship as Feminist Values* (ed. Paula M. Cooey, Sharon A. Farmer, and Mary Ellen Ross; San Francisco: Harper & Row, 1987), 35–49.

11. Schüssler Fiorenza, *But She Said*, 62; Miller, "Arachnologies," 272. Danna Nolan Fewell and David M. Gunn have compared their deconstructive reading of biblical narratives with another textile operation: "'Deconstructive' criticism seeks to expound the gaps, the silences, the contradictions which inhabit all texts, like loose threads in a sweater, waiting to be pulled." *Narrative in the Hebrew Bible* (Oxford Bible Series; Oxford: Oxford University Press, 1993), 10,

12. "Acts does not tell us a single story of a woman preaching the word, leading a congregation, or presiding over a house-church." Schüssler Fiorenza, *But She Said*, 65–66.

13. Brigitte Kahl, "Toward a Materialist-Feminist Reading," in *A Feminist Introduction* (vol. 1 of *Searching the Scriptures;* ed. Elisabeth Schüssler Fiorenza; New York: Crossroad, 1993), 225–40.

14. Ibid., 237.

15. Ibid., 237–38.

16. Hedges, "Needle," 340–41.

17. Hedges, "Needle," 341–42. Gerda Lerner also notes the strong domestic ties maintained by Stowe and other women writers: "When, like so many wives before her, she [Stowe] took up the pen to supplement her husband's inadequate earnings, she did it for the sake of the family." Lerner, *The Female Experience: An American Documentary* (Indianapolis: Bobbs-Merrill, 1977), 58.

18. Ibid., 340.

19. As evidence of his broad familiarity with Greco-Roman culture, Luke actually cites— on the lips of Paul in Athens—snippets from the Greek poets Epimenides and Aratus in Acts 17:28–29.

20. The Lukan writings in Greek were heavily influenced by the Greek-Jewish scriptures in both form and content. As John A. Darr states: "Luke-Acts is saturated with the language, imagery, settings, and flavor of the Septuagint (LXX). It is hard to find a part of Luke's narrative that has not been affected by this intertextual linkage." Darr, *On Character Building: The Reader and the Rhetoric of Characterization in Luke-Acts* (Literary Currents in Biblical Interpretation; Louisville, KY: Westminster/John Knox, 1992), 28.

21. Scholars continue to argue about the precise relationship between Luke and Acts (see Mikeal C. Parsons and Richard I. Pervo, *Rethinking the Unity of Luke and Acts* [Minneapolis: Fortress, 1993]), but no one seriously disputes their common authorship; see I. Howard Marshall, "Acts and the 'Former Treatise," *The Book of Acts in Its First-Century Setting* (vol. 1 of *The Book of Acts in Its Ancient Literary Setting;* ed. Bruce W. Winter and Andrew D. Clarke; Grand Rapids: Eerdmans, 1993), 163–82.

I am focusing here on significant literary "intertexts." A full investigation of relevant contexts would also include a variety of inscriptional and archaeological data. I will hint at some of this information in later notes. For a thorough and careful examination of material as well as literary artifacts pertaining to weaving in Jewish and Greco-Roman antiquity, see Miriam B. Peskowitz, *Spinning Fantasies: Rabbis, Gender, and History* (Berkeley: University of California Press, 1997).

22. Citations from Homer, *The Odyssey* (trans. Robert Fagles; introduction and notes Bernard Knox; New York: Viking Penguin, 1996); on this incident, see the notes by Knox, pp. 50–52, and the parallel scene in 21.389–93.

23. See Helene P. Foley, "Penelope as Moral Agent," in *The Distaff Side: Representing the Female in Homer's* Odyssey (ed. Beth Cohen; New York: Oxford University Press, 1995), 94–97. Note also Peskowitz's discussion of both the popularity and ambiguity of the Penelope tradition in Roman-period Judaism in *Spinning Fantasies,* 1–10.

24. See Ann Rosalind Jones, "Dematerializations: Textile and Textual Properties in Ovid, Sandys, and Spenser," in *Subject and Object in Renaissance Culture* (ed. Margreta de Grazia, Maureen Quilligan, and Peter Stallybrass; Cambridge, UK: Cambridge University Press, 1996), 194–96.

25. Ibid., 195–96.

26. In light of the typical portrayal of sewing elsewhere in the Bible as women's work, one might appropriately envisage God as "seamstress." But "tailor" seems better suited to the Genesis narrative, which consistently employs masculine language for God. Of course, such language is metaphorical and anthropomorphic, not essentialist; the image of "tailor" complements that of potter, gardener, and surgeon in Gen 2.

27. Exod 35:23 also mentions "tanned rams' skins" and "fine leather," but these materials are not specifically linked with women's production in 35:25.

28. On the link between women's weaving and the worship of certain ancient Greek goddesses, see Ross Shepard Kraemer, *Her Share of the Blessings: Women's Religions among Pagans, Jews, and Christians in the Greco-Roman World* (New York: Oxford University Press, 1992), 22–29.

29. The general reference to "all those with skill among the workers" in Exod 36:8 opens the door for a variety of helpers, both male and female. But throughout Exod 35–40, Bezalel is especially singled out as the tabernacle's master builder. See Bird, *Missing Persons,* 95n36.

30. Claudia V. Camp and Carole R. Fontaine, "Proverbs," in *The HarperCollins Study Bible: New Revised Standard Version* (ed. Wayne A. Meeks; New York: HarperCollins, 1993), 984–85.

31. On the wife in Prov 31 as a symbolic representation of Woman Wisdom, see Thomas P. McCreesh, "Wisdom as Wife: Proverbs 31:10–31," *Revue Biblique* 92 (1985): 25–46.

32. The final line in the poem enters a plea that "her works praise her in the city gates" (Prov 31:31), thus calling for public recognition alongside her husband. The fact is, however, that the husband needs no one to trumpet his honor, since he is already known personally as a civic leader, thanks in large measure to his wife's domestic support.

33. As Carey A. Moore observes, "this must have been a bitter pill for Tobit to swallow," particularly if he endorsed the conventional wisdom of Sir 25:22: "There is wrath and impudence and great disgrace when a wife supports her husband." Moore, *Tobit: A New Translation with Introduction and Commentary* [Anchor Bible 40A; New York: Doubleday, 1996), 132–33. Similarly, Amy-Jill Levine correlates Tobit's consternation over Anna's working with a typical scenario in Hellenistic Jewish literature: "when women leave the confines of the home, confusion and marital disharmony result." "Tobit: Teaching Jews How to Live in the Diaspora," *Bible Review* 8 (1992): 51.

34. Cf. Moore's translation of the end of Tob 2:14: "Where are your righteous deeds? Look where they've got you!" *Tobit,* 126.

35. See Tal Ilan, *Jewish Women in Greco-Roman Palestine* (Peabody, MA: Hendrickson, 1995), 184–90.

36. See my earlier studies: "Neglected Widows in Acts 6:1–7," *Catholic Biblical Quarterly* 56 (1994): 728–31; and *The Portrait of Philip in Acts: A Study of Roles and Relations* (Journal for the Study of the New Testament: Supplement Series 67; Sheffield, UK: Sheffield Academic Press, 1992), 199–206.

37. A similar point underlies Jesus' critique of wealthy elites bedecked in "soft robes," "fine clothing," and "purple and fine linen" (16:19), in contrast to the desert prophet John and the diseased beggar Lazarus (Luke 7:24–26; 16:19–23).

38. The only use of a feminine form for "disciple" in the New Testament.

39. Joseph A. Fitzmyer, *The Acts of the Apostles: A New Translation with Introduction and Commentary* (Anchor Bible 31; New York: Doubleday, 1998), 445. The use of the imperfect tense implies a typical, ongoing pattern of conduct.

40. So do most commentators, including feminist interpreters: e.g., Gail R. O'Day, "Acts," in *Women's Bible Commentary* (ed. Carol A. Newsom and Sharon H. Ringe; 2nd ed.; Louisville, KY: Westminster/John Knox, 1998), 309–10; and Turid Karlsen Seim, *The Double Message: Patterns of Gender in Luke and Acts* (Nashville, TN: Abingdon; Edinburgh, UK: T and T Clark, 1994), 242–43.

41. Ivoni Richter Reimer, *Women in the Acts of the Apostles: A Feminist Liberation Perspective* (Minneapolis: Fortress, 1995), 43–44. Robert Tannehill, in "'Cornelius' and 'Tabitha' Encounter Luke's Jesus," *Interpretation* 48 (1994): 354, pictures Tabitha as "one of the poor" but largely because he assumes, without warrant (see below), that she was a widow.

42. John Chrysostom, for example, described Tabitha "as active and wakeful as an antelope." On the whole, the church fathers regarded her name as a positive attribute, except for John Calvin's rather raw rendering of Tabitha/Dorcas as "wild she-goat." See the helpful survey of interpretation in Janice Capel Anderson, "Reading Tabitha: A Feminist Reception History," in *The New Literary Criticism and the New Testament* (ed. Edgar V. McKnight and Elizabeth Struthers Malbon; Valley Forge, PA: Trinity Press International, 1994), 108–44.

43. See Spencer, "Neglected Widows," 732n47.

44. Ibid., 715–33; Seim, *Double Message,* 241–43.

45. Of course, death is much on the mind of Jesus in the Last Supper scene in the upper room, and the account of Eutychus's fall from the upper room in Acts 20 focuses on his death and resuscitation (like Tabitha).

46. *Chitōnas kai himatia* (9:39)—basic under- and outergarments.

47. James M. Arlandson, *Women, Class, and Society in Early Christianity: Models from Luke-Acts* (Peabody, MA: Hendrickson, 1997), 143–44.

48. Tannehill, "'Cornelius' and 'Tabitha,'" 352.

49. Spencer, "Neglected Widows."

50. O'Day, "Acts," 309–10; Clarice J. Martin, "The Acts of the Apostles," in *Feminist Commentary* (vol. 2 of *Searching the Scriptures;* ed. Elisabeth Schüssler Fiorenza; New York: Crossroad, 1994), 782; Mary Rose D'Angelo, "Women in Luke-Acts: A Redactional View," *Journal of Biblical Literature* 109 (1990): 455.

51. See Spencer, "Neglected Widows," 728–31; *Portrait of Philip,* 199–206.

52. See John H. Elliott, "Temple versus Household in Luke-Acts: A Contrast in Social Institutions," in *The Social World of Luke-Acts: Models for Interpretation* (ed. Jerome H. Neyrey; Peabody, MA: Hendrickson, 1991), 211–40.

53. Hedges' phrase cited above. "Needle," 341.

54. Parity between male and female ministers may seem to be suggested in the well-known pattern of pairing incidents involving men and women in Luke-Acts. But juxtaposition does not mean equality. Tabitha's story is sandwiched between similar healing/conversion episodes featuring two men, Aeneas (9:32–35) and Cornelius (10:1–48). Her story is longer than the former's but much shorter than the latter's. But in terms of voice and power, Peter overshadows all of them (see below). See D'Angelo, "(Re)Presentations of Women in The Gospel of Matthew and Luke-Acts," in Kraemer and D'Angelo, eds., *Women and Christian Origins,* 180–91.

55. Reimer, *Women in the Acts of the Apostles,* 54.

56. See the trenchant analysis of the "dark side" of Henry's interpretation in Anderson, "Reading Tabitha," 120.

57. See the discussion of various possibilities in Bradley Blue, "Acts and the House Church," in *The Book of Acts in Its Graeco-Roman Setting* (vol. 2 of *The Book of Acts in Its First-Century Setting;* ed. David W. J. Gill and Conrad Gempf; Grand Rapids: Eerdmans, 1994), 184–86.

58. We do well to remember the sage caution of Shelly Matthews: "It is difficult to ascertain Lydia's status on the basis of four words, *Lydia, porphyropōlis poleōs Thyateirōn* [Lydia, a purple-dealer of the city of Thyatira]." Matthews, *First Converts: Rich Pagan Women and the Rhetoric of Mission in Early Judaism and Christianity* (Stanford, CA: Stanford University Press, 2001), 86.

59. Wayne A. Meeks, *The First Urban Christians: The Social World of the Apostle Paul* (New Haven, CN: Yale University Press, 1983), 203n93; see the discussion in Colin J. Hemer, *The Book of Acts in the Setting of Hellenistic History* (ed. Conrad H. Gempf; Winona Lake, IN: Eisenbrauns, 1990), 114–15, 231; Luise Schottroff, "Lydia: A New Quality of Power," in *Let the Oppressed Go Free: Feminist Perspectives on the New Testament* (Gender and the Biblical Tradition; Louisville, KY: Westminster/John Knox, 1993), 132–33.

60. Ben Witherington III, *The Acts of the Apostles: A Socio-Rhetorical Commentary* (Grand Rapids: Eerdmans, 1998), 491–92; cf. Hemer, *Book of Acts,* 114, 231; Florence M. Gillman, *Women Who Knew Paul* (Zacchaeus Studies; Collegeville, MN: Liturgical Press, 1992), 31.

61. See Karen Jo Torjesen, *When Women Were Priests: Women's Leadership in the Early Church and the Scandal of Their Subordination in the Rise of Christianity* (San Francisco: HarperSanFrancisco, 1993), 14–15, 54–56.

62. See Reimer, *Women in the Acts of the Apostles,* 99–100.

63. Witherington, *Acts,* 492. While the processing and management of luxury purple dye derived from the Tyrian mollusk was an imperial monopoly, less expensive sources of purple, like the madder plant, were not under government control. See Hemer, *Book of Acts,* 114–15; Gillman, *Women Who Knew Paul,* 34–35.

64. Lillian Portefaix, *Sisters Rejoice: Paul's Letter to the Philippians and Luke-Acts as Seen by First-Century Philippian Women* (Stockholm: Almqvist & Wiksell International, 1988), 170–71; cf. Gillman, *Women Who Knew Paul,* 34.

65. Schottroff, "Lydia: A New Quality of Power," 131–37; Reimer, *Women in the Acts of the Apostles,* 101–9.

66. Plutarch, *Pericles* 1.3–4; cited in Reimer, *Women in the Acts of the Apostles,* 107.

67. Public honor—a "pivotal value" in the ancient Mediterranean world—had more to do with family heritage and patronal networks than with sheer accumulation of wealth. To be sure, generous sharing of wealth could enhance one's public standing, but money made at a "dirty" profession like dyeing would not have compensated for its lowly reputation. Bruce J. Malina, *The New Testament World: Insights from Cultural Anthropology* (rev. ed.; Louisville, KY: Westminster/John Knox, 1993), 28–62.

68. This possibility of Lydia's dual role as both merchant and manufacturer is hotly debated in recent scholarship. In *First Converts: Rich Pagan Women,* 86–88, Shelly Matthews places Lydia "squarely among the urban elite" (although perhaps the "quasi-elite" by virtue of her profiting from a lowly craft) and finds Schottroff's and Reimer's "arguments that trade in purple necessarily involved work in manufacturing . . . less than compelling." Rosalie Ryan, "Lydia, A Dealer in Purple Goods," *Bible Today* 2 (1984): 287–89, assumes that Lydia was only a prosperous merchant, with no involvement in manufacturing. She cites the parallel of the famous Stoic philosopher, Zeno, who made a fortune in the purple trade. Similarly, David W. J. Gill observes that "frequently it was the men who dealt with purple who were able to become members of the civic councils and therefore have a major role in the life of their communities." In Hierapolis, for example, an inscription identified one M. Aurelius Alexander Moschianus as

both "purple-seller" and "town councilor." Gill, "Acts and the Urban Elites," in Gill and Gempf, eds., *The Book of Acts in Its Graeco-Roman Setting,* 114–15. In Lydia's case, however, we have no evidence concerning any possible involvement in local politics, and the fact that she is situated *outside* the city gates may suggest a degree of marginalization (see more below).

69. Schottroff, "Lydia: A New Quality of Power," 132–34.

70. Cf. Matthews, *First Converts: Rich Pagan Women,* 55–61. Matthews especially notes the parallel between Cornelius in Acts 10–11 and Lydia in Acts 16: "One can recognize her story along with Cornelius's as a male-female pair of significant Gentile converts" (p. 59).

71. Bernadette J. Brooten, *Women Leaders in the Ancient Synagogue* (Brown Judaic Studies 36; Atlanta, GA: Scholars Press, 1982), 139–41.

72. See John Gillman, "Hospitality in Acts 16," *Louvain Studies* 17 (1992): 189–91.

73. See Luke 2:1–7; 5:27–32; 7:36–50; 10:38–42; 11:37–52; 14:1–24; 22:14–27; 24:28–30, 36–43; Acts 9:10–19; 16:27–34; 17:5–9; 18:2–3; 28:7–10, 30–31; John Koenig, *New Testament Hospitality: Partnership with Strangers as Promise and Mission* (Overtures to Biblical Theology 17; Philadelphia: Fortress, 1985), 85–123; Spencer, *Portrait of Philip,* 253–62.

74. Schottroff, "Lydia: A New Quality of Power," 135–36.

75. See F. Scott Spencer, *Acts* (Readings: A New Biblical Commentary; Sheffield, UK: Sheffield Academic Press, 1997), 165–66.

76. See Luke 10:42; Barbara E. Reid, *Choosing the Better Part?: Women in the Gospel of Luke* (Collegeville, MN: Liturgical Press, 1996); and the previous chapter in this book.

77. Cf. Gillman, "Hospitality," 188–89.

78. In Rom 16:3 and 2 Tim 4:19, Prisca (Priscilla's more formal name) appears first; she is listed after Aquila only in 1 Cor 16:19. Luke's use of the diminutive "Priscilla" more likely reflects a term of endearment or familiarity than "a put-down," as Jerome Murphy-O'Connor suggests in "Prisca and Aquila: Traveling Tentmakers and Church Builders," *Bible Review* 8 (1992): 40.

79. Her name recalls the *gens Prisca,* a venerable Roman family, perhaps suggesting her elite background. Her inclusion in the Jews' expulsion from Rome under Claudius (Acts 18:2) may owe more to her marital tie with Aquila than her ancestry. Only Aquila is specifically labeled "a Jew . . . a native of Pontus" (18:2); we know nothing of Priscilla's origins. See F. F. Bruce, *The Pauline Circle* (Grand Rapids: Eerdmans, 1985), 45–47.

80. As part of an apparent agenda "to reduce the prominence of Priscilla," the Western reviser (in codex D) adds Aquila's name in 18:3, 18, 21—without also mentioning Priscilla—and reverses the order to put Aquila first in 18:26. Bruce M. Metzger, *A Textual Commentary on the Greek New Testament* (2nd ed.; Stuttgart: Deutsche Bibelgesellschaft, 1994), 460–61, 466–67. See also Ben Witherington III, "The Anti-Feminist Tendencies of the 'Western' Text in Acts," *JBL* 103 (1984): 82–84.

81. See Acts 5:1–2—"But a man named Ananias, *with the consent of his wife Sapphira,* sold a piece of property; *with his wife's knowledge,* he kept back some of the proceeds" (cf. 5:7–10).

82. Ronald F. Hock, *The Social Context of Paul's Ministry: Tentmaking and Apostleship* (Philadelphia: Fortress, 1980), 81n46. Throughout this study, Hock typically refers only to Aquila the tentmaker, thus effacing Priscilla's potential contribution to the family business (see, e.g., pp. 31, 50, 59, 67).

83. See a similar critique in Gillman, *Women Who Knew Paul,* 18, 51–52. In two studies, Luise Schottroff suggests that wives were often required to assist their husbands in difficult manual trades like tent making, simply to make ends meet: "Women as Followers of Jesus in New Testament Times," in *The Bible and Liberation: Political and Social Hermeneutics* (ed. Norman K. Gottwalk and Richard A. Horsley; rev. ed.; Maryknoll, NY: Orbis, 1993), 458–59; and "Women as Disciples of Jesus in New Testament Times," in *Let the Oppressed Go Free,* 90–91.

84. Jerome Murphy-O'Connor, *Paul: A Critical Life* (New York: Oxford University Press, 1997), 86–87, citing Pliny, *Natural History* 19.22–24; cf. Murphy-O'Connor, "Prisca and Aquila," 43–49.

85. Murphy-O'Connor, *Paul: A Critical Life,* 87–88.